IMAGES
*of America*

# NORTH AND WEST CHELMSFORD

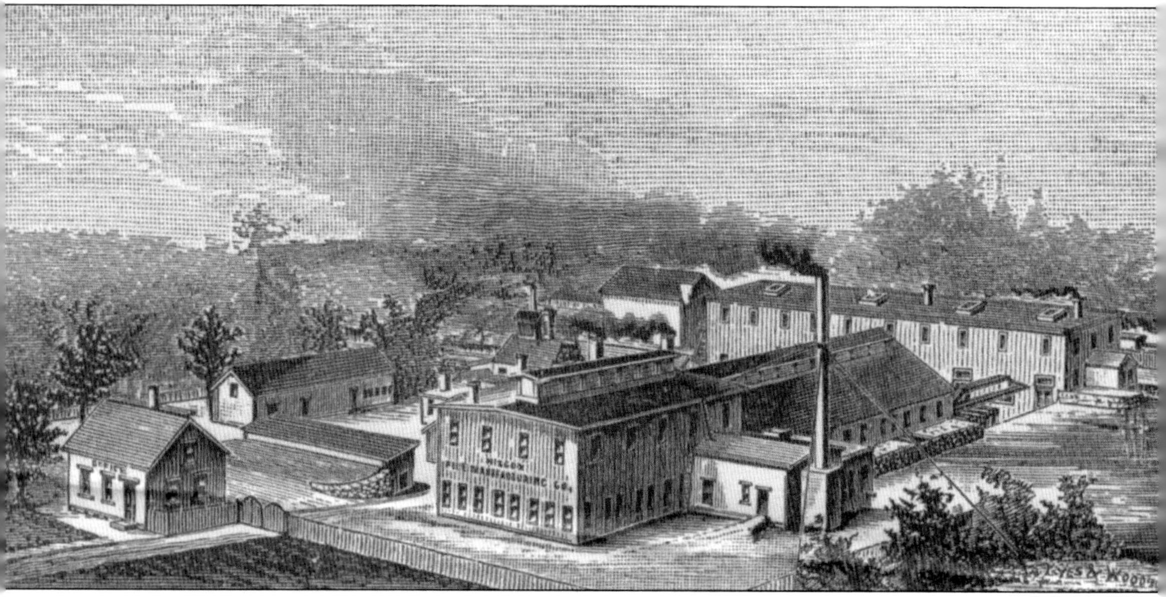

Deacon John Farwell built and operated a scythe factory in West Chelmsford from 1820 to 1846. Christopher Roby continued scythe production but switched to military swords during the Civil War. Although he went bankrupt in 1867, the Roby Manufacturing Company continued making industrial knives and swords until 1875. This block print is from an 1880s letterhead of the Hiscox File Manufacturing Company, which owned the factory until 1889. (Bernie Ready.)

**On the Cover:** In 1906, leather belts were still critical for distribution of power to all kinds of mill equipment. This North Chelmsford Supply Company shop produced oak-tanned leather belting, advertising "First-Class Work Guaranteed" and "Special attention given to repairing." In the back right section of the shop, pins were set into various industrial combs. T. Richard Davis, who is wearing a tie and standing behind a scrap bin, eventually became company superintendent. See page 40 for more information. (Chelmsford Historical Society.)

IMAGES
*of America*

# NORTH AND WEST CHELMSFORD

Fred Merriam

ARCADIA
PUBLISHING

ISBN 978-1-4671-2391-4

Published by Arcadia Publishing
Charleston, South Carolina

Printed in the United States of America

Library of Congress Control Number: 2016935147

For all general information, please contact Arcadia Publishing:
Telephone 843-853-2070
Fax 843-853-0044
E-mail sales@arcadiapublishing.com
For customer service and orders:
Toll-Free 1-888-313-2665

Visit us on the Internet at www.arcadiapublishing.com

*This book is dedicated to the residents of North and West Chelmsford who take pride in their communities and are curious about their past.*

# Contents

# ACKNOWLEDGMENTS

This book would not have been possible without the work of photographer Simon Towle (1834–1910), who shared a studio with his brother-in-law, the first daguerreotype artist in Lowell, George C. Gilchrest. Towle was responsible for many of the earliest stereopticon photographs taken in Chelmsford in the 1860s and 1870s, and when his niece Ella J. Gilchrest married industrialist George C. Moore in 1872, he was positioned to become Moore's in-house photographer. After Moore's death in 1923, the photograph print collection followed three different paths over the next 90 years.

The majority of prints were handed down through the Moore family. Thanks go to Moore's great-grandson William Johnston Jr. for providing electronic copies of the collection along with family history and vintage news articles.

A second set of prints went to Royal Shawcross, who organized the Varney Playground Association in 1930 and owned the Brookside Mill in Westford after 1944. When he died in 1980, these prints went to the Chelmsford Public Library. The library's Brian Herzog granted access to the Shawcross collection.

A third set of prints went to T. Richard Davis, an employee of the North Chelmsford Machine & Supply and Crysler companies from 1898 until 1951. His daughter Mabelle donated his collection to the Chelmsford Historical Society, where the author is a volunteer, in 1985.

These people were instrumental in the discovery or loan of the remaining vintage photographs used in this book: Donna Bulka, Thomas Collins, William and Katherine Davis, Bradford Emerson, Tim Tyler Fraize, Lynne Hershey, Liliana Lucas, Shawn and Jenny Lynch, George Merrill, Francis Miskell, John and Patricia Parow, Donald Peterson, Linda Prescott, James Quinn Jr., Peter Ricciardi, Matthew Saxton, Janet Shipman, and Chris Ware.

Richard McLaughlin, who currently owns the Moore residence once occupied by the Nabnasset Pond Farm manager in Westford, provided significant Moore research material.

Stephen Kochersperger, senior research analyst for postal history in Washington, DC, provided details on the closure of the West Chelmsford post office.

Special thanks go to my wife, Carol, for sharing her opinions, making sure the necessary time was available, and keeping the household running in the present.

# INTRODUCTION

The villages of North and West Chelmsford evolved soon after the town was incorporated in 1655 around farming, granite quarries, and mills harnessing the power of Stony Brook. In 1875, the arrival of future industrialist George C. Moore started a period of steady expansion and prosperity. A December 23, 1897, news article recovered from the Princeton Street School time capsule around 1954 sets the scene for Moore's early career:

> Mr. Moore was born at Brookside, a rather picturesque little hamlet on the banks of Stony Brook, about six miles above North Chelmsford. While he was not born in poverty, by any means, there was still no silver spoon within reach that might have been inserted between his lips at the time of his dawning upon the world. His father at the time, ran a wool scouring business in a most unpretentious little shanty that was dignified with the name of the Brookside mill. Young George went to school for a while, but when a youngster decided that the only way in which to make money was to get out and hustle for it and at the age of 15 years when most boys are still romping the streets, he entered his father's employ and was given the not easy task of scouring 100 pounds at a time, with no 20th century inventions to assist him.
>
> From about 1867 to 1875 he scoured wool and made good money which he held on to, his ambition being to own a mill of his own. In 1875 he went to North Chelmsford and started the first of the Moore's mills of North Chelmsford. It was a 200-foot structure, three stories high. He saw it completed and he saw it all ready for opening.

Here is what happened next, as printed in the August 12, 1923, edition of the *Lowell Sunday Telegram*:

> A big Australian wool sorter in his employ had been giving him a lot of trouble and one day the quarrel came to hard words and blows. "My father had always taught me that in trouble of that kind to get in the first blow and get in a hard one. The Australian was much bigger than I was, but I let him have it and knocked him cold. That night the mill burned, and I am sure the Australian did it. He told at the store how he was going to do it, but we never found him. I was under-insured and lost a lot of money but began to rebuild the very next day."
>
> One of the secrets of Mr. Moore's success is the fact that he is one of the hardest and steadiest workers in the mills. In fact, he takes too little recreation, for a young man. His hobby is to make money and spend it again on his plant, improving it all the time, and as a result while his bank account may not be that of the usual run of mill owners, none has a finer plant than he. He works from morning until night. Shut-downs, cut-downs and strikes are unknown quantities in Moore's mills and at present the plant is running in many departments until 9:30 o'clock at night, so great is the rush of business.

Moore's business activities in North and West Chelmsford were so extensive that a timeline may be helpful:

1863: Left school at age 15 to work with his father, George, and uncle Seth at Brookside Mill
1872: Married Ella J. Gilchrest, purchased old foundry site from George T. Sheldon, rented out existing two-story brick building on foundry site
1874: Purchased Nabnasset Pond Farm and Nabnasset Grove in Westford
1875: Constructed a three-story mill on the old foundry site; when this burned, constructed a temporary wooden building and leased Baldwin Mill for a year
1877: Replaced temporary wooden building with one-story brick mill
1882: Purchased half interest in Brookside Mill in Westford
1885: Built two-story brick addition onto his one-story brick mill
1887: Purchased grist and sawmill property near the mouth of Stony Brook
1888: More than doubled the size of his brick mill for worsted wool processing
1892: Inherited the other half of Brookside Mill from his late father
1893: Purchased former Roby Manufacturing/Hiscox File Mill in West Chelmsford
1895: Purchased the Baldwin Mill from George T. Sheldon
1896: Built five-story Middlesex Street storehouse above Stony Brook
1897: Started North Chelmsford Supply Company inside Silver & Gay Company
1898: Purchased Silver & Gay Company from Ziba Gay, renamed it North Chelmsford Machine Company
1901: Rebuilt North Chelmsford Machine and Supply Companies after a massive fire
1902: Sold his worsted mill and five-story storehouse to Moore Spinning Company for $1.6 million and continued working as its agent
1903: Started construction of wool scouring mill on Baldwin Mill property
1905: Combined two companies into North Chelmsford Machine & Supply Company
1908: Purchased George T. Sheldon estate on Princeton Street for office space
1909: Wool scouring mill burned; shifted production to Baldwin Mill buildings
1910: Opened newly designed wool scouring mill
1913: Sold wool scouring business—but not land and buildings—to Edgar Dixon
1917: Rebuilt the Hiscox File Mill dam and Freeman Lake canal control dam

Moore had his share of personal tragedy. His wife, Ella, passed away on July 12, 1901, at age 49, less than three months after the fire that destroyed his North Chelmsford Machine and Supply Companies. In August 1920, Moore gave his Nabnasset Pond properties to his daughter, Bessie (Moore) Griffin, whose husband, Harry, was an executive with the Woolworth Company in New York. Moore was devastated to learn that 40-year-old Bessie had died on April 24, 1923, and he passed away at age 75 on November 6 that same year.

In the late 1800s, when many of these photographs were taken, street names had been assigned independently within each village, so there was some duplication, and house numbers did not exist. In the early 1900s, duplications were eliminated, and house numbers were assigned to aid the fire department in responding to fires reported on the new and expanding telephone system. For example, Main Street in North Chelmsford was changed to Middlesex Street; after that, the only Main Street in town was the one in West Chelmsford. Fletcher Street in North Chelmsford was changed to Canal Street in the 1800s and to Newfield Street in the 1900s. In this book, all street addresses and lake names are referred to by their current designations, not their historical names.

# *One*

# Moore Spinning Company

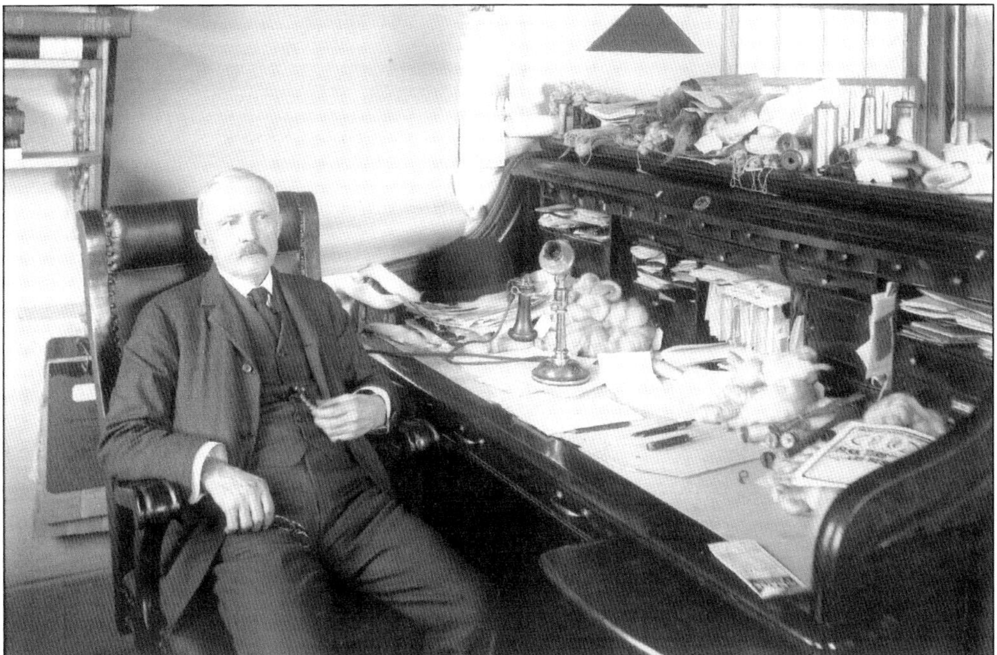

George C. Moore was a natural businessman with the ability to identify a process in need of improvement—in this case, conversion of raw wool and camel's hair into yarn—and the courage to take the risks necessary to capture a significant percentage of the world's market. His father, George R. Moore, was a mill owner on a smaller scale and a creative inventor on the side. (Chelmsford Historical Society.)

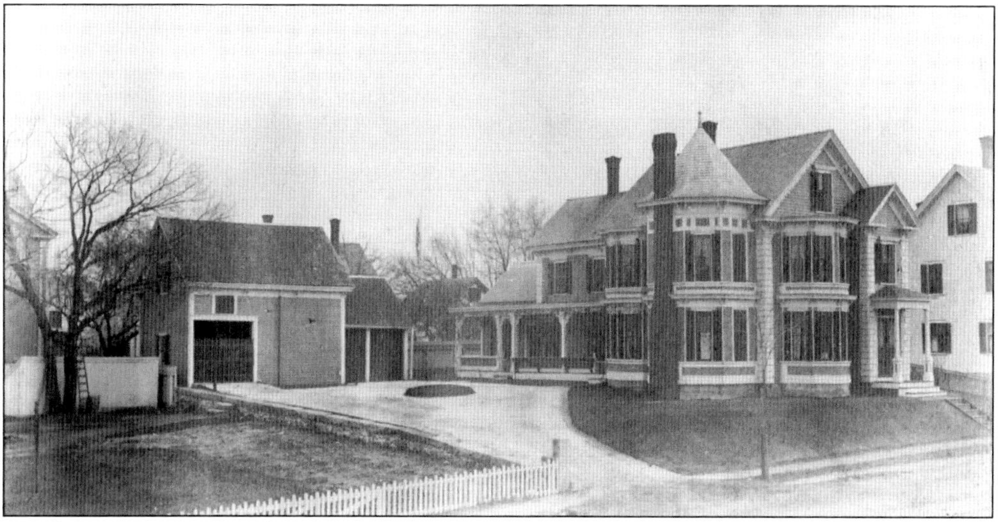

This house at 16–20 Wright Street was the home of George C. and Ella J. Moore from 1882 until George's death in 1923. The small lot was subdivided by neighbor Samuel T. Wright from a larger parcel he purchased from Thomas J. Adams in 1869. North Town Hall, built in 1852, is to the left of the carriage house. The house now contains four apartment units. (William Johnston Jr.)

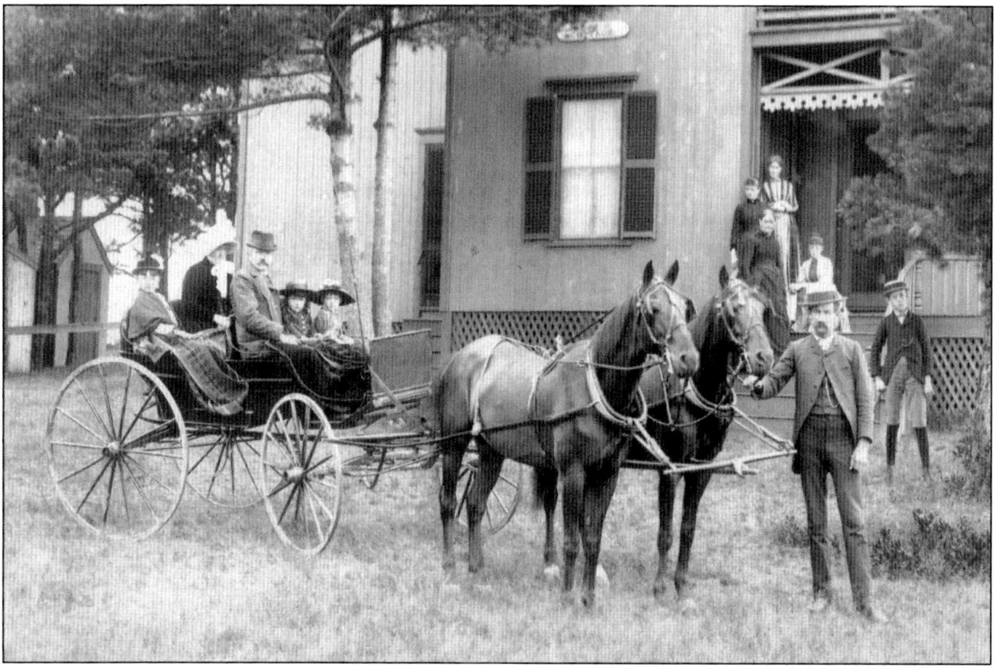

Simon Towle took this photograph around 1890 at the Gilchrest family summer home, Primrose Cottage, near Old Orchard Beach. Moore family members in the buggy are, from left to right, Bessie, Ella, George Sr., George Jr., and an unidentified relative. Ella's brother George E. Gilchrest is holding the horses' reins, and their mother, Nancy (Towle) Gilchrest, is standing on the highest step. Nancy was Simon Towle's sister. (William Johnston Jr.)

This portrait of Simon Towle, taken around 1890, shows him at age 57. Towle lived in Lowell with his sister Nancy and her photographer husband, George C. Gilchrest, with whom Towle shared a photograph studio on Merrimack Street. Towle was a prolific professional photographer on the east coast of New England and was responsible for all photographs within this book that are credited to the Chelmsford Public Library and William Johnston Jr. (Tim Tyler Fraize.)

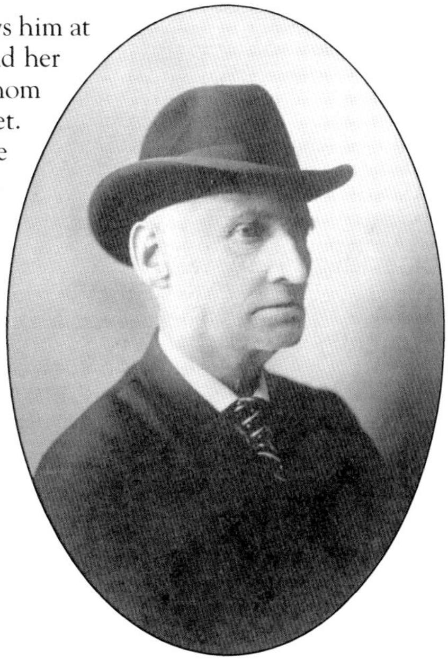

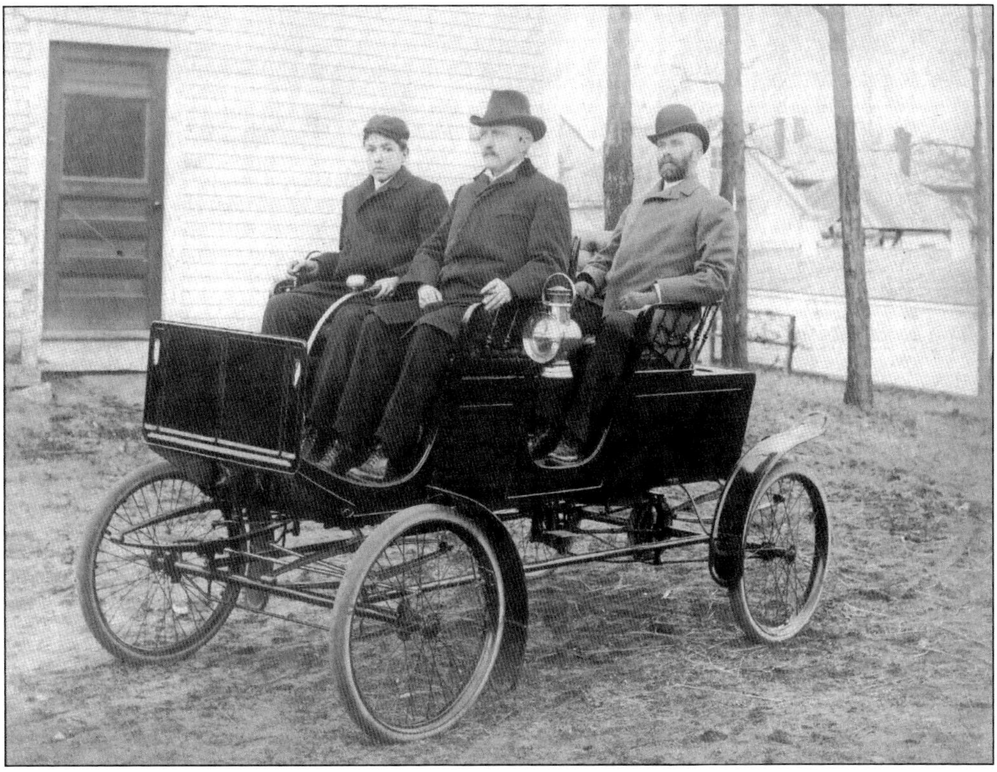

From left to right, George C. Moore Jr. (holding the steering tiller), George C. Moore Sr., and George Sr.'s first cousin Harry Moore pose in a new 1899 Locomobile steam car built in Newton, Massachusetts. This was a rare extended model with a second bench seat. George Sr. was a lifelong automobile enthusiast—called "autoists" at the time—and one of the first people in Chelmsford to own a car. (William Johnston Jr.)

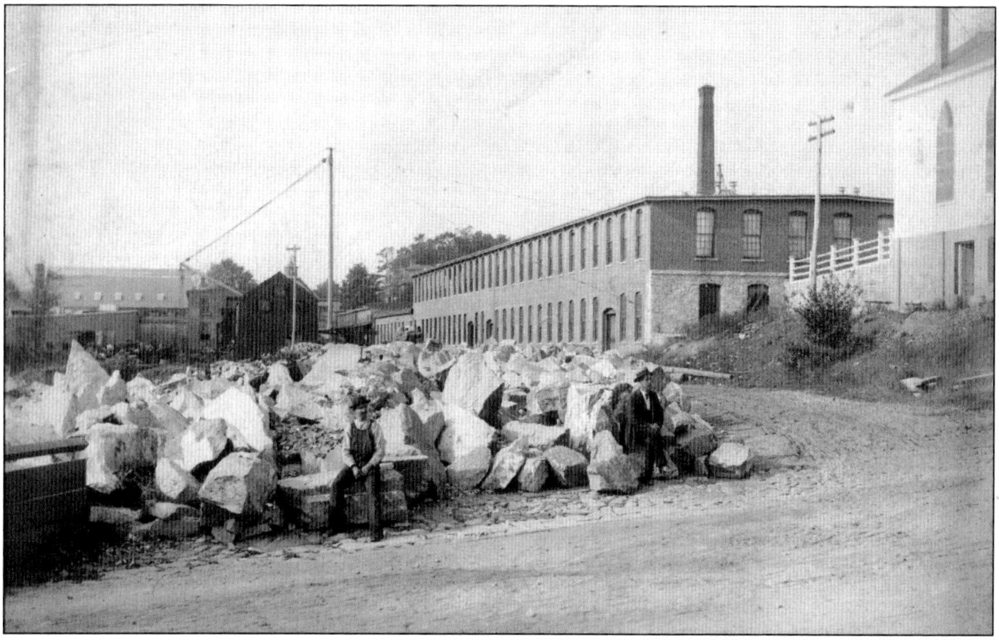

The one-story section of George C. Moore's mill (pictured) was built in 1877 on the site of a disastrous 1875 fire. The right half of the two-story section was built in 1885, and the left half in 1888, replacing a one-story section. The Chelmsford Foundry Company is at left, and the Second Congregational Church is at far right, with the E.H. Shaw and Sons store underneath. (William Johnston Jr.)

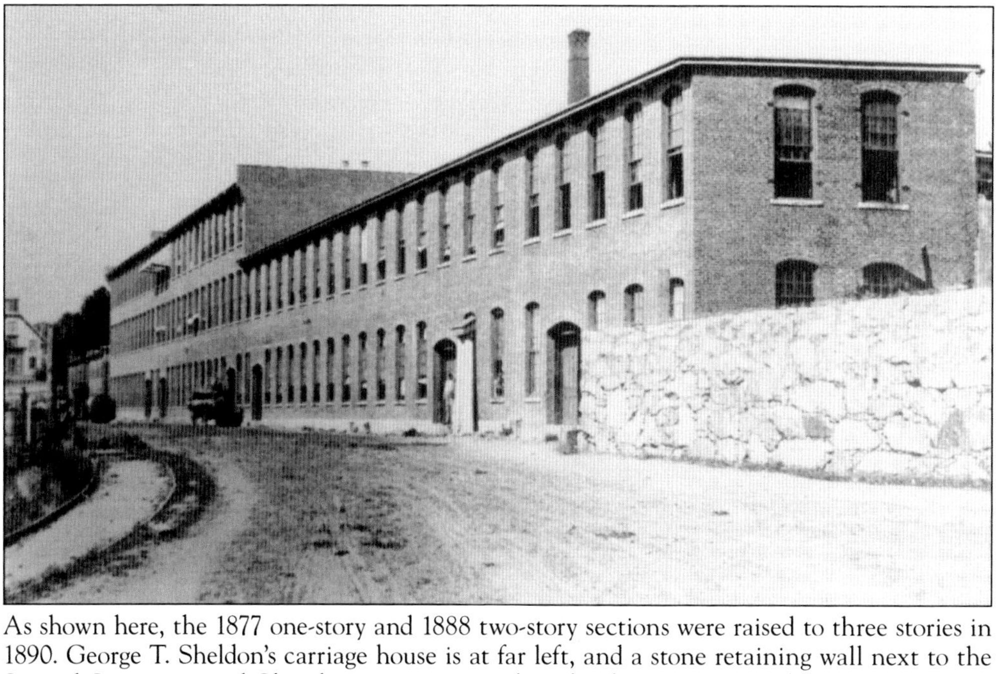

As shown here, the 1877 one-story and 1888 two-story sections were raised to three stories in 1890. George T. Sheldon's carriage house is at far left, and a stone retaining wall next to the Second Congregational Church property is at right. The short two-story addition by the stone wall was built late in 1888 and housed offices upstairs and a carpenter shop below. (Chelmsford Historical Society.)

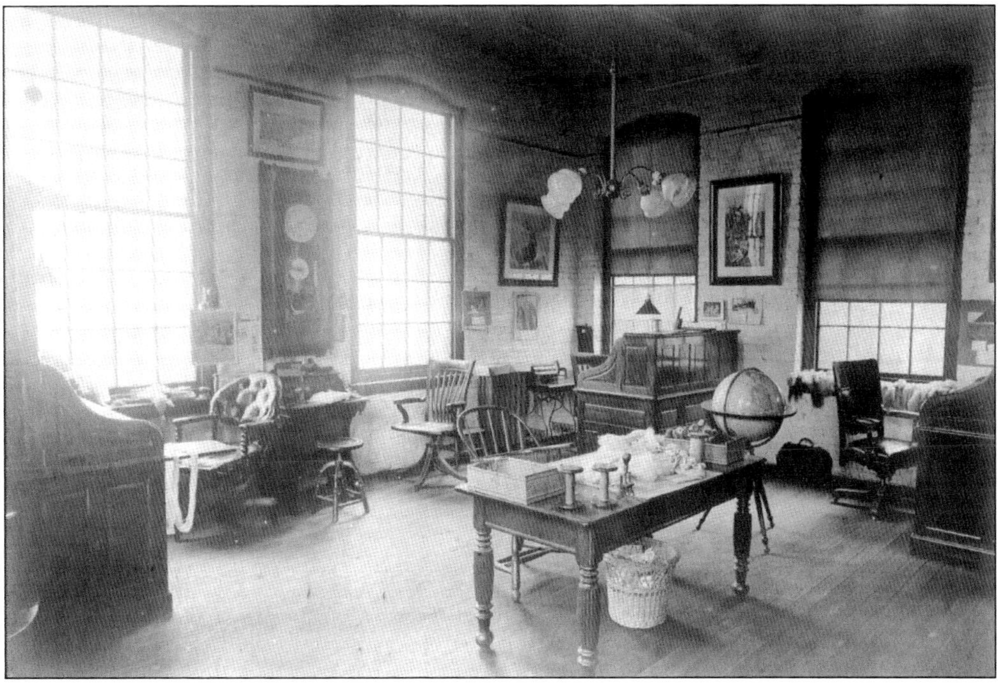

This c. 1889 photograph shows the private office located behind the Second Congregational Church. These desks could have belonged to George C. Moore, bookkeeper L.S. Hastings, and paymaster William Brown, who was a former Lowell newspaperman. The "watch clock" located between the windows synchronized all company operations. Moore, an early adopter of telephone service, connected through the small switchboard underneath the clock. (William Johnston Jr.)

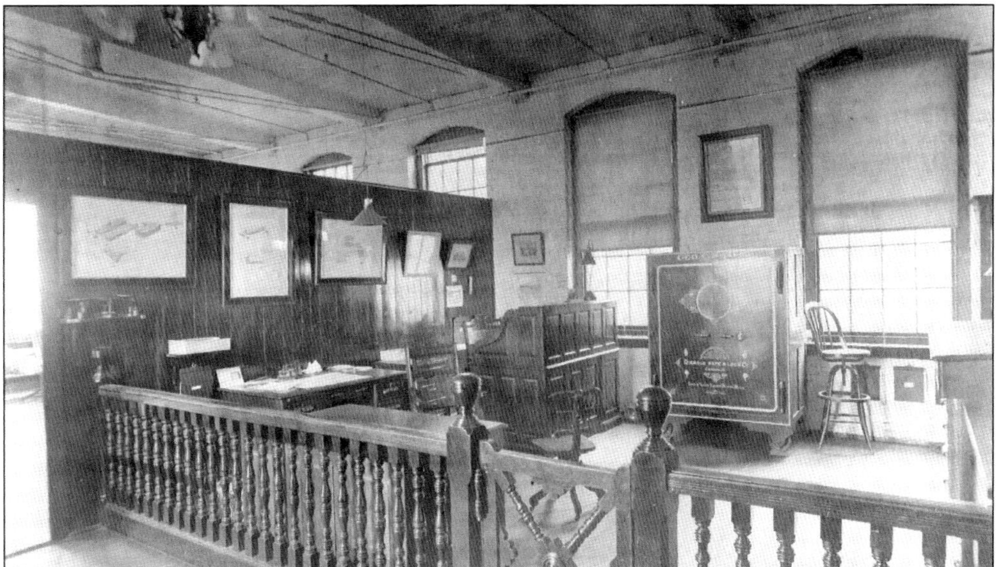

The main office, where John O'Connor presided as superintendent of Moore's mill, included a new Diebold safe. It was described in the September 21, 1888, *Lowell Daily Courier* as "the large new anti-dynamite safe in the main office . . . as complete a coffer for the puzzling of cracksmen and the resisting of fire as the latest and most ingenious inventions can secure." (William Johnston Jr.)

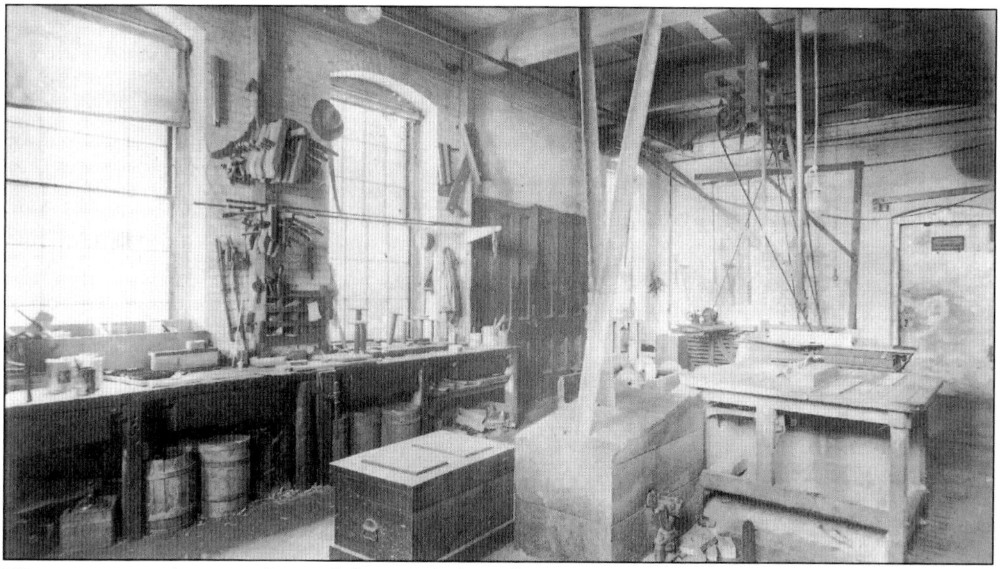

This carpenter shop was located directly below the superintendent's office until the office was moved up one story in 1980. The table saw, small lathe, and planer were all connected to a line shaft by a complicated system of belts and pulleys. Exposed fast moving belts were a hazard that employees had to be wary of throughout the mill. Serious injuries did occasionally happen. (William Johnston Jr.)

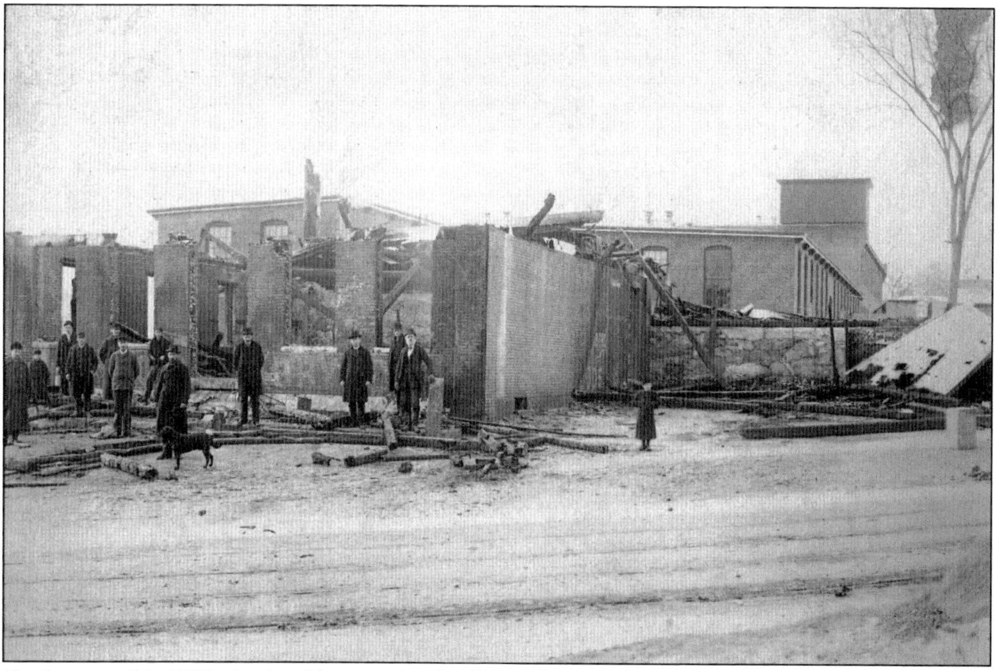

On January 20, 1893, the bookkeeper for the E.H. Shaw and Sons store had a kerosene lantern on the floor to keep warm when a dog ran through and knocked it over, spilling the fuel. The Lowell fire department prevented the flames from spreading to George C. Moore's nearby office wing, but the store and church above it were lost. The boy at far right is Bill Tobin, who later became a well-known railroad employee. (Chelmsford Public Library.)

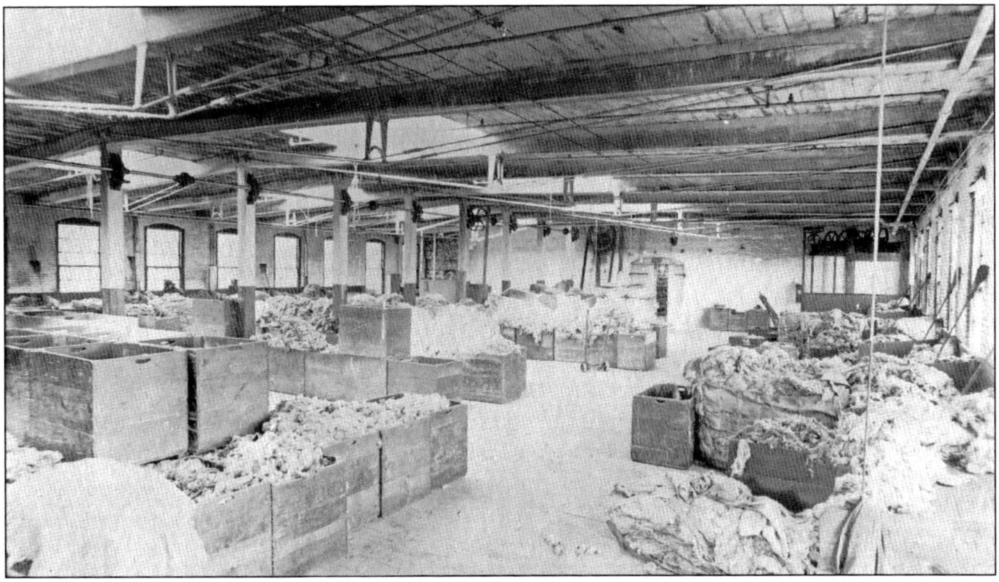

This is a series of seven photographs taken inside Moore's No. 1 Mill around 1897 showing the various stages of wool production. Wool was first delivered to the third floor of Section 1 for sorting into several different grades, with wool from a sheep's upper back and sides being the best. Edgar A. Dixon was the supervisor of this department. Note the elevator in the right rear corner. (William Johnston Jr.)

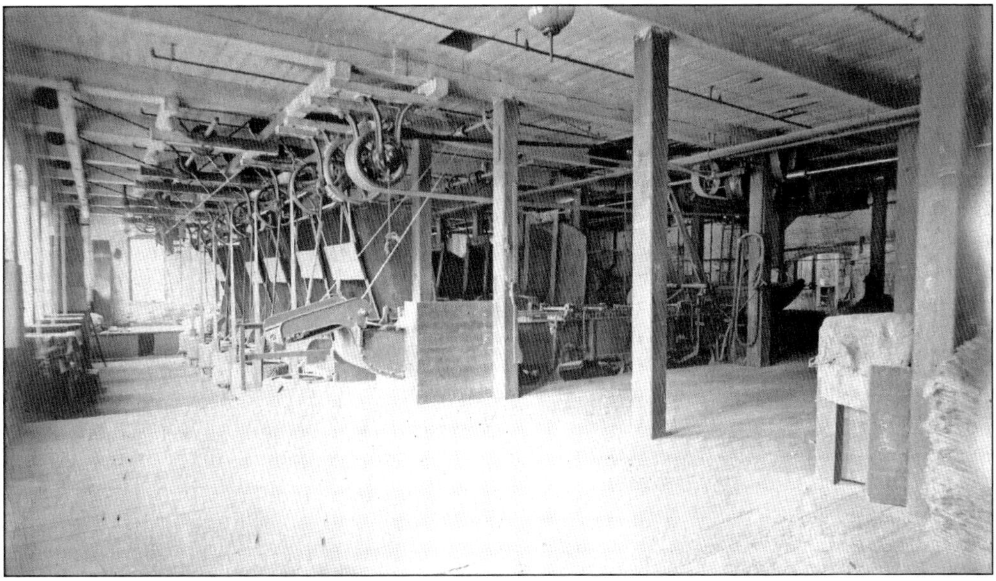

The second step in wool processing was scouring. At least half the weight of incoming wool was grease and dirt. In this scouring room on the first floor of Section 1, wool was tipped into a hot water and soap bath from a hopper on the right, run through stages of washing and rinsing, and finished up in a spin dryer on the left. George C. Moore himself designed the equipment. (William Johnston Jr.)

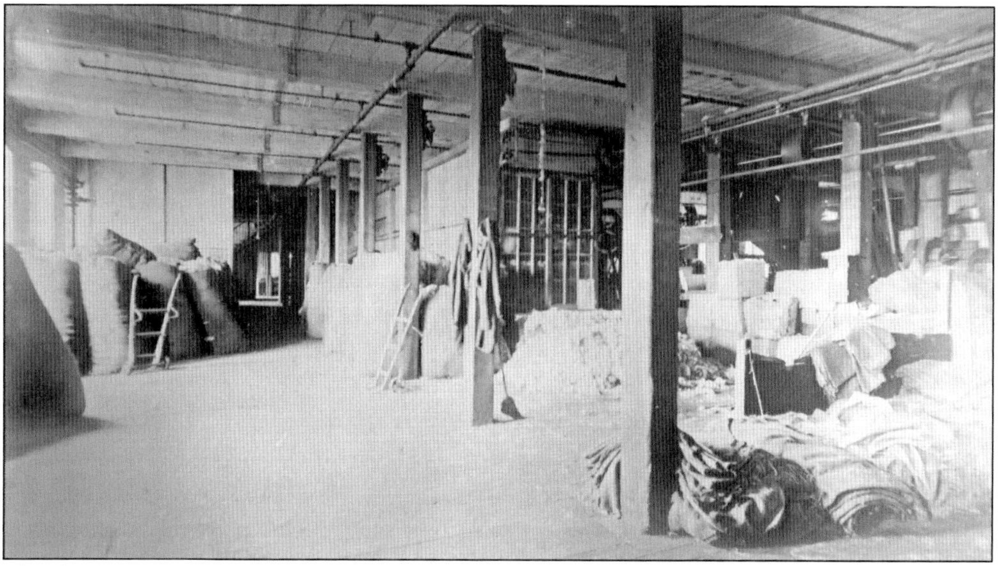

The third step in wool processing was to dry the wool and beat it into a fluffy mass. This dryer, also designed by George C. Moore, was capable of drying 25,000 pounds of clean wool per day by conveying wool through air heated by steam. This dryer was on the first floor of Section 2, and plans indicate there were two additional dryers in the third-floor Section 1 sorting room. (William Johnston Jr.)

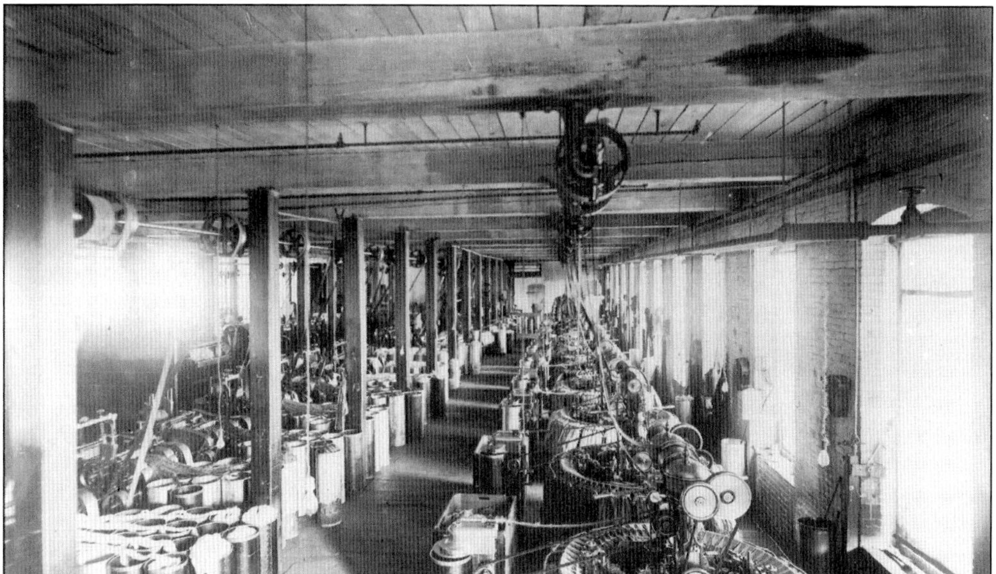

The fourth, fifth, and sixth steps in the processing of worsted yarn were carding, drawing, and combing. Woolen yarn did not go through this drawing and combing process. The carding machinery is in the overexposed left background, the drawing machinery is at left center, and the combing machinery is at center. This was the first floor of Section 3, where John H. McEnaney supervised carding and Jerimiah O'Connor supervised combing. (William Johnston Jr.)

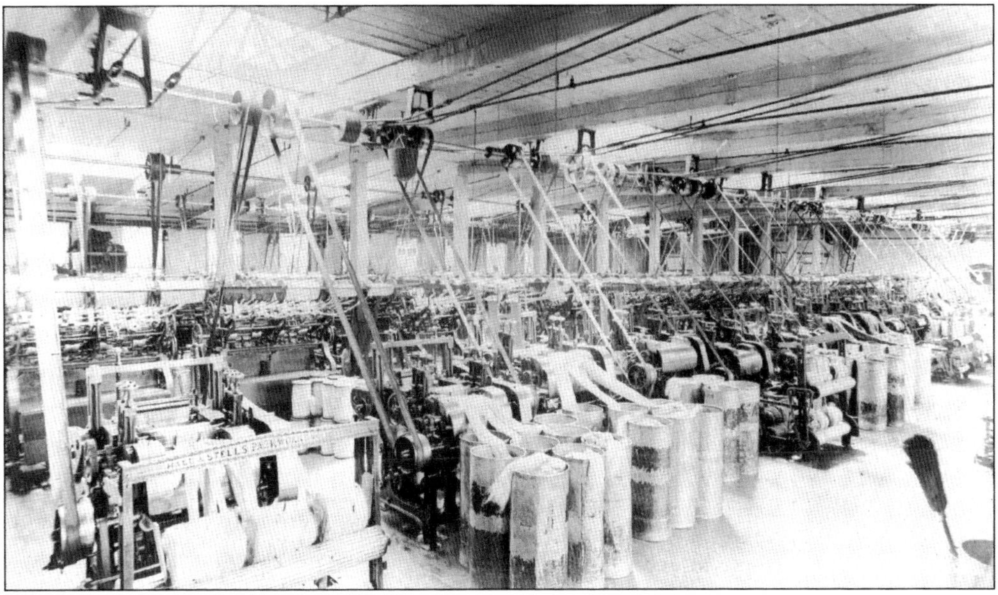

The fifth step for woolen yarn was to combine and stretch out loose sliver (rhymes with diver) resulting from carding. The equipment in the foreground combines sliver from several cans, stretching and lightly twisting the result into thick roving on large spools. Drawing equipment in the background stretches four to seven spools of roving onto one spool. This room was on the third floor of Section 2. (William Johnston Jr.)

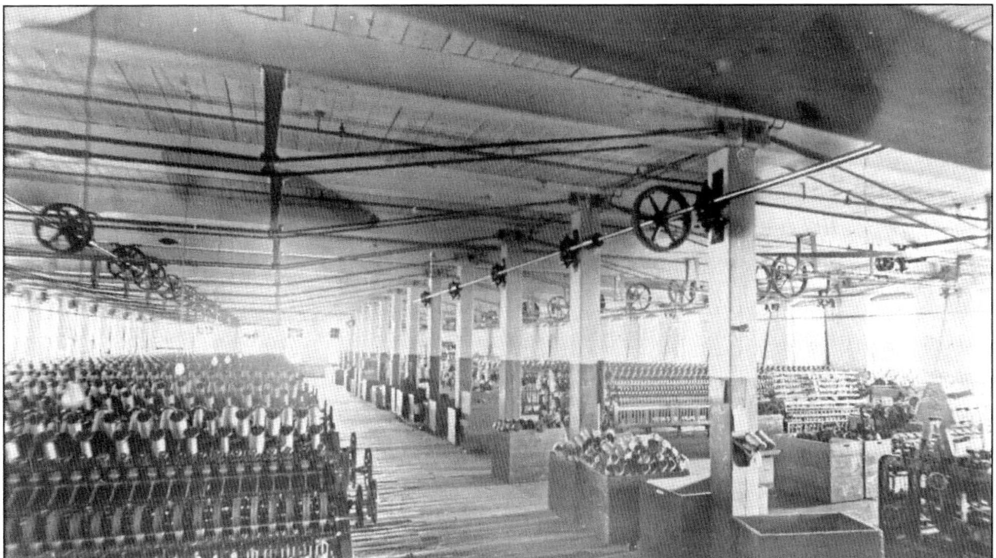

The final step for both worsted and woolen yarn was the spinning process, which stretched and twisted the combed or uncombed roving into yarn for delivery to the customer. There were mechanical adjustments on the machines to control the thickness and twist density of the yarn depending on the customer's requirements. This spinning room was on the second floor of Section 3, where Michael J. Gallagher worked as overseer. (William Johnston Jr.)

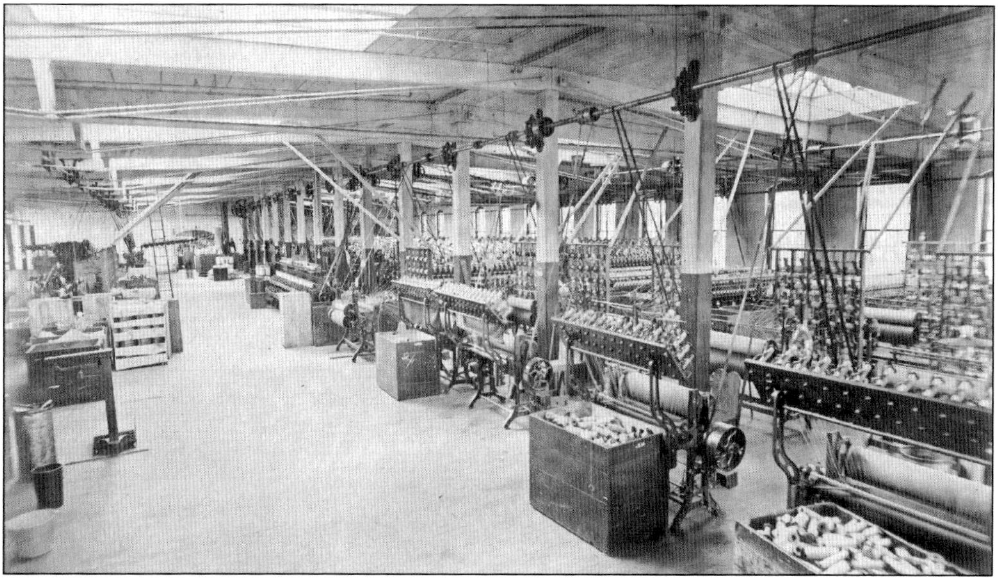

Woolen yarn was most commonly used in making tufted carpet, woven carpet, woven fabric, or knitted fabric. In preparation for weaving fabric, multiple spools of yarn are simultaneously wound onto a long reel with the thread count and spacing set up to match the destination loom, as shown in this room. This reeling room was located on the third floor of Section 3. (William Johnston Jr.)

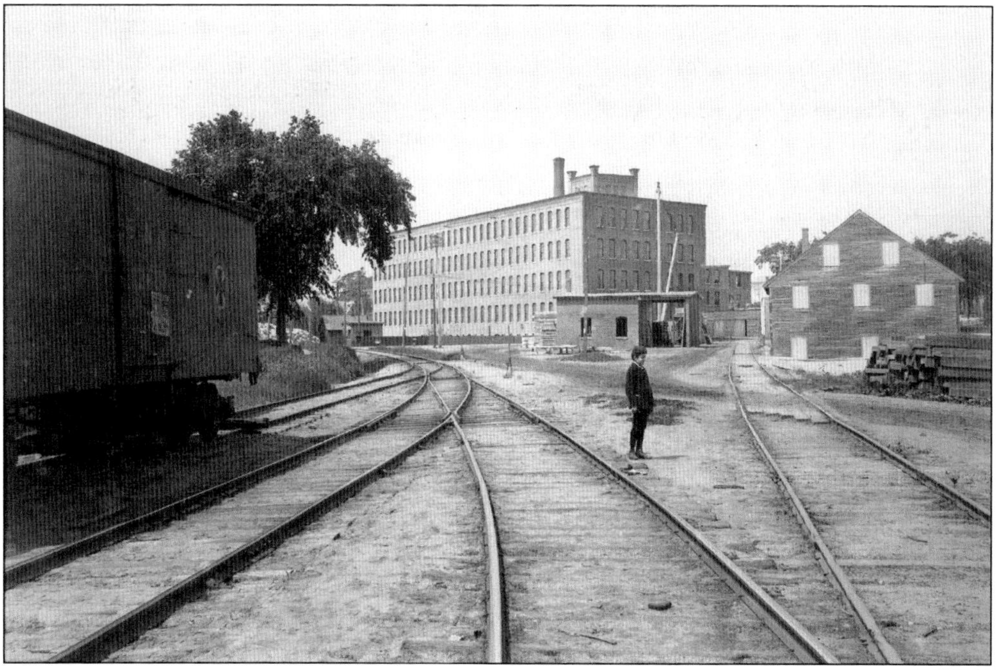

The wooden storehouse building at right was purchased by George C. Moore in 1887 as part of a grist and sawmill property. In 1896, he completed the five-story brick storehouse at center, which had five acres of floor space and a storage capacity of 12 million pounds. The foundation straddled Stony Brook, making use of previously wasted real estate. The boy in the foreground is George C. Moore Jr. (Chelmsford Public Library.)

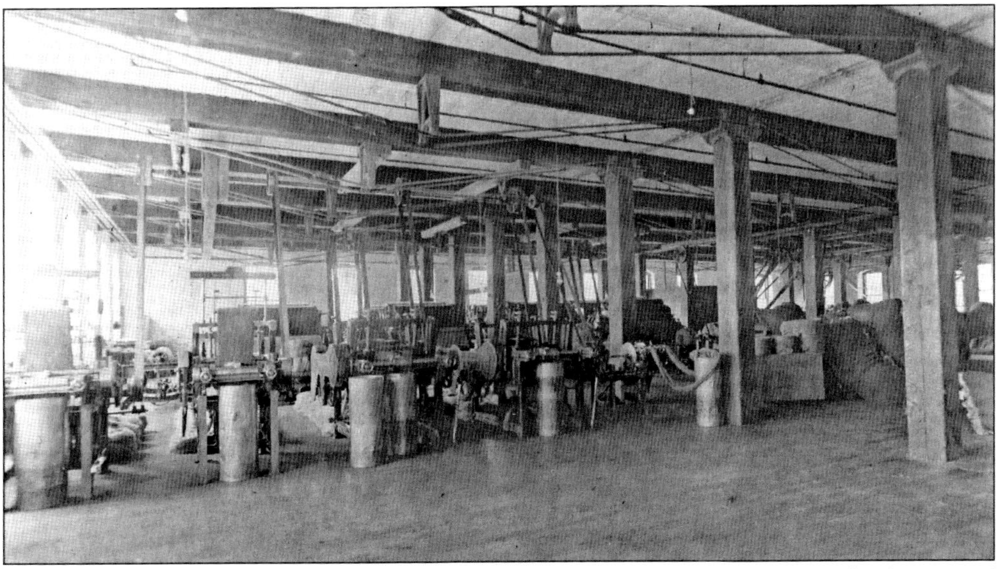

This picture of the first floor of the storehouse shows some drawing frames in the foreground and carding machines in the background. Each post could support a 700,000-pound load, and each beam could support 90,000 pounds with the iron trusses shown here. The building had a sprinkler system (supplied by four 20,000-gallon tanks in the top of the tower), steam heat, and a state-of-the-art freight elevator. (William Johnston Jr.)

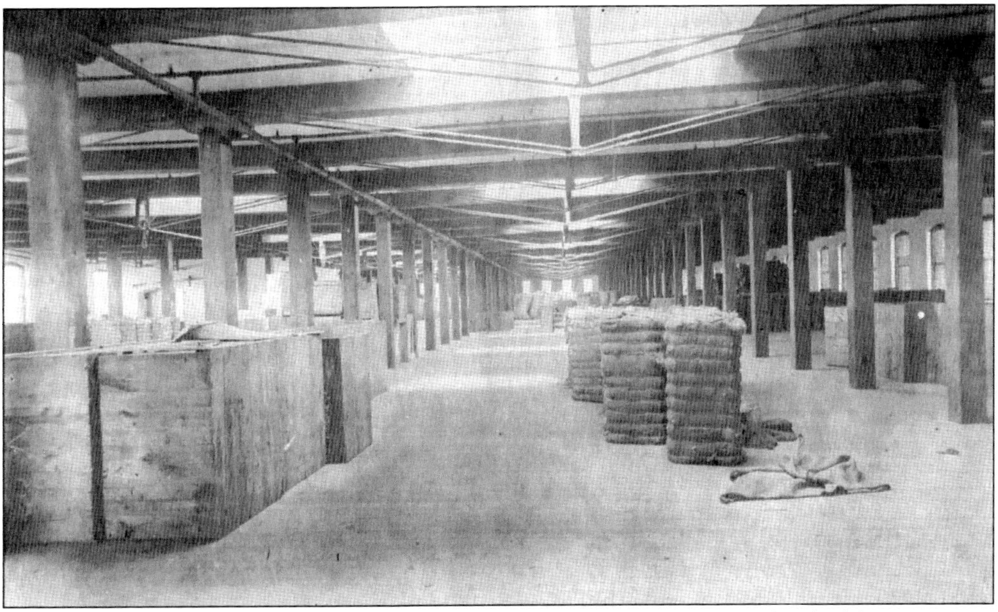

This was the fifth floor of the storehouse. Wool was shipped to North Chelmsford for processing from countries all over the world. By 1897, Moore was processing 24 million pounds of grease wool for traders in Boston and 10 million pounds of his own every year. The inside of the repurposed storehouse looks the same 120 years later, but the skylights are gone, and two freight-only elevators replaced the original. (William Johnston Jr.)

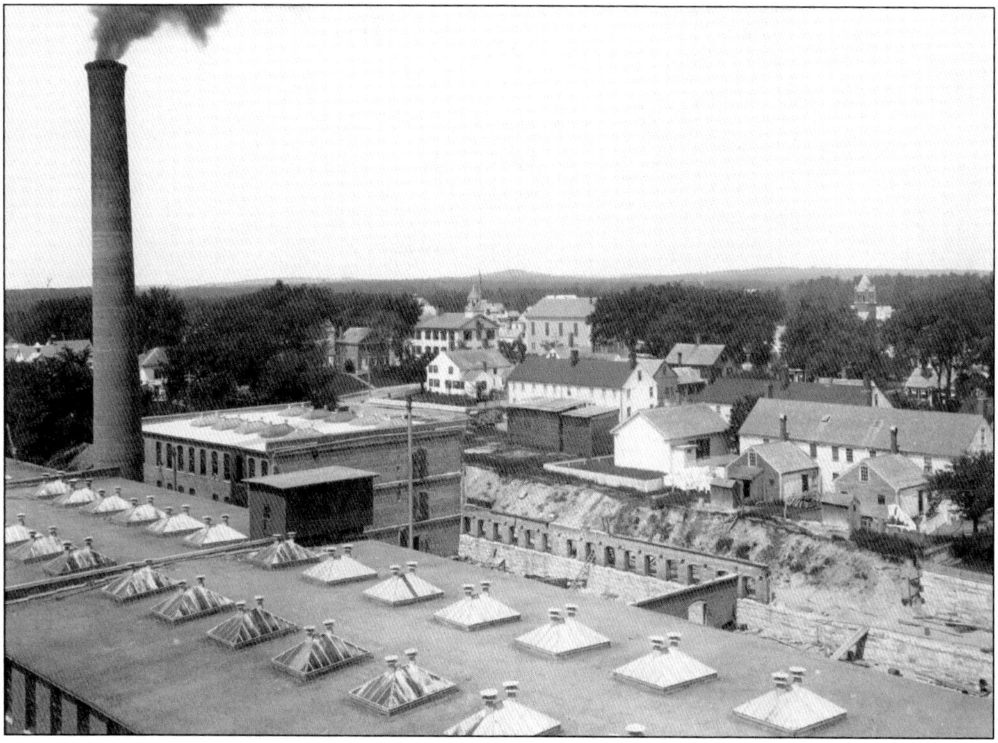

The above photograph was taken from the tower on the five-story storehouse around 1898. Sections 1, 2, and 3 of the No. 1 Mill are pictured from left to right in the foreground, and the completed Section 4 and unfinished Sections 5 and 6 of the No. 2 Mill are directly behind. The Princeton Street School and town hall are in the center background, and Gay Street Library is at the left end of the row house at right. The below photograph shows the completed sections 5 and 6 of the No. 2 Mill and the smokestack bristling with cellphone antennas in 2015. North Fire Station replaced the Princeton Street School, and North Town Hall was fully restored and is now listed in the National Register of Historic Places. The Gay Street Library site is now a parking lot. (Above, Chelmsford Public Library; below, photograph by the author.)

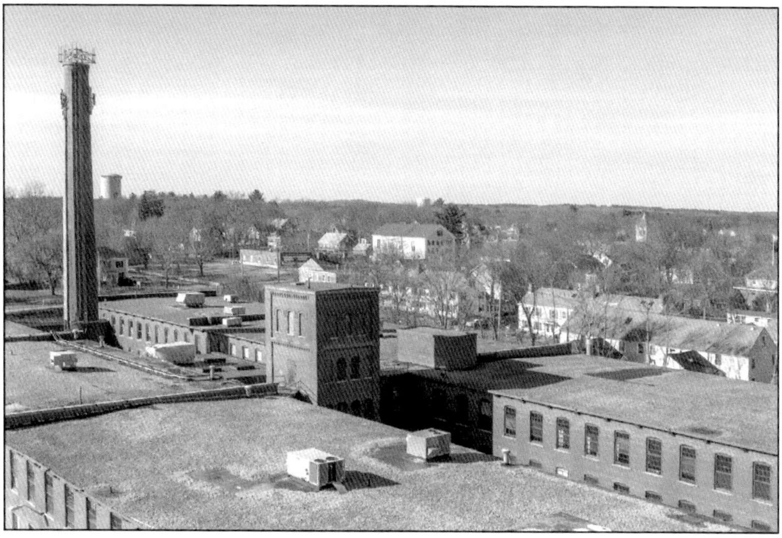

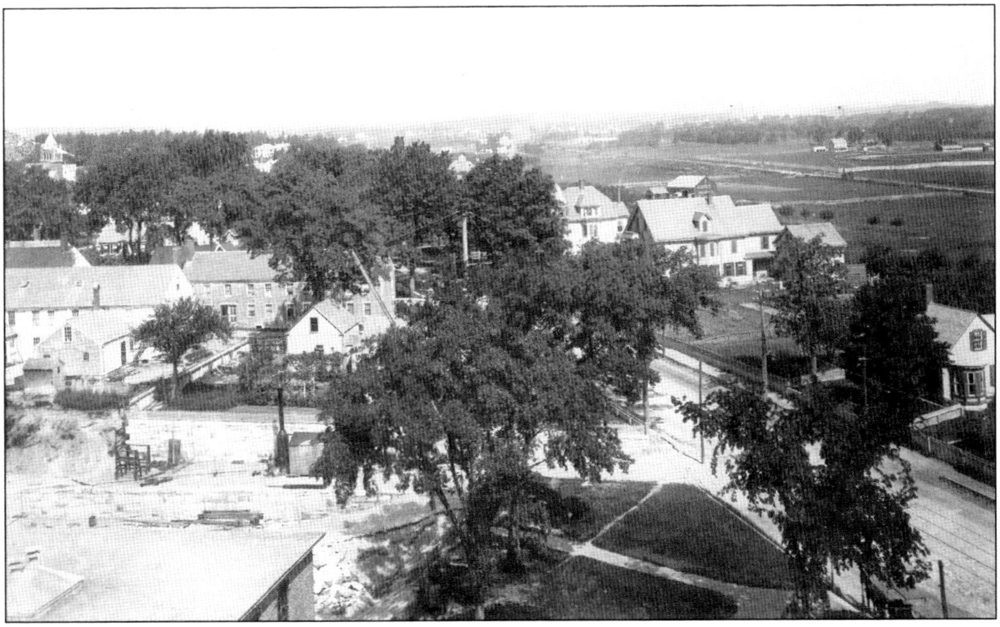

Another photograph from the storehouse tower shows the Second Congregational Church at top left, the No. 2 Mill construction site at left center, and the lawn and paths of the former church property at lower center. Wannalancit Park, at top right, was a popular horse- and dog-racing track operated by Frank H. Harris in the late 1890s. No sign of the track or buildings remains today. (Chelmsford Public Library.)

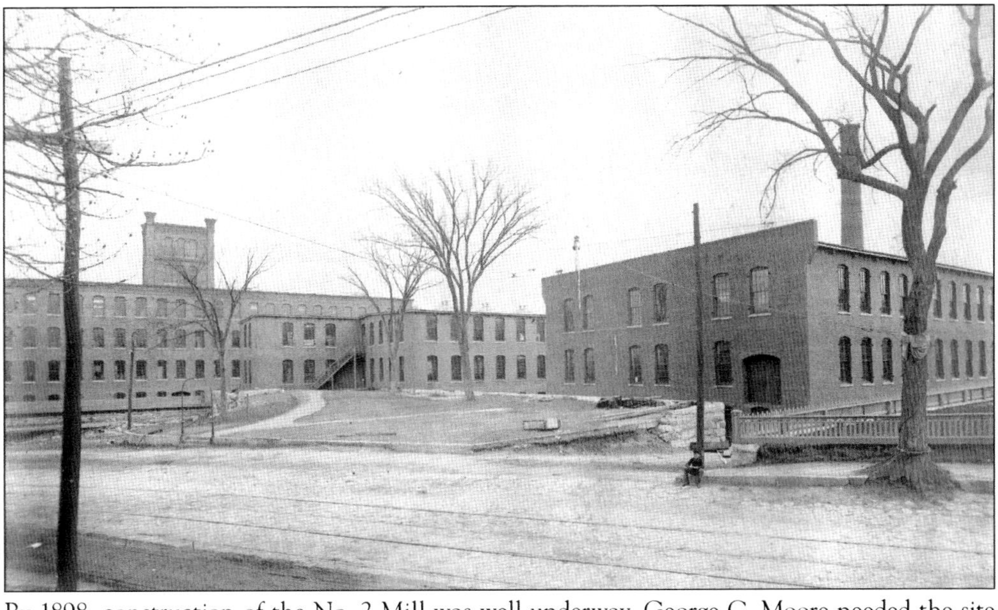

By 1898, construction of the No. 2 Mill was well underway. George C. Moore needed the site of the 1893 church fire, shown here, to complete plans for the front of the two buildings, but Elisha H. Shaw, owner of the site, would not sell it. Shaw tragically died on November 24, 1898, at only 51 years old, and his widow, Harriott, sold the land to Moore on March 2, 1899. (William Johnston Jr.)

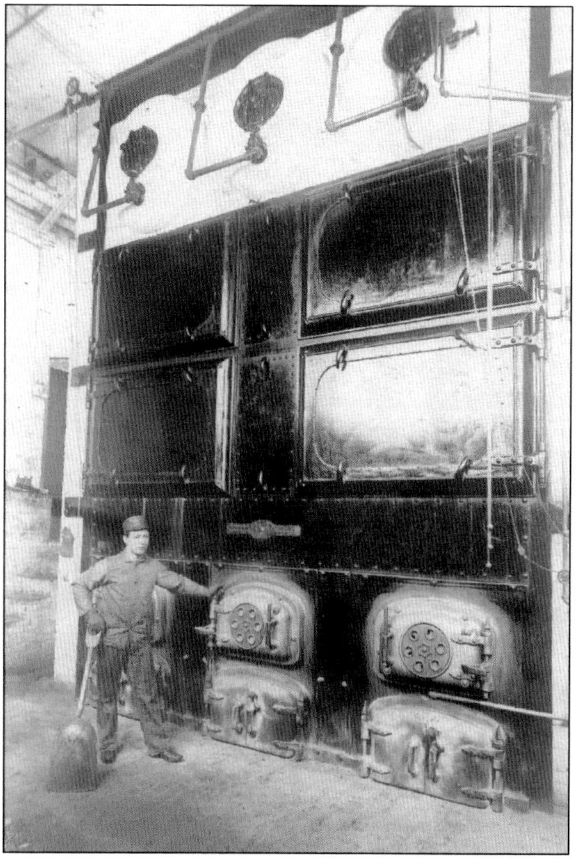

The Babcock and Wilcox boiler at left, designated as No. 3 in the boiler room located between the mills near the smokestack, was installed around 1899 to provide steam for a new 1,200-horsepower steam engine driving line shafts in the No. 2 Mill. Abner E. Hemlow, Moore's fireman, machinist, and—later—engineer, might be the man with the shovel. The No. 3 boiler was later removed and replaced, but the No. 2 boiler (below), of similar vintage but smaller, sits unused today in its original location. Starting in 1919, the mill began a transition from steam engine and water turbine power to 25-, 50-, 100-, and 150-horsepower 550-volt three-phase General Electric motors. The bankruptcy inventory of the United States Worsted Corporation's Silesia Mill in 1931 listed General Electric motors totaling about 2,000 horsepower. (Left, William Johnston Jr.; below, photograph by the author.)

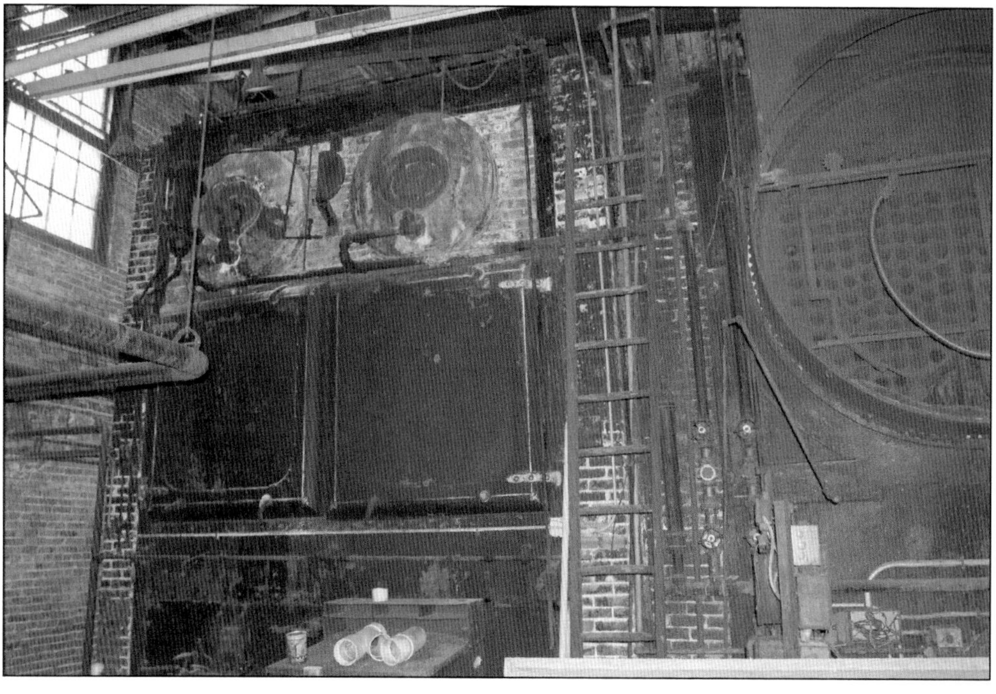

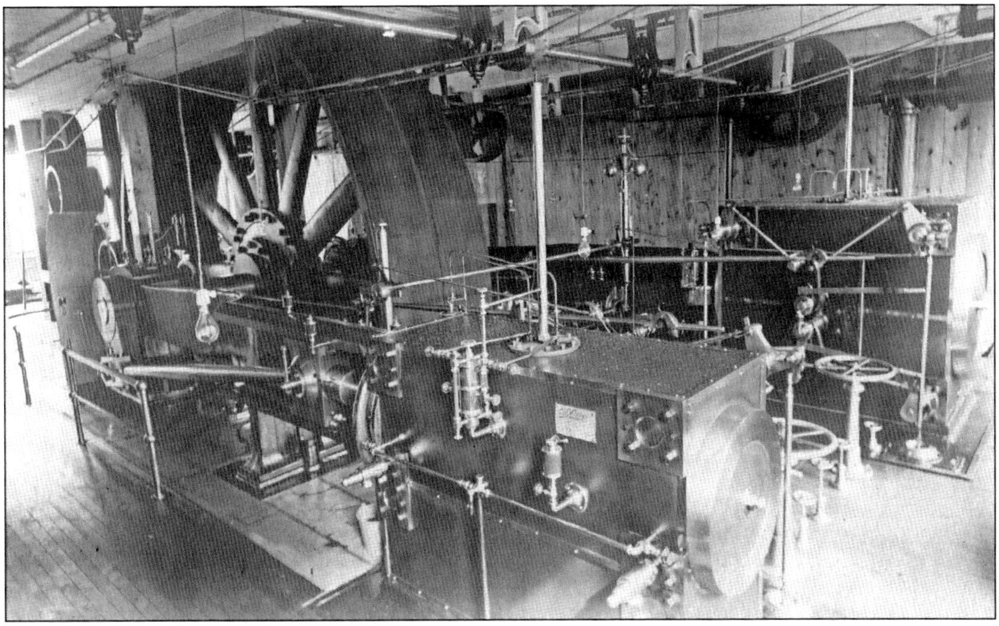

This 1,200-horsepower C. & G. Cooper double expansion horizontal engine spanned three floors of the No. 2 Mill. Exhaust steam from the high-pressure cylinder on the left powered the larger low-pressure cylinder. The rod and lever valve control system was patented by George H. Corliss of Rhode Island in 1849 and was so efficient that his design was universally adopted once the patent expired. (William Johnston Jr.)

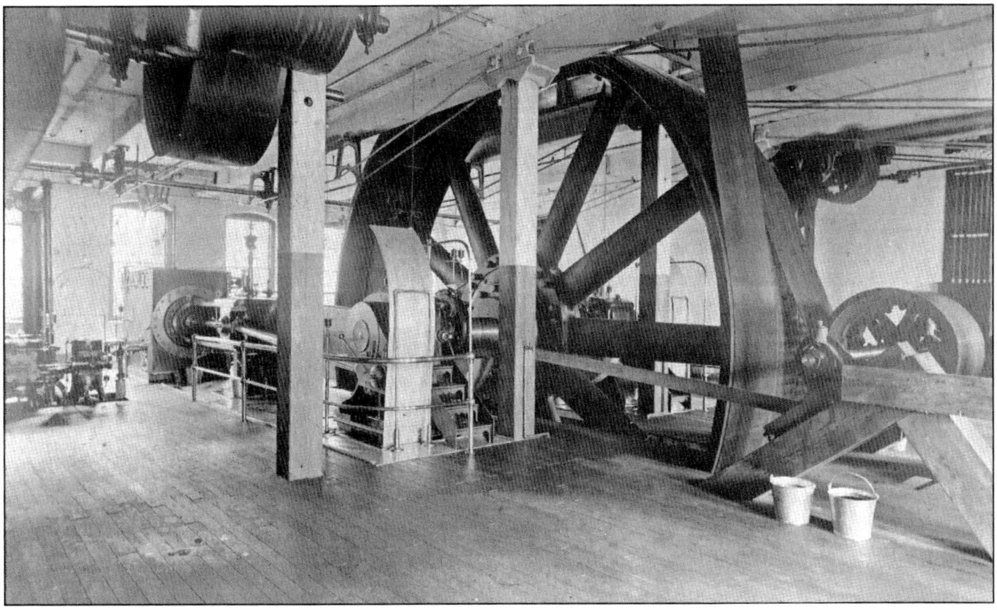

Power was coupled to line shafts distributed throughout the building via the two massive leather belts shown here on the flywheel. A fly ball governor located between the cylinders coupled into the Corliss valve gear to regulate speed, and a steam pump in the floor at left forced water from condensed steam back to the boiler. Glass and brass oilers were placed wherever a bearing needed lubrication. (William Johnston Jr.)

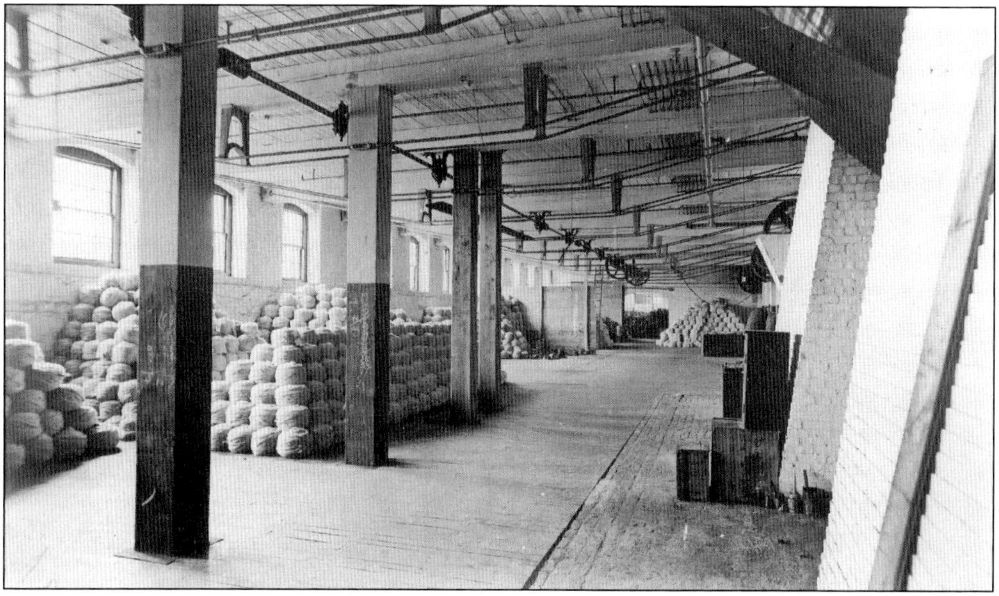

Without the solid brick structures at right supporting the main engine bearings, the huge unbalanced cranks on the Cooper engine could shake the entire building. The bottom of the flywheel, with its two leather belts, is at upper right, the electric generator line shaft is just beyond the brick towers, and "knob and tube" electric distribution wiring from the generator is on the ceiling. (William Johnston Jr.)

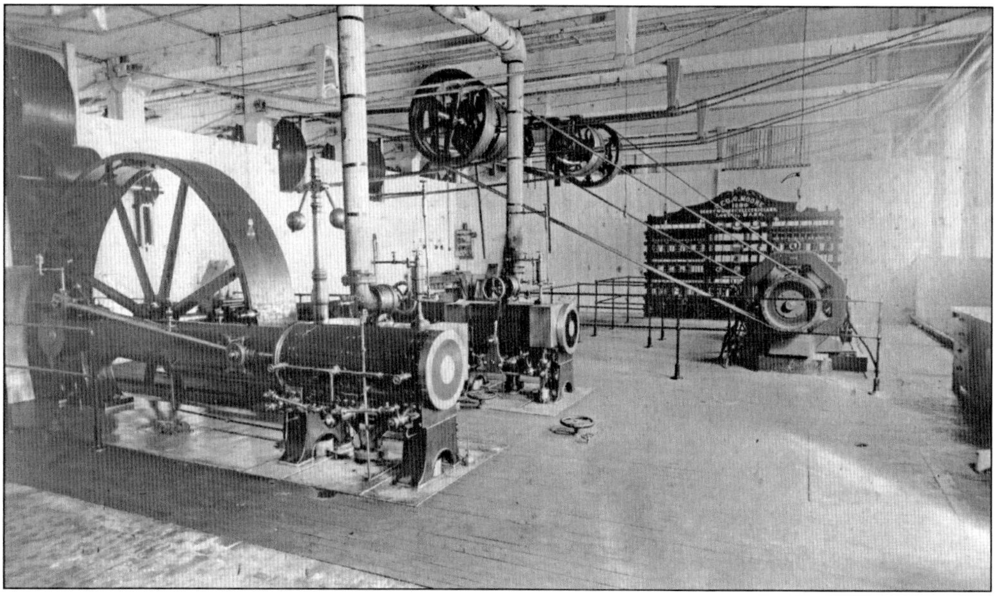

This 300-horsepower single expansion twin cylinder engine built by the Rollins Engine Company of Nashua was used to generate electricity for lighting purposes. The fly-ball governor and belt and pulley system coupling the engine to a pair of generators are clearly seen here. The custom switching and meter panel on the far wall was built for George C. Moore in 1899 by Derby & Morse Electricians of Lowell. (William Johnston Jr.)

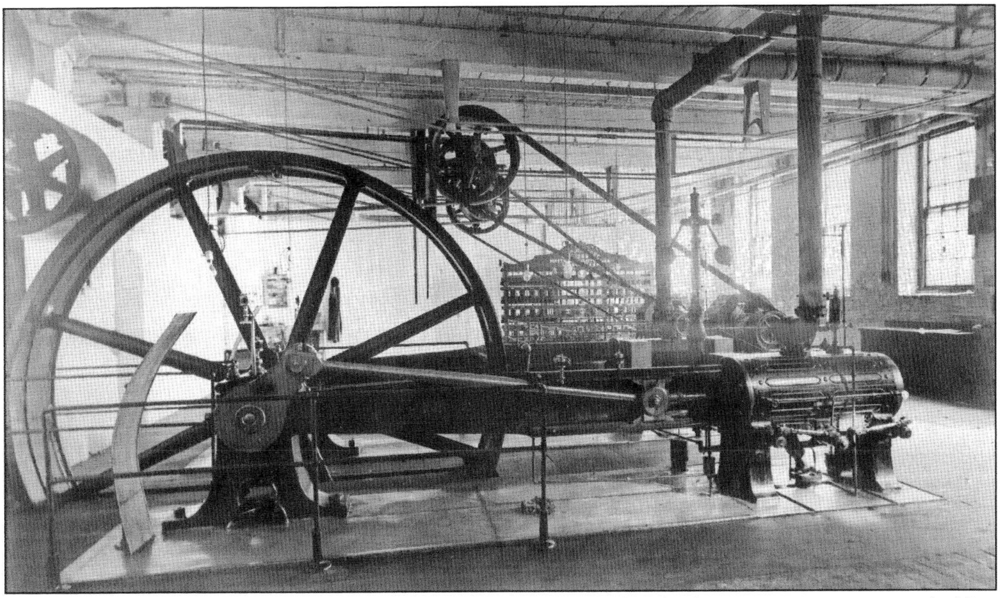

Prior to approval of a municipal water supply for North Chelmsford in 1906, Moore provided his own water supply for fire protection. Steam engines such as this one were not suitable for pumping water for fire protection 24 hours a day on short notice, so mill canal water was used to power a 100-horsepower, locally designed Swain Turbine coupled to a pair of 1,000-gallon-per-minute pumps to provide water pressure. (William Johnston Jr.)

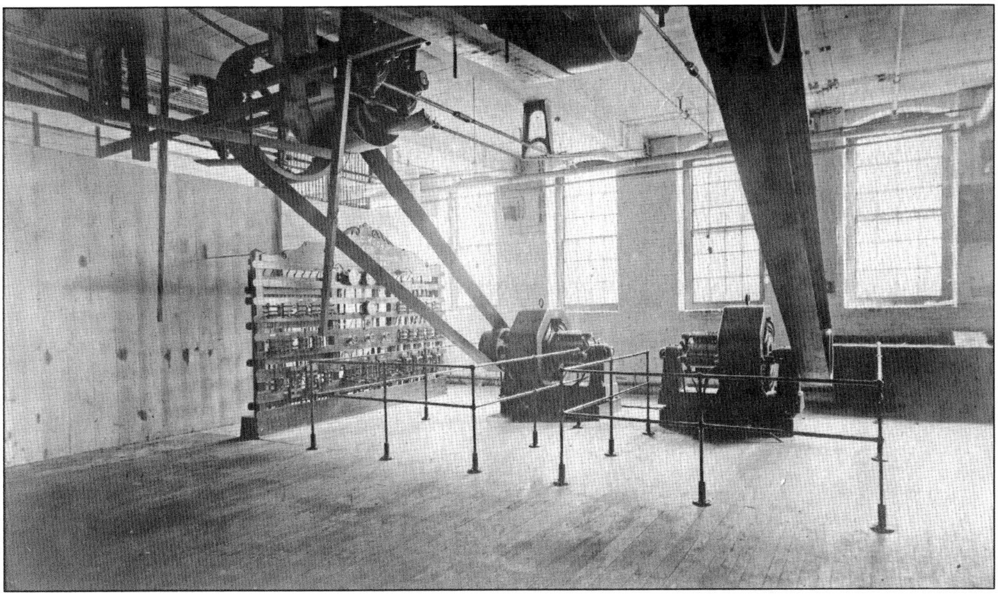

The two levers hanging from the ceiling in this image were used to push leather belts from an idler pulley onto an active pulley coupled to a generator. It was reported in the April 5, 1919, issue of *Textile World Journal* that the US Worsted Company's Silesia Mill was constructing a transformer building that would make electricity from outside utilities available for lighting and large motors in the mill complex. (William Johnston Jr.)

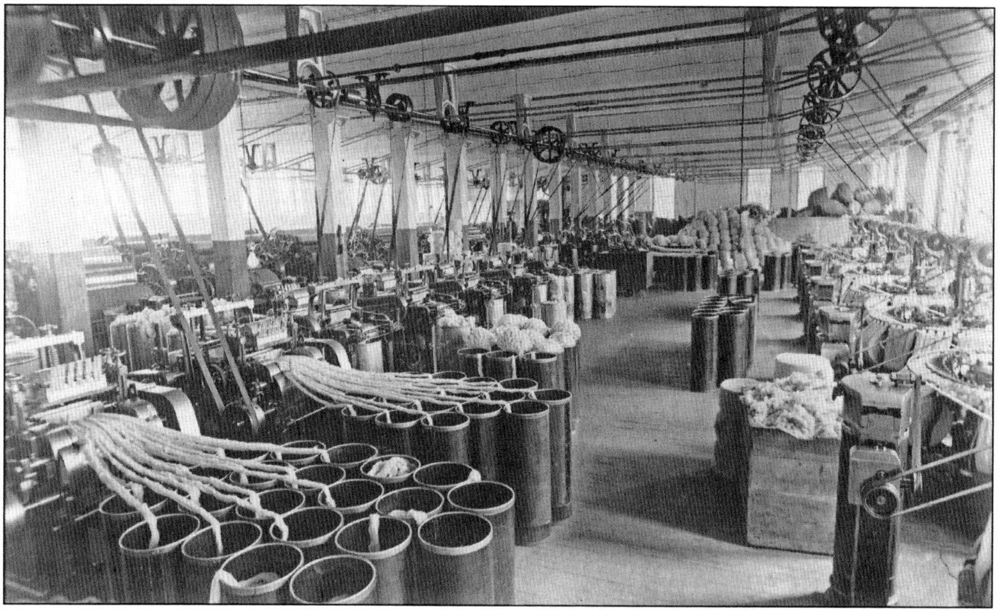

George C. Moore sold his mill complex in 1902 to the Moore Spinning Company for $1.6 million. The next 12 images show workers and machinery inside the No. 2 Mill around 1902. In the above photograph, carding machines beyond the center posts at left disentangled and separated scoured wool fibers into a gauze-like sheet that was cut into slivers and loaded into cans. Drawing frames at left stretched and lightly twisted four or more slivers into roving. The combing machines at right separated out short fibers, called noil, leaving roving suitable for worsted yarn. Balls of combed roving, called tops, were drawn and twisted again onto a large spool. This room was on the first floor of Section 6. Men traditionally worked as carders, and the group below was no exception. (Above, William Johnston Jr.; below, Chelmsford Historical Society.)

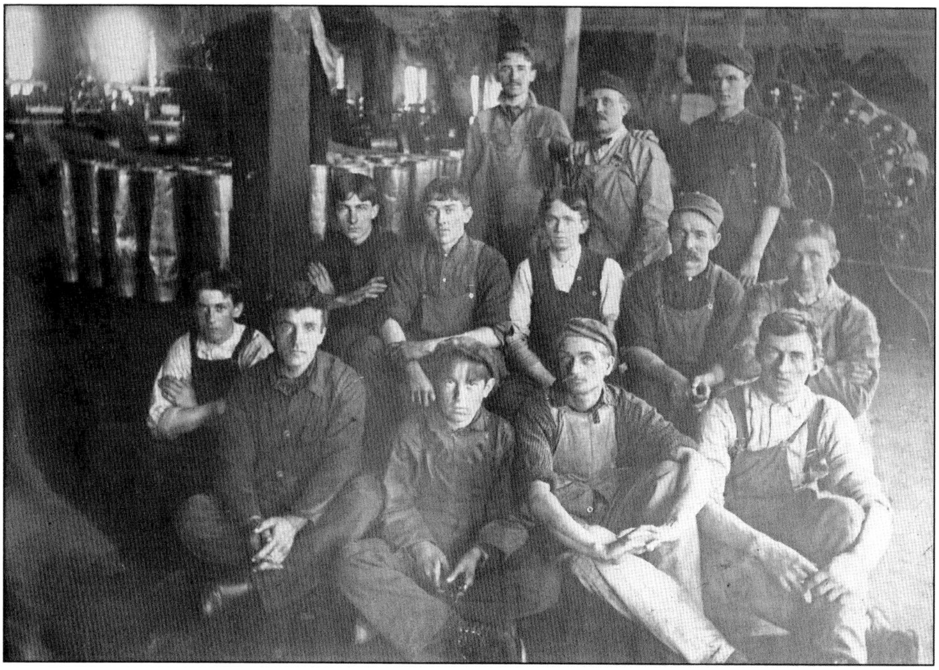

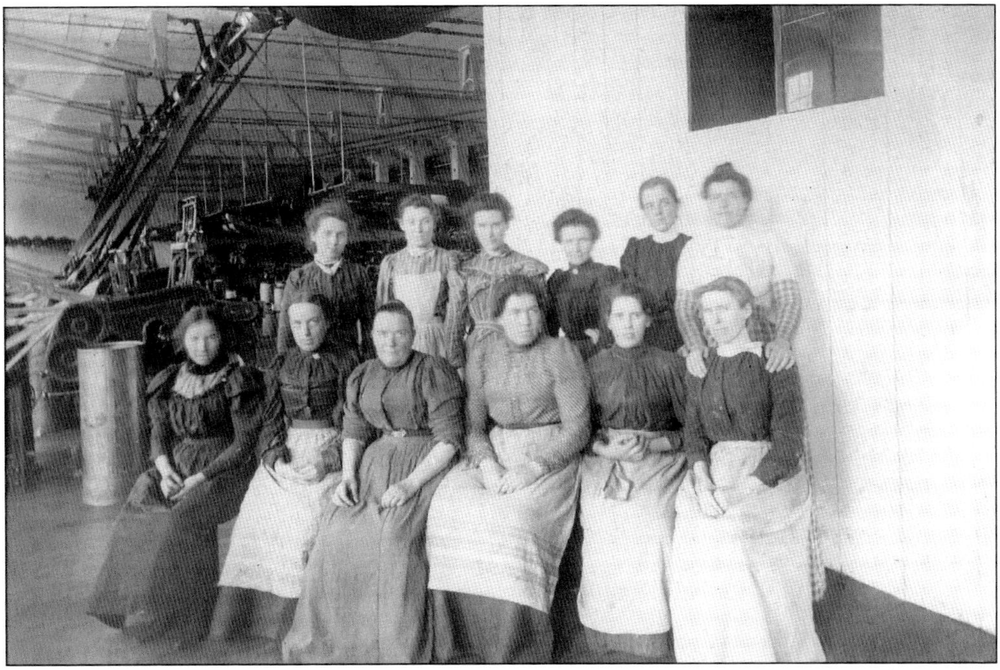

These photographs show two separate groups of hands who worked in a small drawing department on the second floor of Section 5. The Cooper steam engine occupied the other half of this floor. The drawing frames at left above are set up to unroll eight tops of combed wool, stretching them out and gently twisting them onto large roving spools. The drawing frames behind the ladies below are set up to take eight spools of roving, stretching and lightly twisting them together onto another spool for spinning into worsted yarn in another room. A broken strand of sliver or roving could be repaired by twisting the fibers together, but after this process it had to be tied with a knot. Boys could legally start working at age 12. (Both, Chelmsford Historical Society.)

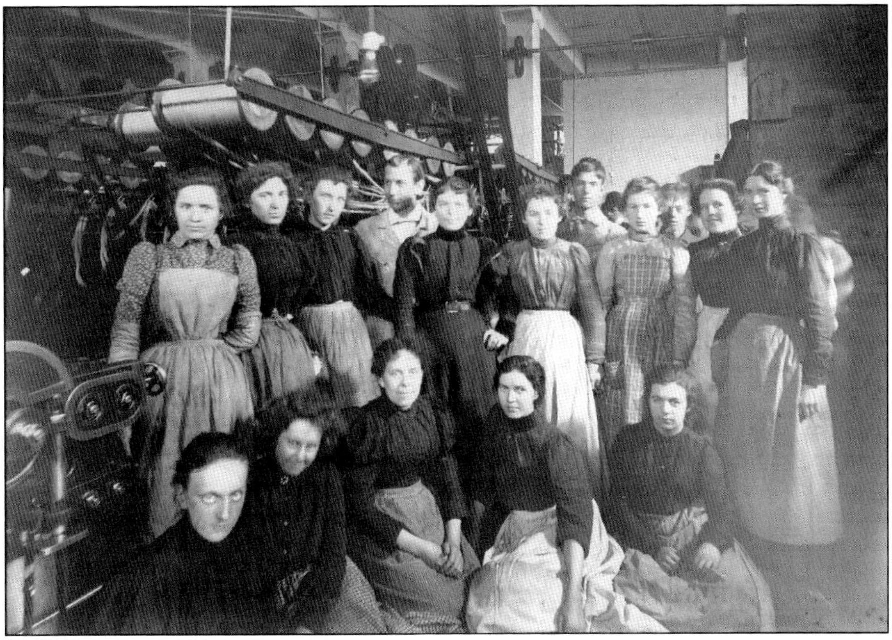

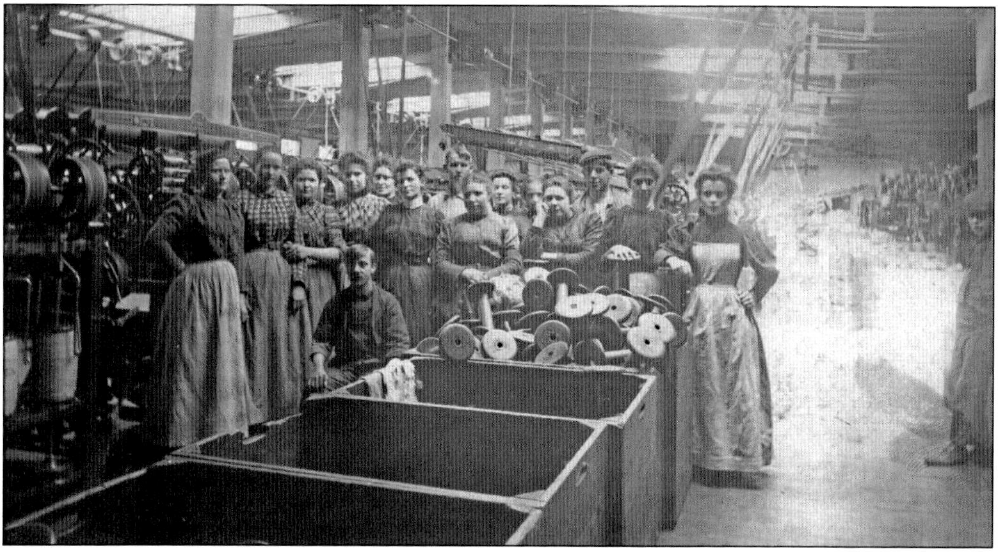

The drawing department shown here was on the third floor of the No. 1 Mill. The twisting end of a drawing frame is visible at far left, and someone walking through sunlight at right during the long exposure washed out the image on that side. George C. Moore kept his workers happy; many of them commuted by trolley from Lowell, and Moore matched salaries negotiated in the Lowell mills. (Chelmsford Historical Society.)

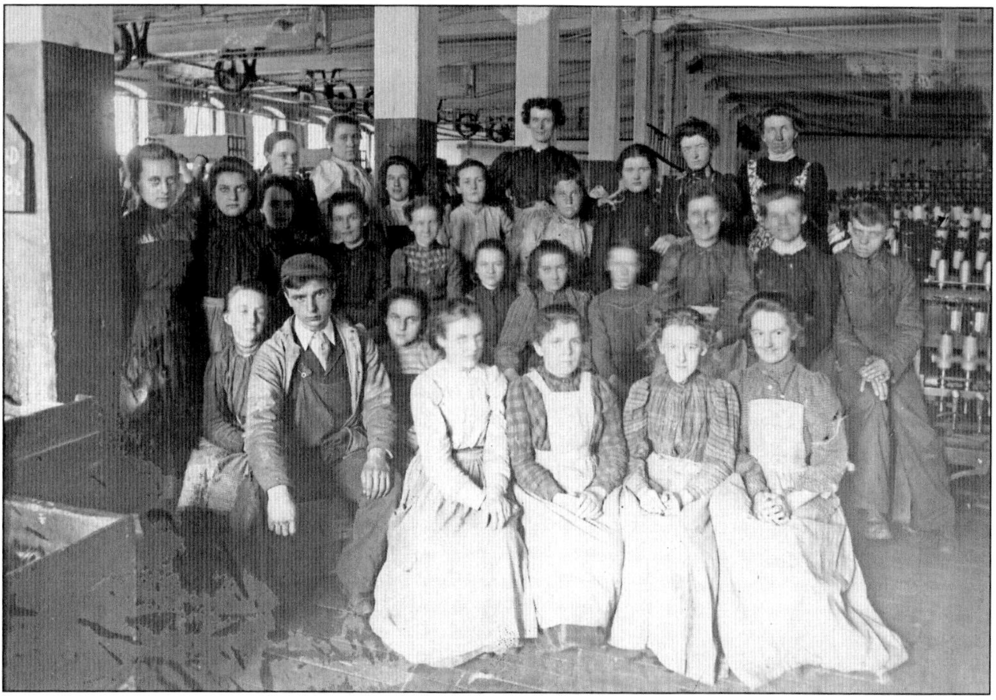

This spinning and twisting room was on the second floor of Section 6. This equipment stretched and twisted the roving into yarn with diameter and density that met customers' requirements. Spinners, sweepers, piecers, and doffers were often younger, as speed and dexterity were needed to perform their tasks. Girls usually started as spinners and boys as doffers and sweepers. Piecers tied broken threads together. (Chelmsford Historical Society.)

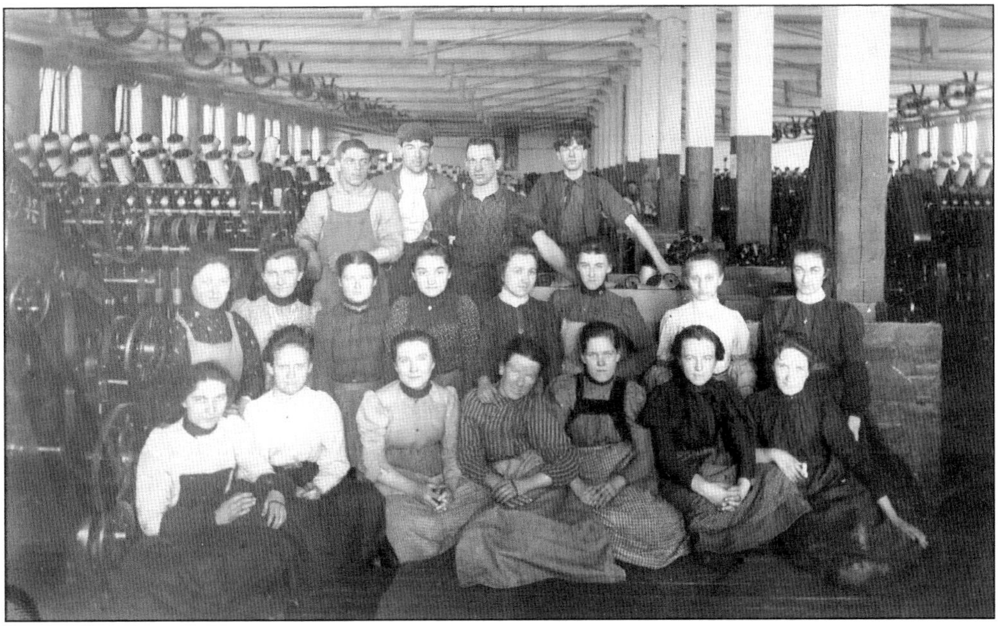

Additional spinning and twisting rooms were located on the second and third floors of Section 4. The spinning frames were shut down when their bobbins were full, and young doffers, like the boys shown below, would scramble in to remove and replace them with empties. Underage family members occasionally worked in the spinning rooms, and if anyone asked, they had to remember to say they were 12 years old. In 1904, the National Child Labor Committee was founded, and in 1907, it received a charter from Congress. In 1908, they hired photographer Lewis Hine to document child workers in Southern textile mills. Hine's compelling photographs helped a drive to reform employment laws in the United States, and by 1914, there were few children under the age of 12 working in the mills. (Both, Chelmsford Historical Society.)

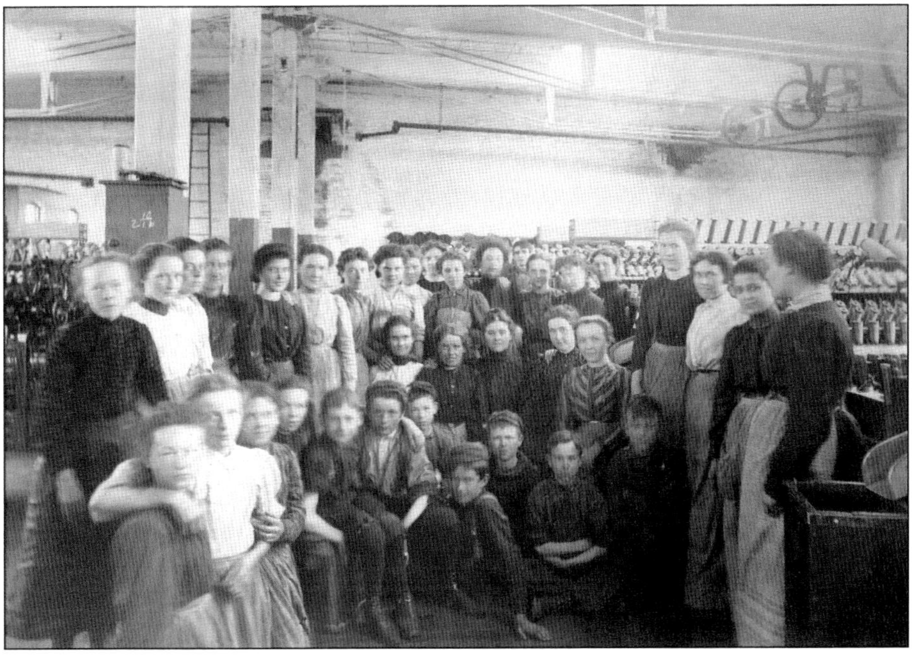

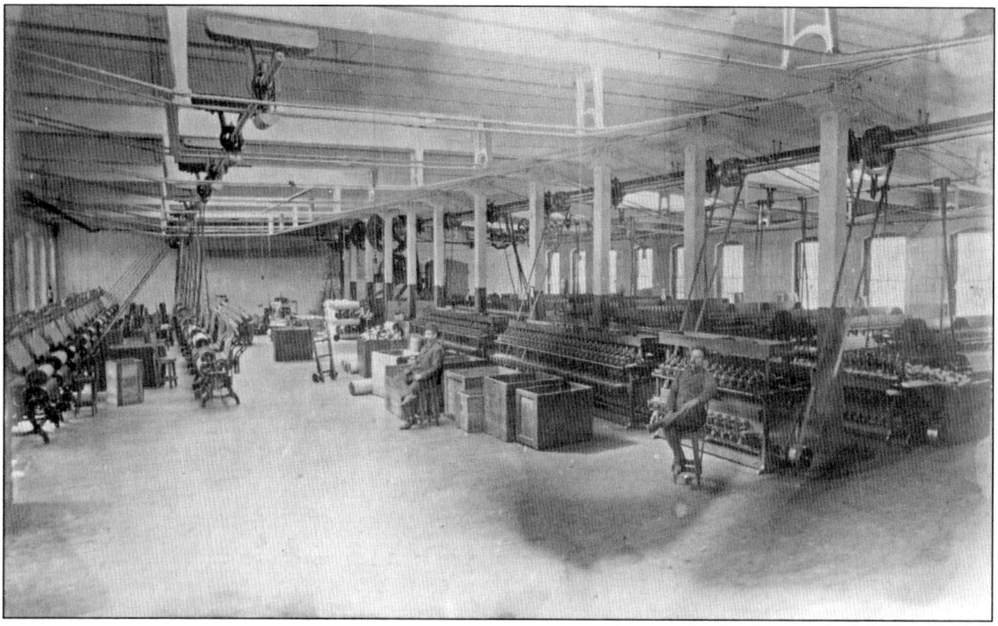

This spooling and reeling room was on the third floor of Section 5. The drive belt from the Cooper engine is visible toward the rear of the room, where it connected to the line shaft running behind the center posts. George C. Moore's businesses did not include the capability of weaving textiles, but at the time these photographs were taken, there was a weaving company next door (in Section 6) using reels of yarn produced here. One of Moore's specialties was yarn made from camel's hair, and Donald Cameron, at his Sugden Press Bagging Company in West Chelmsford, used camel's hair to make specialized cloth for pressing oil out of seeds. Although the connection is not confirmed, it would have been logical for Moore to supply camel's hair products to Cameron. (Above, William Johnston Jr.; below, Chelmsford Historical Society.)

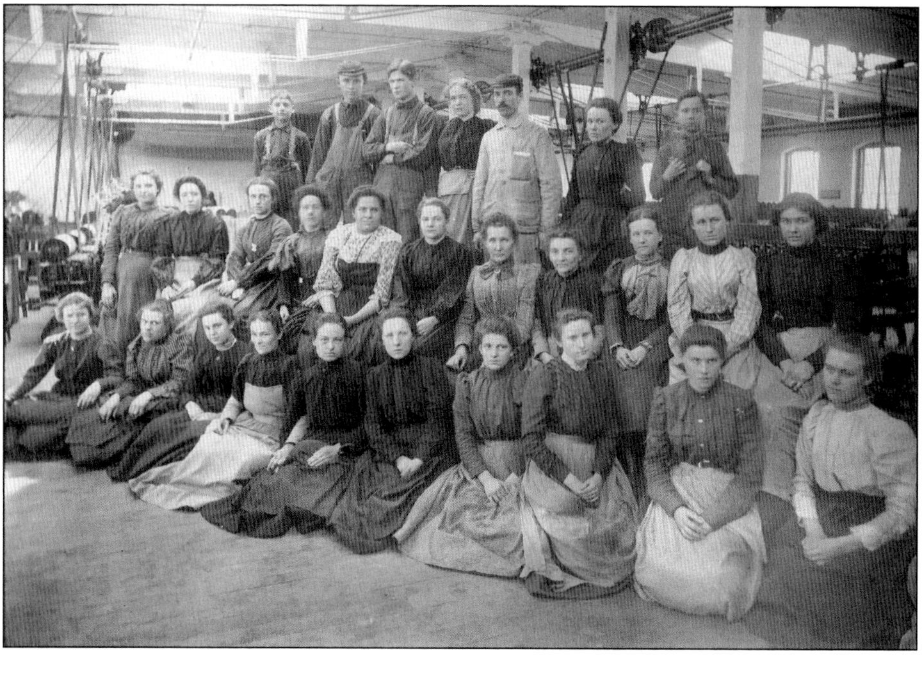

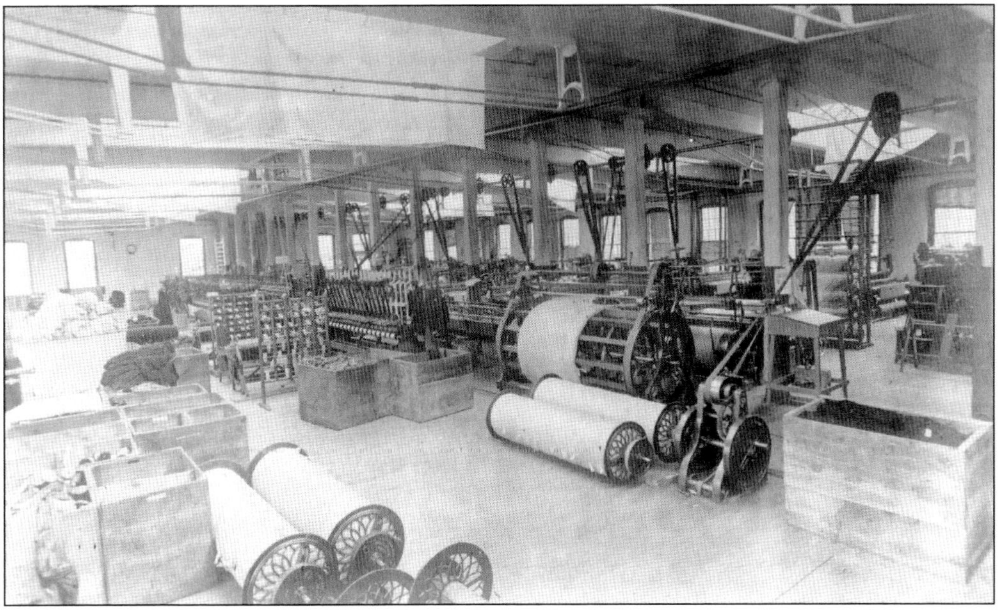

In 1901, John Shirreffs rented this space on the third floor of Section 6 and organized the Success Worsted Company with his brother David as manager. The company produced woven worsted products and later changed its name to the Shirreffs Worsted Company. In 1902, Moore sold the Geo. C. Moore Company to the Moore Spinning Company, and in 1903, the Shirreffs moved their company from North Chelmsford to Fitchburg. Another George C. Moore in the elastic textile business in Worcester at the time incorporated as the George C. Moore Company in 1909. North Chelmsford's Moore likely used the "Geo." abbreviation to avoid confusion. The Worcester namesake is still in business as George C. Moore, a division of the Moore Company, with operations in Westerly, Rhode Island, and El Salvador in Central America. (Above, William Johnston Jr.; below, Chelmsford Historical Society.)

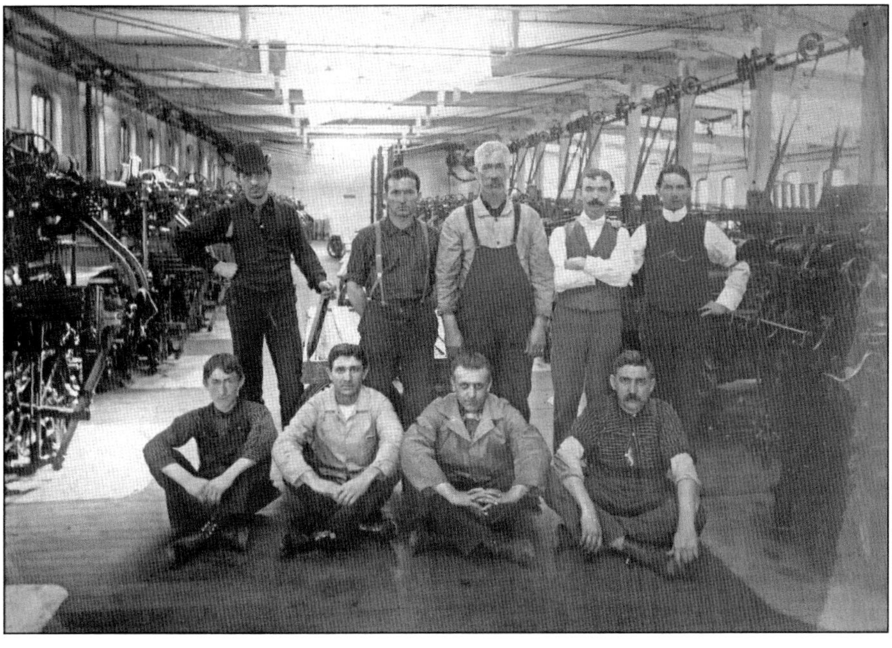

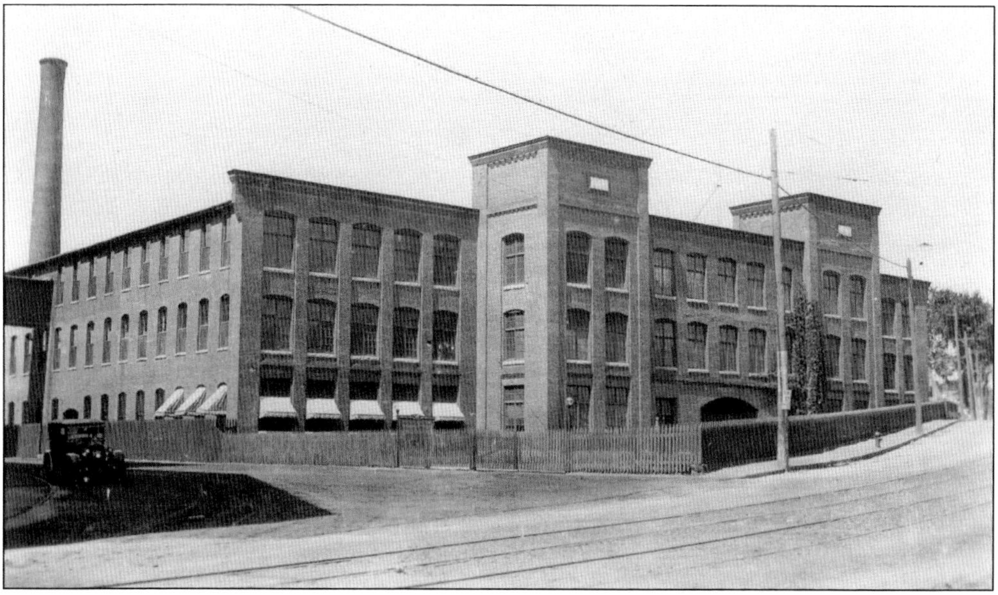

In 1910, the Moore Spinning Company connected the No. 1 and No. 2 mills with this 20-foot-deep arch and tower structure, as George C. Moore had planned to do many years before. The logo at the top of the left tower reads "SWM" (Silesia Worsted Mill), and the logo on the right tower reads "1910." In 1912, the United States Worsted Corporation purchased the mill complex for $3 million. The above photograph was taken around 1929, during the Great Depression. The United States Worsted Corporation went into receivership and was auctioned off on November 3–5, 1931. The Geo. C. Moore Wool Scouring Company purchased the five-story storehouse, and the Southwell Wool Combing Company on Wotton Street purchased the Silesia No. 1 and No. 2 mills. The below photograph shows how the buildings looked in 2015. (Above, Chelmsford Historical Society; below, photograph by the author.)

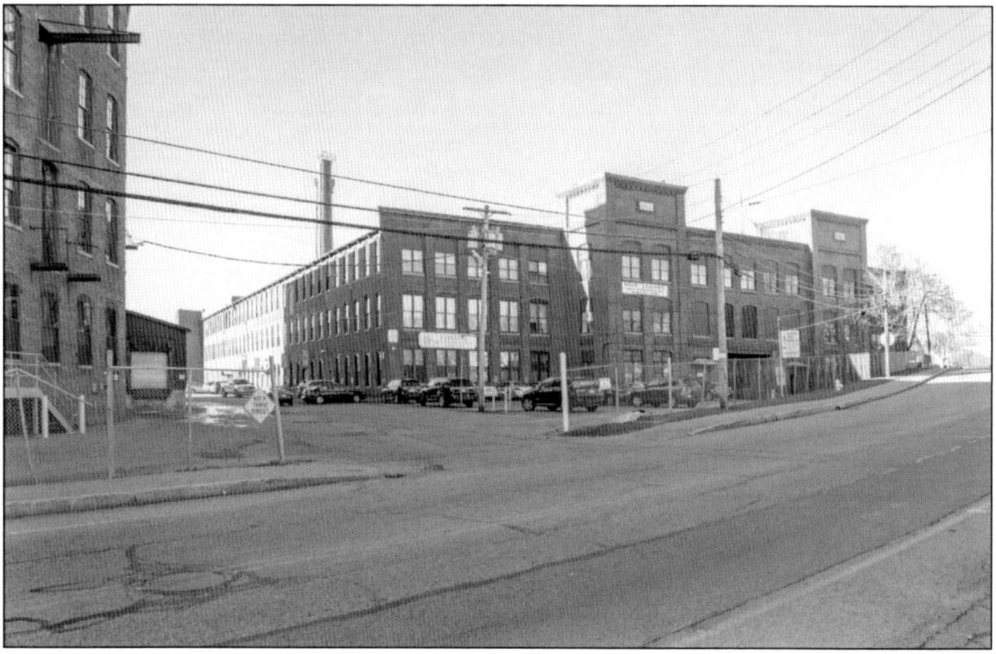

# *Two*

# Silver & Gay Company

This is the view looking across Princeton Street from George C. Moore's new wool scouring mill around 1904. The former Silver & Gay Company, lined up parallel to Princeton Street, had become the North Chelmsford Machine and North Chelmsford Supply Companies by this time. The houses in the foreground were later torn down to make room for expansion of Moore's scouring mill. (William Johnston Jr.)

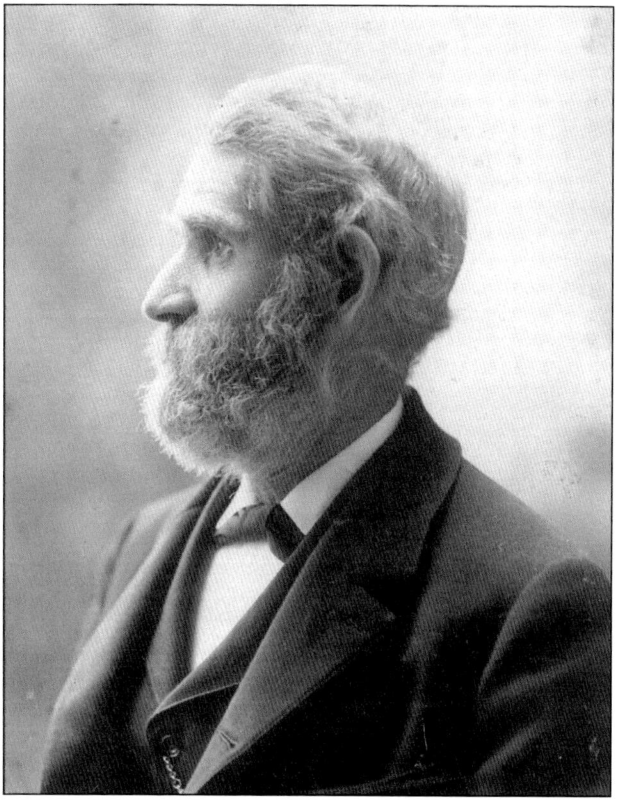

Ziba Gay Jr. ran the Silver & Gay Company from 1859 until George C. Moore purchased it in 1898. The company was started in 1830 as the Ira & Ziba Gay Company by Ziba's father, Ziba Gay Sr., and uncle Ira, who died in 1837. Ziba Sr. reorganized as Gay, Silver & Co with Harvey Silver in 1841, and again in 1857 as Silver & Gay Company. (Chelmsford Historical Society.)

George C. Moore started the North Chelmsford Supply Company in this rear wing of the Silver & Gay Company in 1897. In this photograph, each man is holding or wearing one of the supplies manufactured by the new company. The ring was used on wool combing machines. James S. Turner, the manager at this time, later opened a clothing and shoe store in Vinal Square. (Chelmsford Historical Society.)

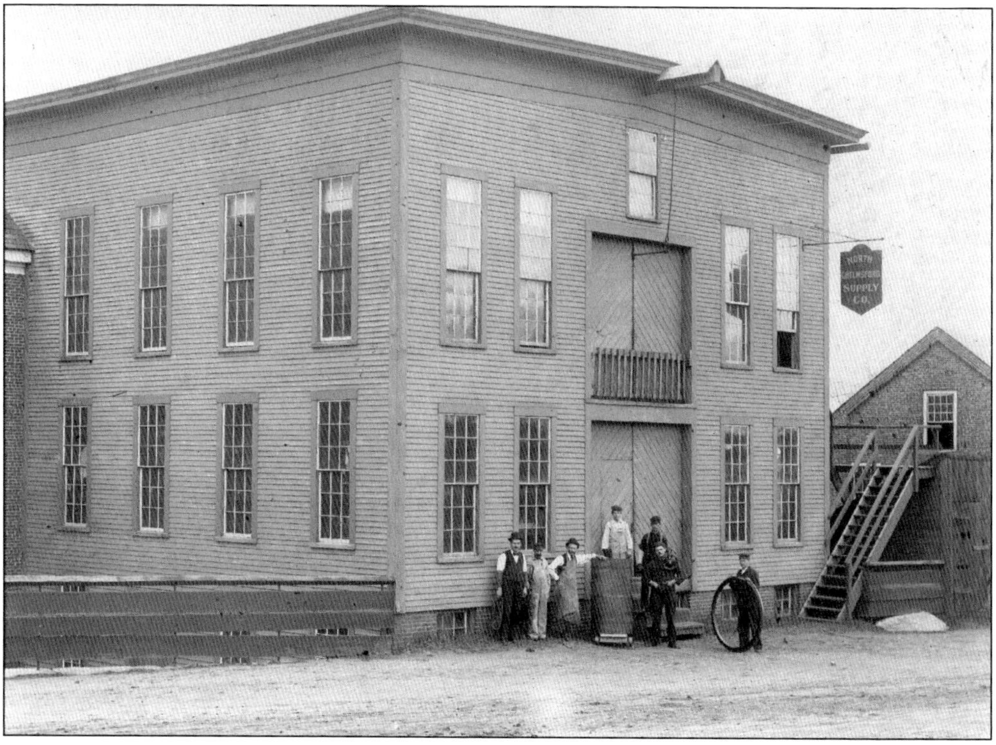

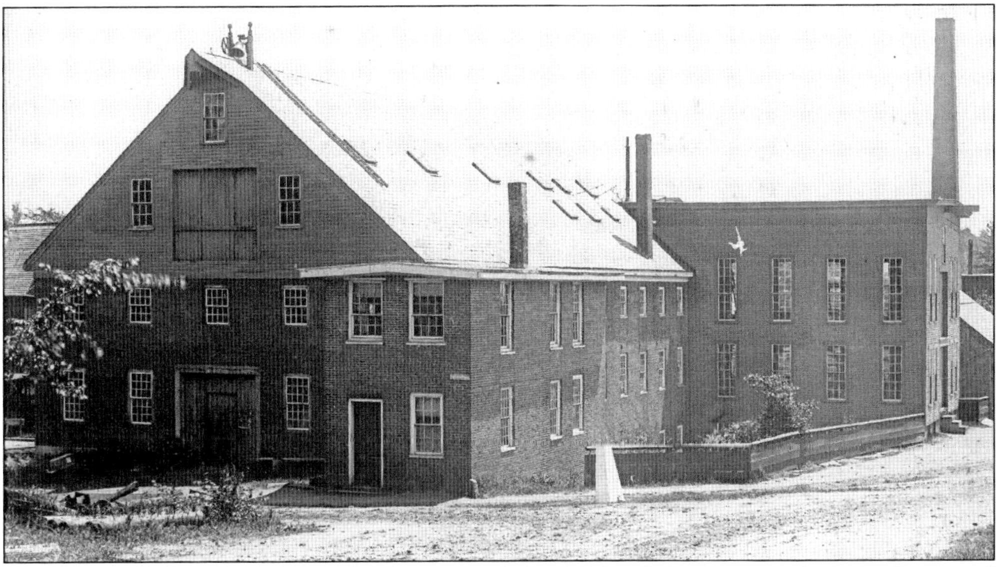

George C. Moore purchased the Silver & Gay Company from Ziba Gay in April 1898 and renamed it the North Chelmsford Machine Company. In this view, Princeton Street passes through the foreground, and Foundry Street goes to the left. The square smokestack served the boiler house and blacksmith shop next to Stony Brook. The bell on the roof marked the beginning and end of each workday. (Chelmsford Public Library.)

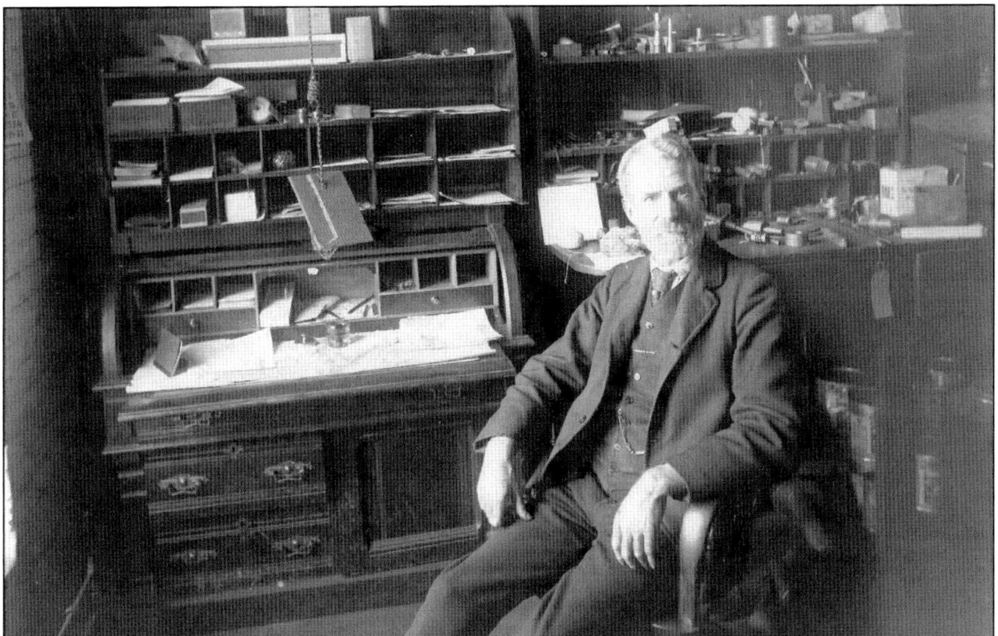

Otis P. Wheeler was the foreman of the North Chelmsford Machine Company for its entire existence—from 1898 until his death at age 74 in 1923, the same year that George C. Moore died. Wheeler was also secretary of the North Chelmsford Library Association during that time. His son Arthur O. served as clerk, assistant station agent, telephone operator, then station agent at the North Chelmsford railroad depot. (Chelmsford Historical Society.)

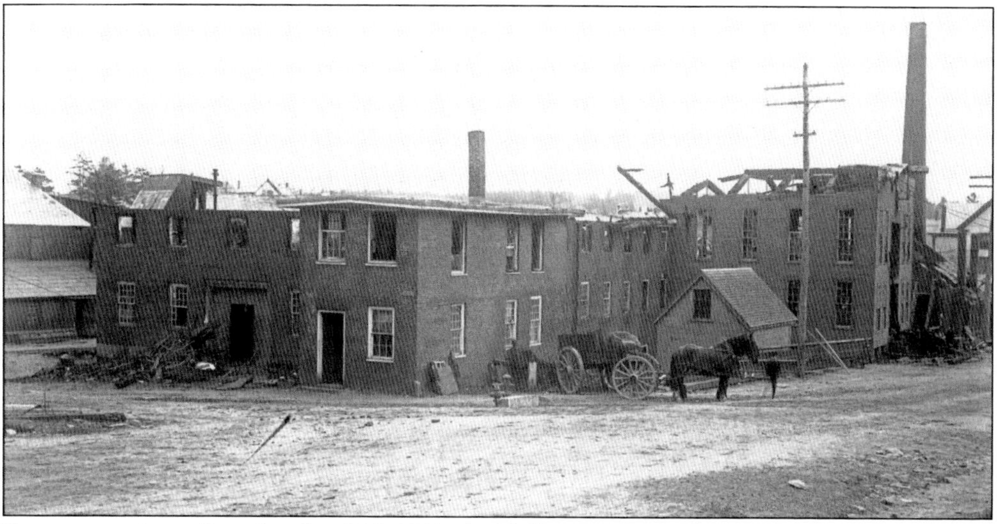

Disaster struck on Saturday April 27, 1901. At 12:57 p.m., passers-by saw smoke forcing its way through the third-floor roof and alerted employees, who all got out safely. The North Chelmsford Machine Company bell was rung, and the nearby worsted mill horn blasted. The fire was thought to have started from electric wiring or a spark from the nearby Chelmsford Foundry Company furnace, but the cause was never conclusively determined. (Chelmsford Public Library.)

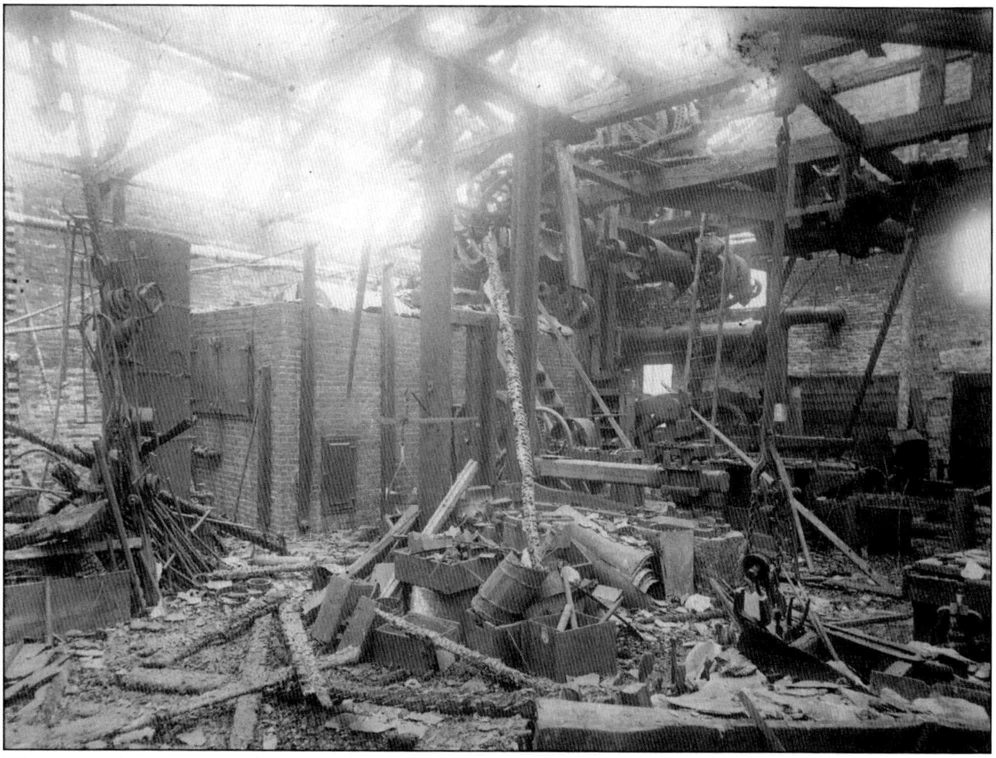

These are the remains of the inside of the boiler house and blacksmith shop. The main boiler is inside the brick structure at center, and there are two large trip hammers with granite bases at right center. Fuel for the boiler was provided by wood shavings swept out the rear of the pattern shop and by coal hand-carried from a shed out back next to Stony Brook. (Chelmsford Public Library.)

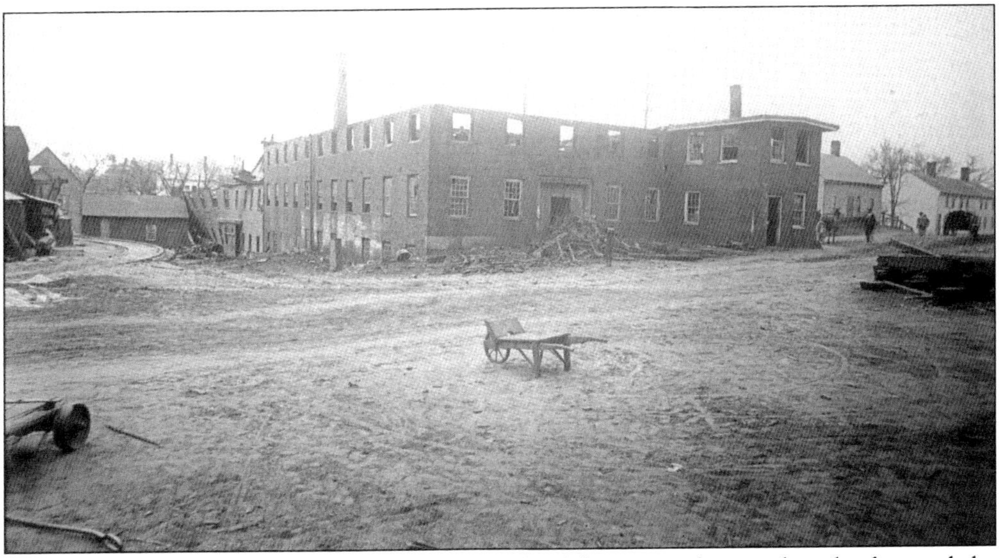

All the valuable wooden patterns stored on the third floor were destroyed in the fire, and the slate roof collapsed. In this view, workers have shoveled debris out the front door for pickup, and a man is looking out a top-floor window. Buildings on the far left side were part of the Chelmsford Foundry Company, and the houses on the far right were part of the Baldwin Mill property. (Chelmsford Public Library.)

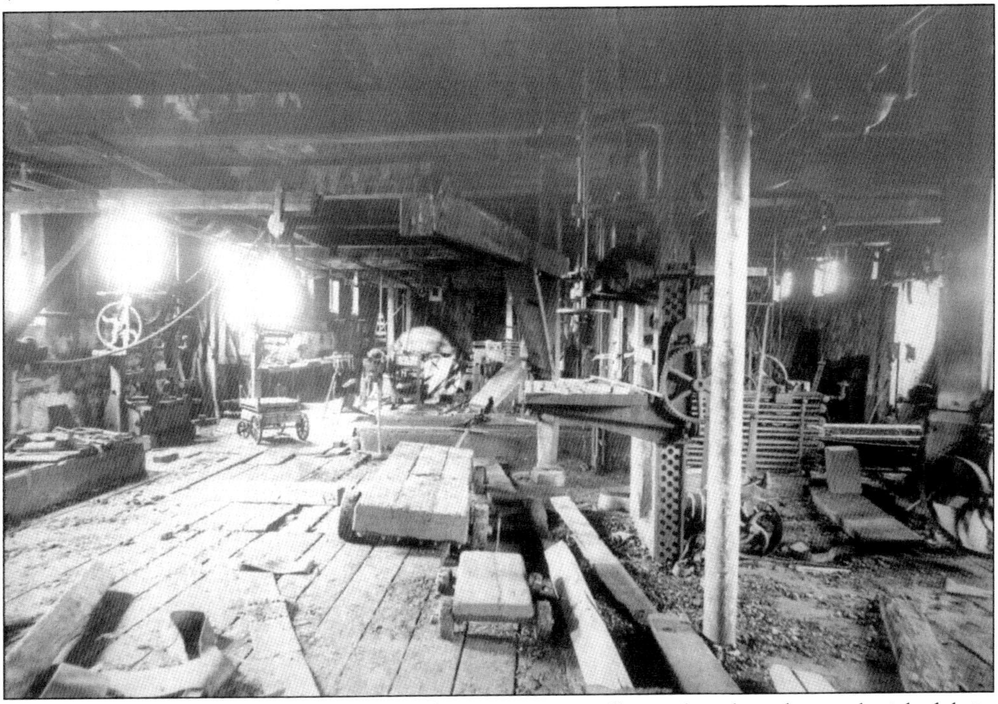

After the fire, the machine shop in the basement was still standing but cluttered with debris. The wooden overhead lifting arms, balance scale, drill press, lathe, exposed heating coils, and dollies appear to be very old technology. A water turbine in the basement powered a water pump used for pressurizing fire hydrants. The first floor was used for setting up new machinery, and the second floor was for making patterns. (Chelmsford Public Library.)

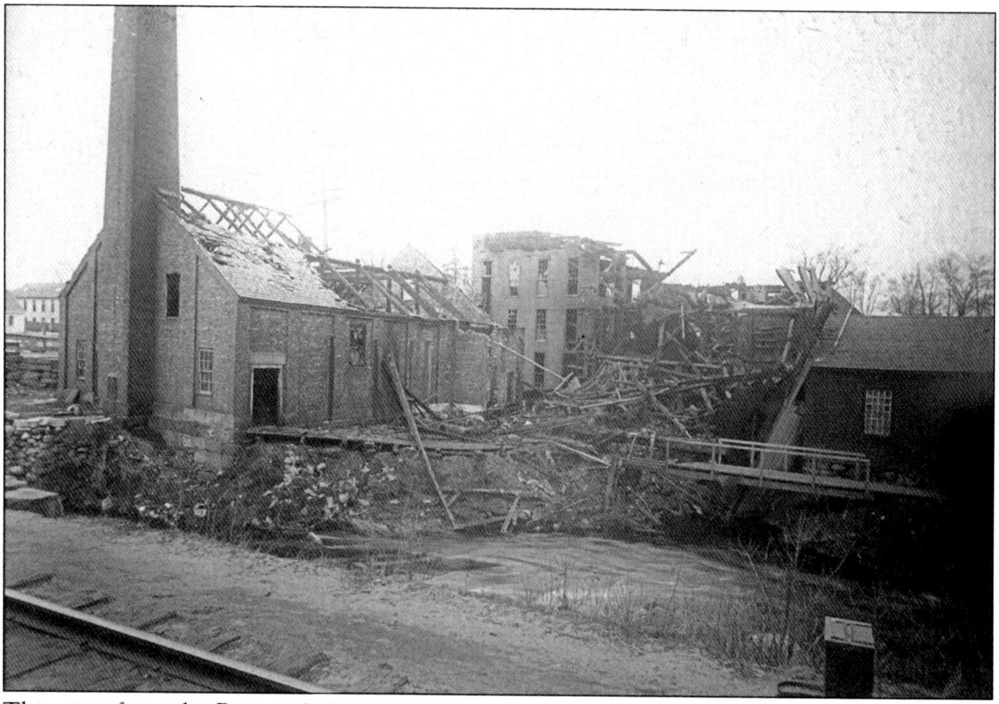

This view from the Boston & Maine Railroad tracks shows the boiler house and blacksmith shop, with its square smokestack, on the left. The wooden North Chelmsford Supply building at center is still standing but gutted. The wooden extension of the main brick building was totally destroyed, and its side is leaning onto the coal and pattern storage building, which survived, at right. (Chelmsford Public Library.)

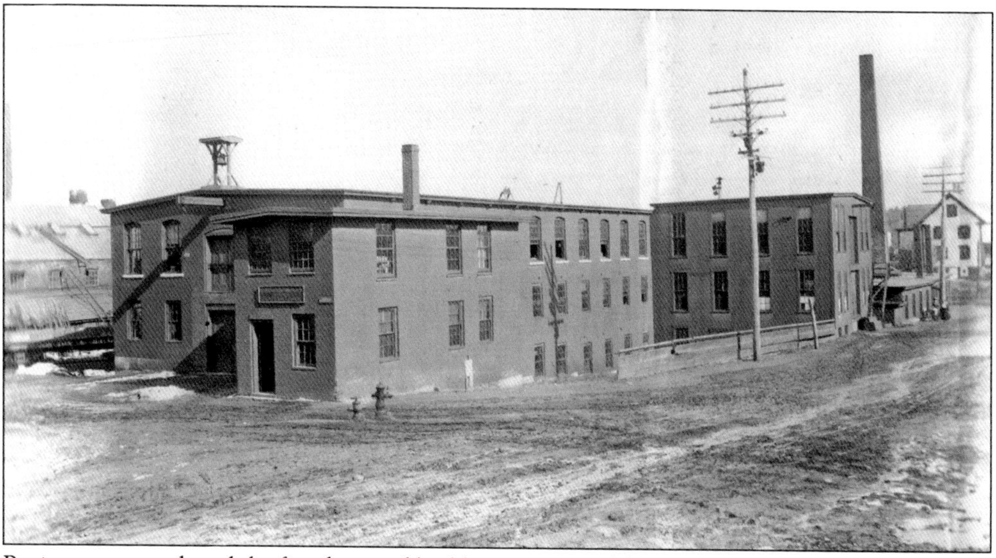

Business was good, and the fire-damaged buildings were quickly rebuilt and outfitted with modern machinery. In 1905, George C. Moore combined his Machine Company and Supply Company into one, officially known as the North Chelmsford Machine & Supply Company. The Machine & Supply Company is shown here in 1906 with a new bell tower and lower pitched roofs. The Chelmsford Foundry Company is at far left. (William Johnston Jr.)

In this c. 1902 image, the brick boiler house and blacksmith shop have been rebuilt with a lower roofline, and a man is painting the exterior wall. Houses on the other side of Princeton Street are visible in the background. The brick three-story main building, extended back where there used to be a wooden structure, is still under construction with staging attached to the outside wall. (Chelmsford Historical Society.)

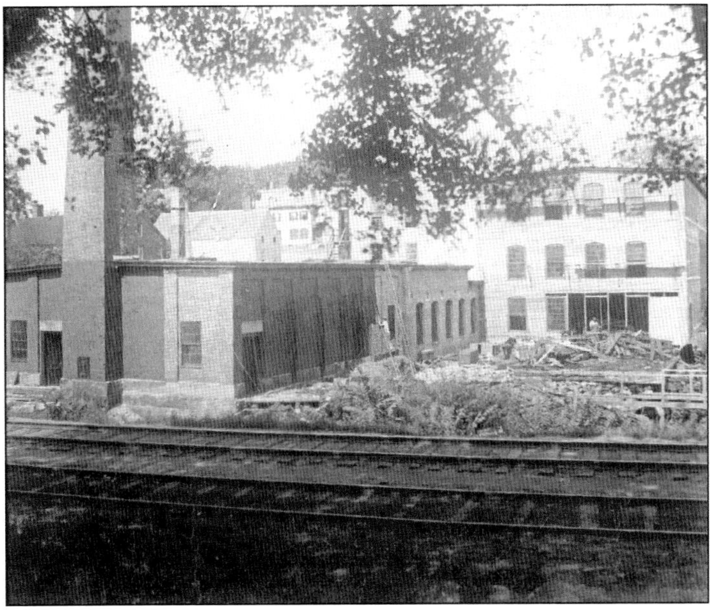

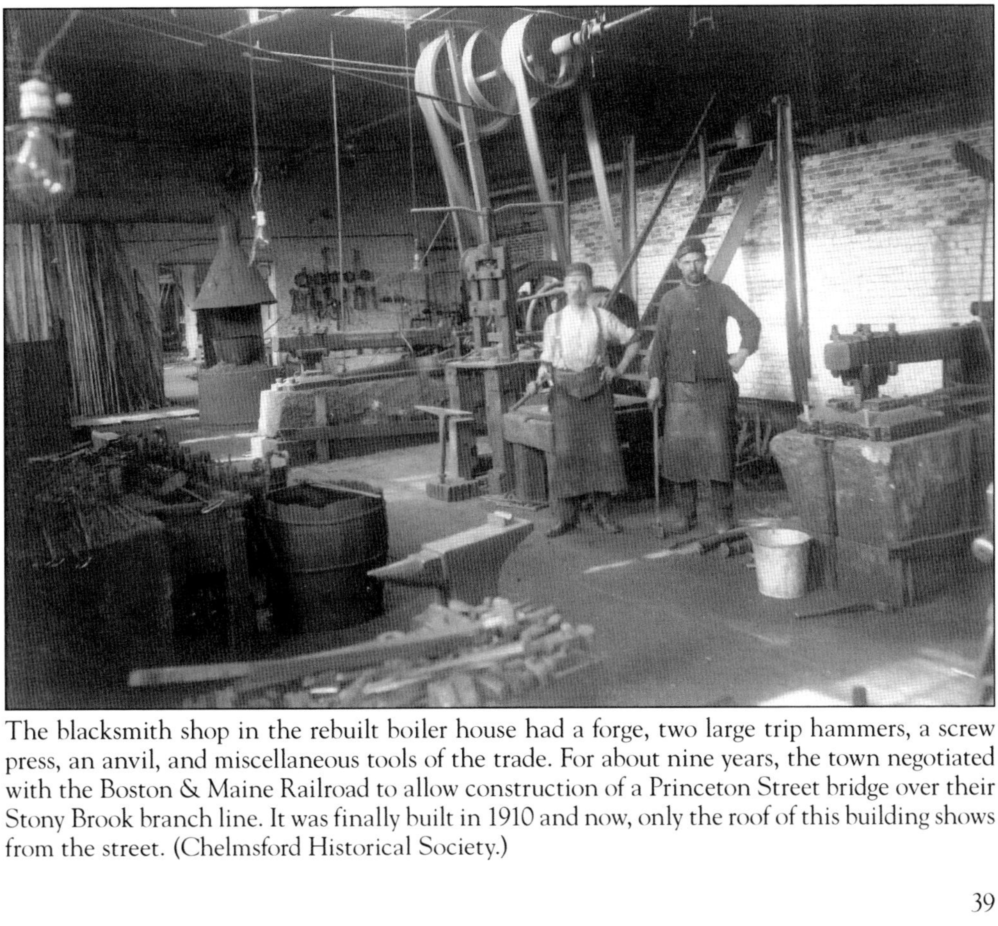

The blacksmith shop in the rebuilt boiler house had a forge, two large trip hammers, a screw press, an anvil, and miscellaneous tools of the trade. For about nine years, the town negotiated with the Boston & Maine Railroad to allow construction of a Princeton Street bridge over their Stony Brook branch line. It was finally built in 1910 and now, only the roof of this building shows from the street. (Chelmsford Historical Society.)

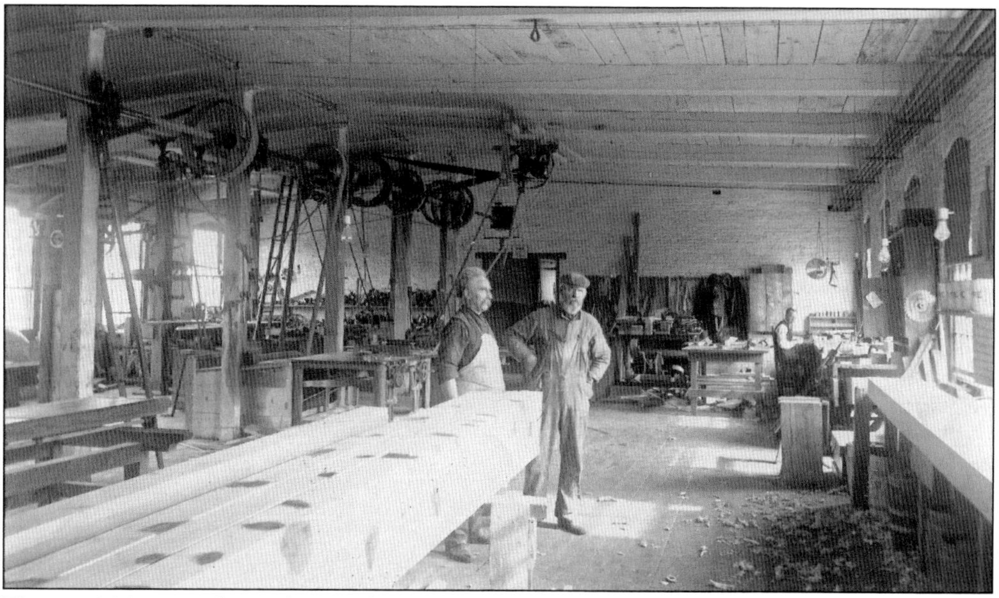

This c. 1906 image shows the woodworking and pattern shop on the second floor of the main building. The exposed ceiling reveals the gentle pitch of the roof, and the line shaft that powers the tools is rotating at full speed. Electric trolley service from Lowell arrived in 1892, and many of the tradesmen working at the North Chelmsford Machine and Supply Company commuted from Lowell. (Chelmsford Historical Society.)

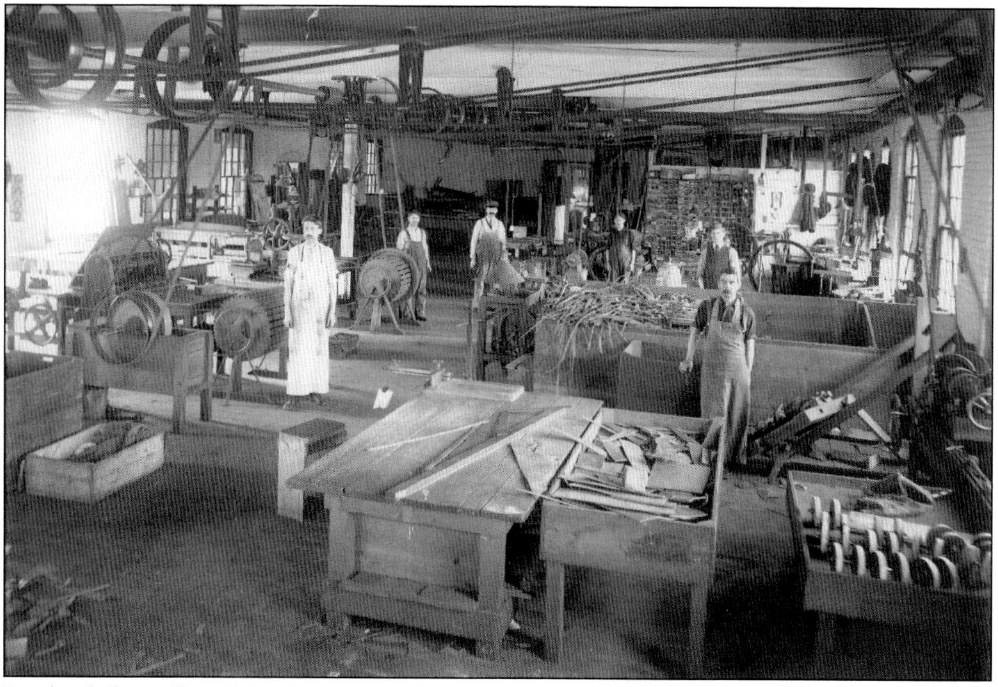

Leather belts, still used in 1906 to transmit power to and from line shafts, were manufactured and repaired in this first-floor shop. The machines at left were used to cut leather and attach links joining sections of belt. The pin-setting area in the right rear of the shop was the domain of T. Richard Davis, who is wearing a tie and standing behind a scrap bin. (Chelmsford Historical Society.)

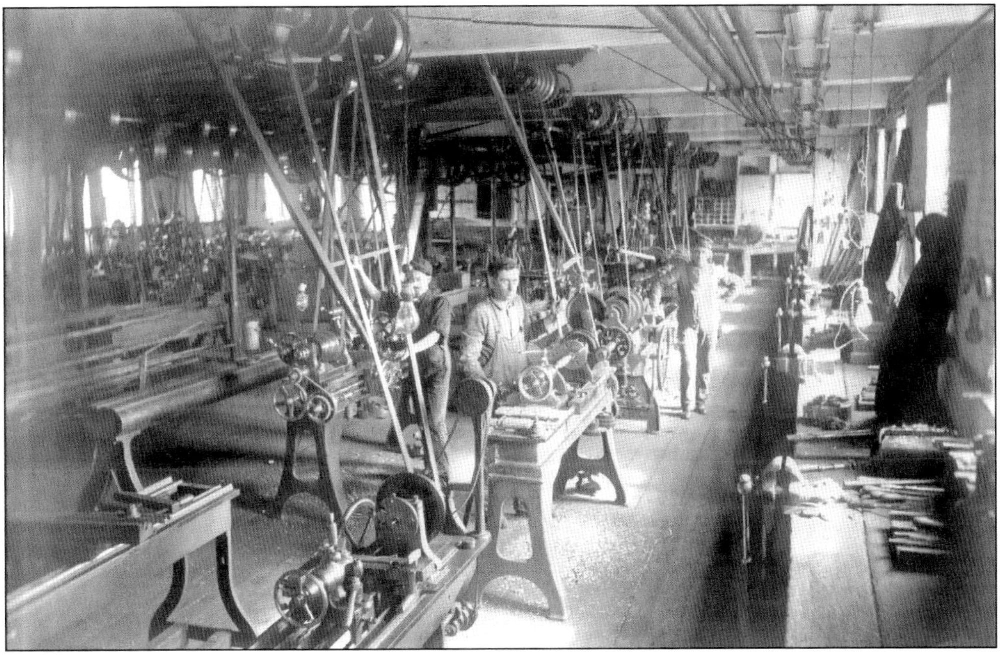

The new basement machine shop was outfitted with the latest metalworking machinery, and each man had his own bench space and tools. The Lowell Model Company, a manufacturer of small gasoline engines, had moved from Lowell into the basement of the Machine Company just three months before the 1901 fire. After the fire, the company moved to Brookside Mill in Westford. (William Johnston Jr.)

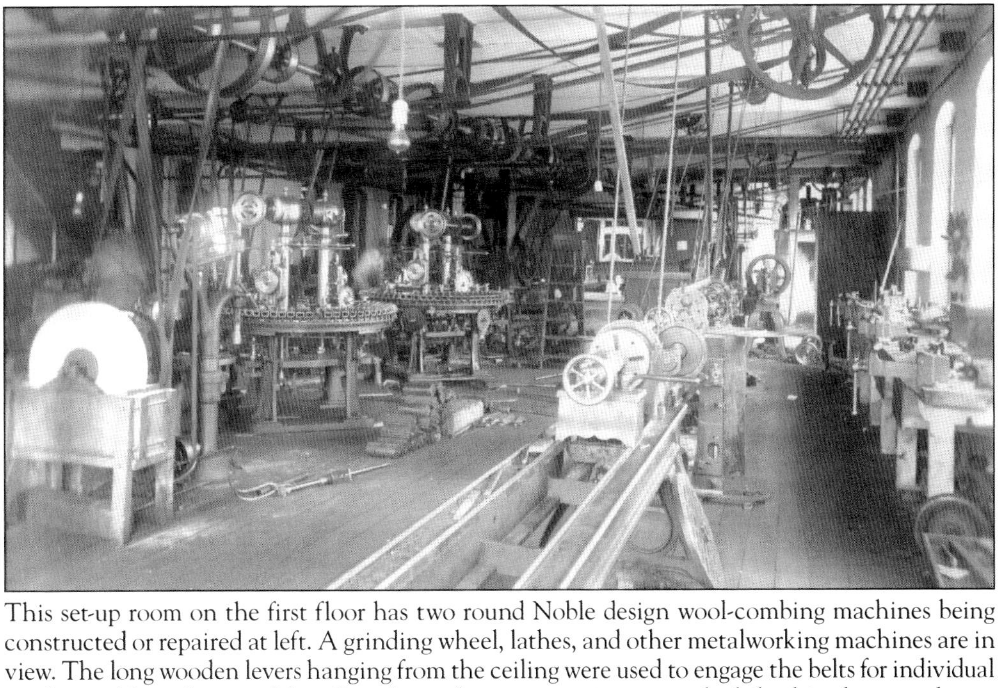

This set-up room on the first floor has two round Noble design wool-combing machines being constructed or repaired at left. A grinding wheel, lathes, and other metalworking machines are in view. The long wooden levers hanging from the ceiling were used to engage the belts for individual machines. Note the two "ghost" workers who were moving around while this photograph was being exposed. (William Johnston Jr.)

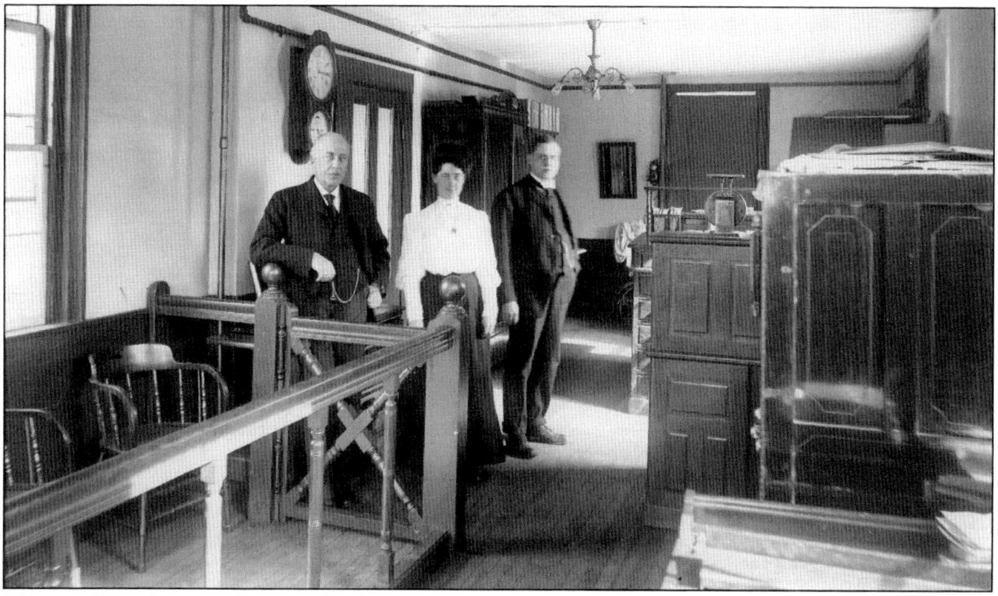

The small brick appendage on the front of the main building contained this business office, with its visitor waiting pen and safe, around 1906. Although those pictured here are not identified, key employees at this time were (at Machine Company) H. Stanley Crysler, manager; George C. Moore, treasurer; Otis P. Wheeler, foreman; and Clarence L. Deroehn, assistant foreman. At Supply Company, key employees included Henry Woods, manager and treasurer; John Austin, foreman; and George W. McKittrick, clerk. (Chelmsford Historical Society.)

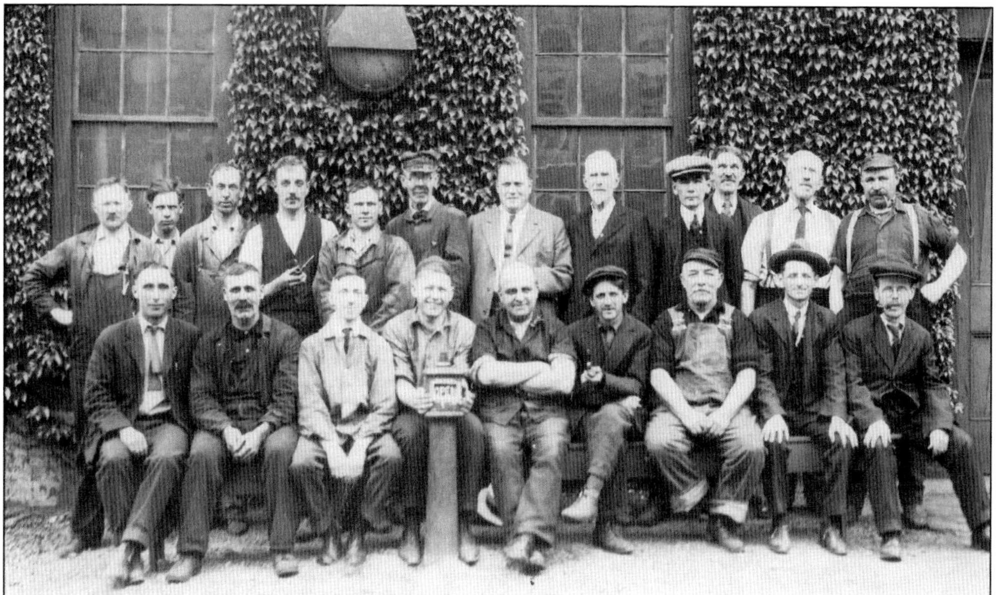

The North Chelmsford Machine and Supply Company closed after George C. Moore's death on November 6, 1923. H. Stanley Crysler, the manager, formed the Crysler Company in 1924, and this photograph was taken about that time. T. Richard Davis (second from right in the front row) became the superintendent of the new company. His brother Edwin E. Davis (fourth from right in the front row) was a machinist. (Chelmsford Historical Society.)

# *Three*

# Geo. C. Moore Wool Scouring Company

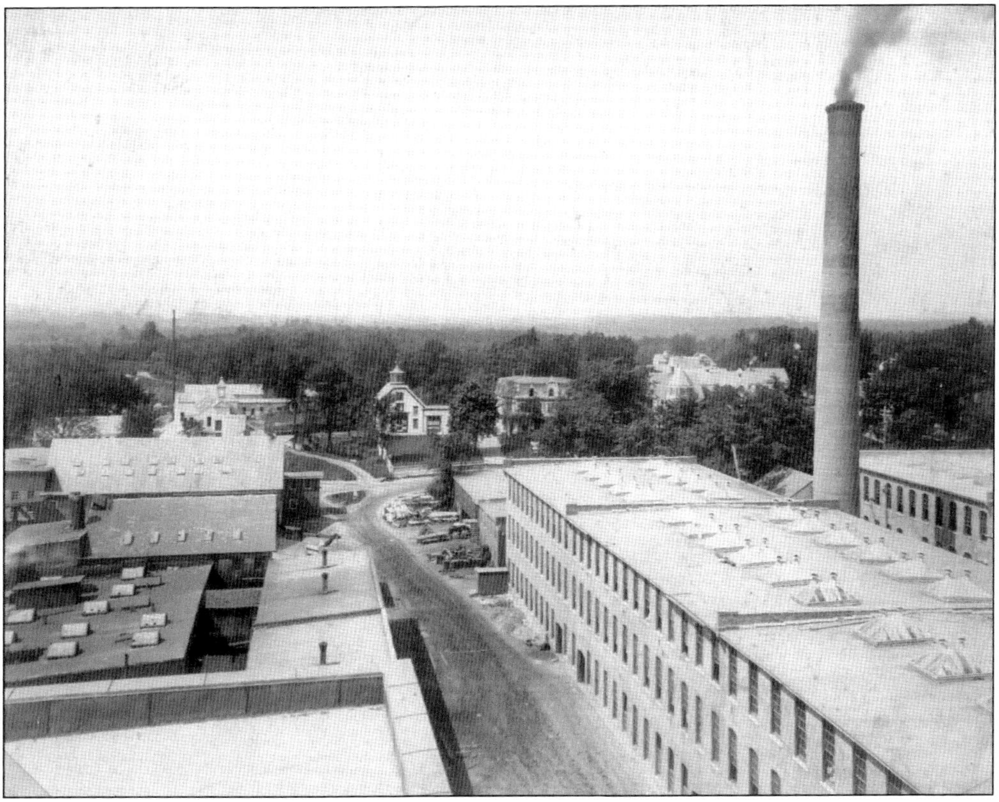

In this view from the tower on top of the five-story storehouse, the buildings on the left are, from nearest to farthest: corner of the storehouse, storehouse expansion, Chelmsford Foundry Company, North Chelmsford Machine Company, and the Baldwin Mill (prior to construction of George C. Moore's new wool scouring mill). Moore's No. 1 and No. 2 mills are at right. (William Johnston Jr.)

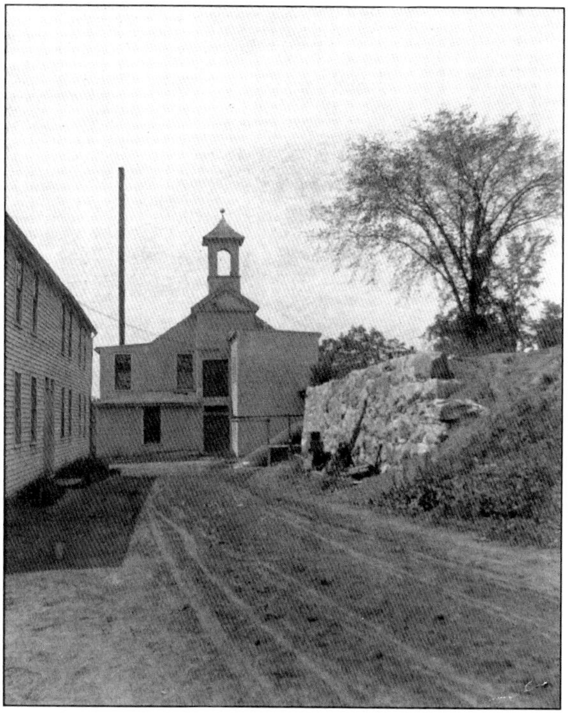

The mill canal from Freeman Lake is behind the stone wall on the right of the main entrance to the Baldwin Mill in this c. 1900 photograph. The tenement house at left was part of the mill property. George C. Moore purchased the complex from George T. Sheldon on October 2, 1895, but did not start construction of his new mill until about 1902. (Chelmsford Public Library.)

Another view of the Baldwin Mill shows the wool house next to the brook and the empty bell tower on the main building. This mill, originally constructed in 1842, was powered by water from the canal that flowed under the center of the main building, then to a machine shop behind the trees at left. Water power was later supplemented by steam power using the smokestack shown here. (Chelmsford Public Library.)

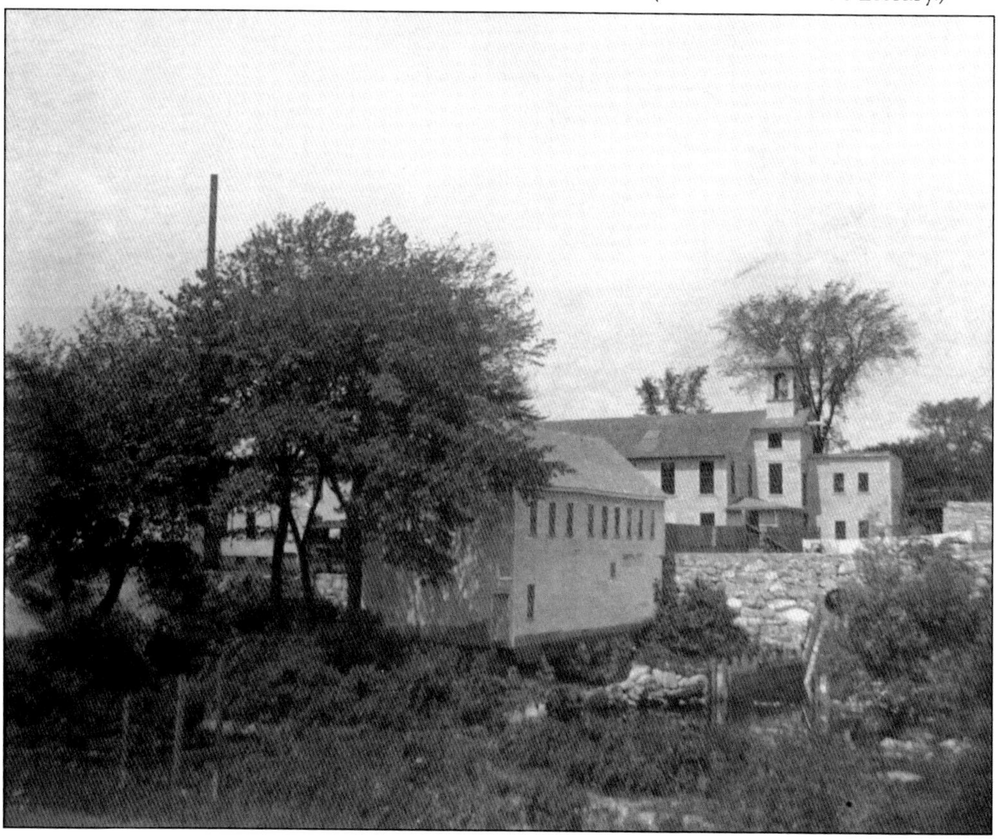

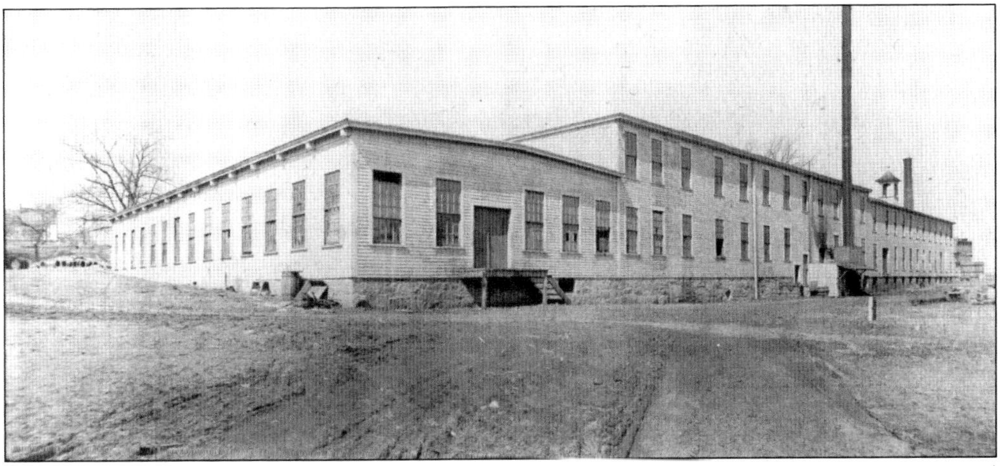

The Baldwin Mill remained relatively unmodified until George C. Moore sold his mill complex and five-story storehouse to the Moore Spinning Company in 1902 for $1.6 million to get relief from a huge inventory of wool and crushing debt. He continued to support Moore Spinning Company as an agent, using his extensive knowledge and contacts, and used the proceeds to embark on a new commission-based wool scouring business. (William Johnston Jr.)

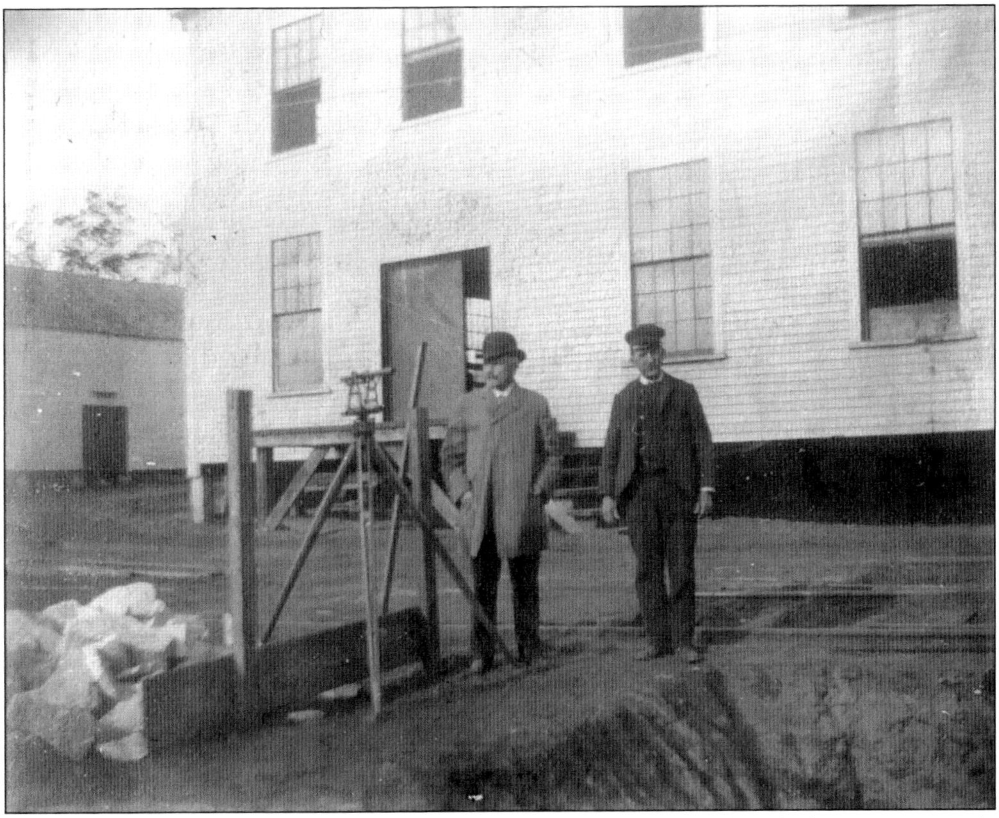

George C. Moore, at left, is touring his construction site with an unidentified associate in early 1904. The building directly behind the men was the one-story section at the end of the original Baldwin Mill, which Moore had recently expanded to two stories. The excavation for westward expansion of his new wool scouring building is in the foreground. (William Johnston Jr.)

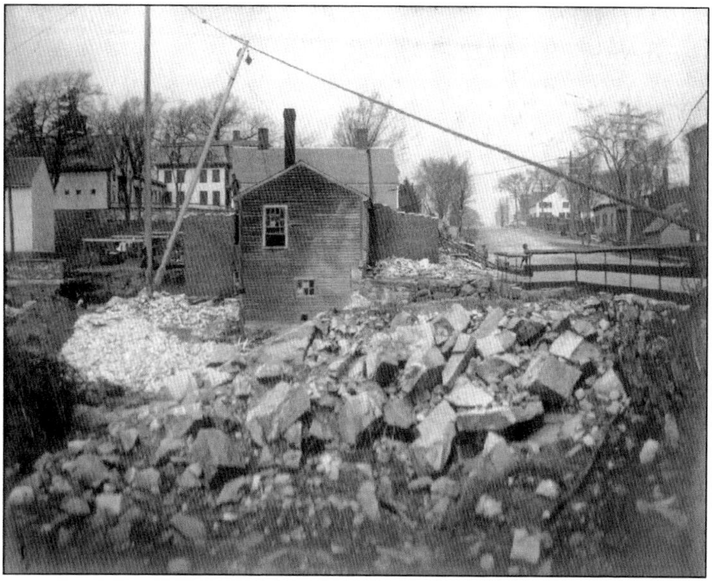

Here, several boarding houses belonging to Moore after his 1898 purchase of the Silver & Gay Company are being torn down around 1902 to make room for eastward expansion of the scouring mill. George T. Sheldon's estate is in the upper left background, and the former Silver & Gay building is at far right. Granite blocks (to be recycled into new construction) are stockpiled in the foreground. (William Johnston Jr.)

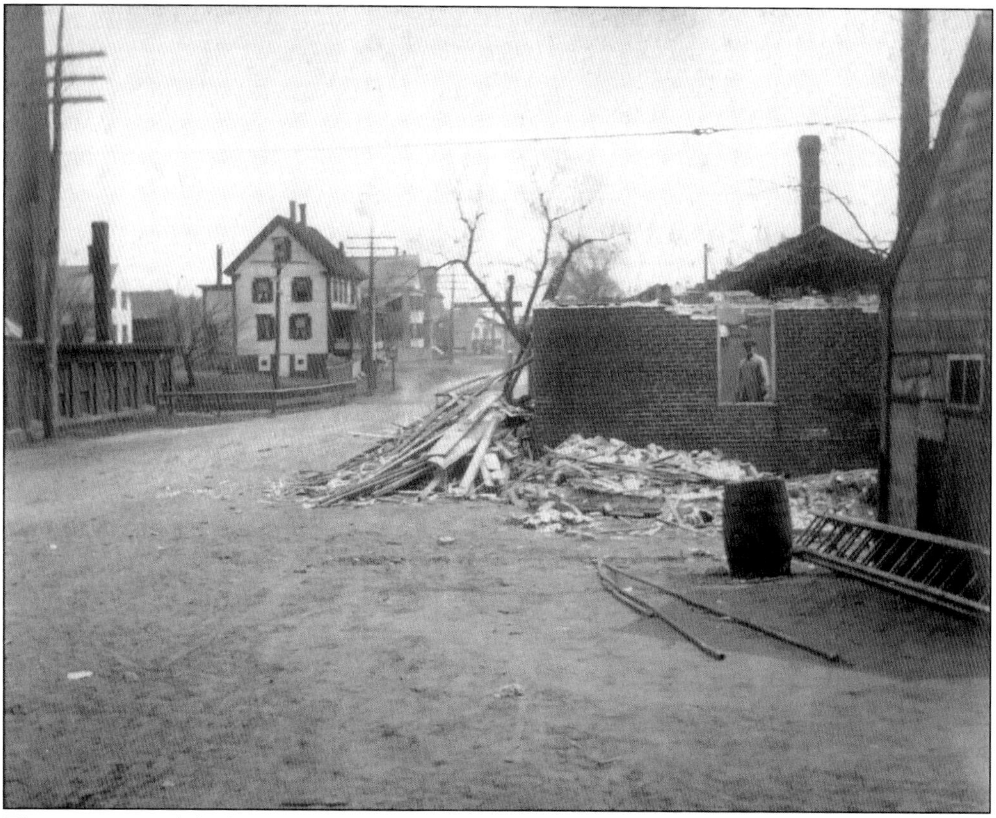

This is a view of the house demolition from the opposite direction on Princeton Street. The two houses next to the railroad tracks on the other side of the Stony Brook bridge were removed after the bridge was raised up over the tracks. The property is now owned by the New England Power Company. The North Chelmsford Machine Company building at far left is now below street level. (William Johnston Jr.)

The first phase of the wool scouring plant consisted of this four-story building with six- and seven-story elevator towers. The two-story section extending toward Princeton Street is half-finished, and there is a gin pole crane and pile of granite foundation stones at right. The grade crossing for the Boston & Maine Railroad is in the foreground, along with a kerosene streetlamp and the flagman's shack. (William Johnston Jr.)

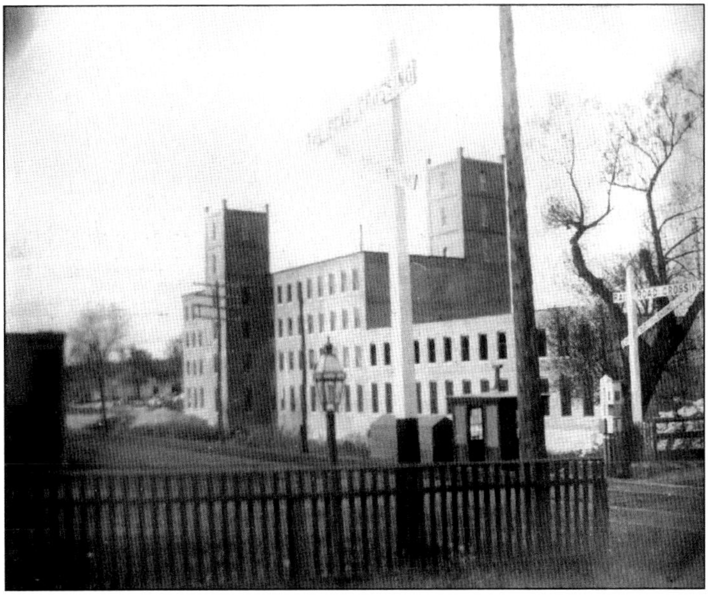

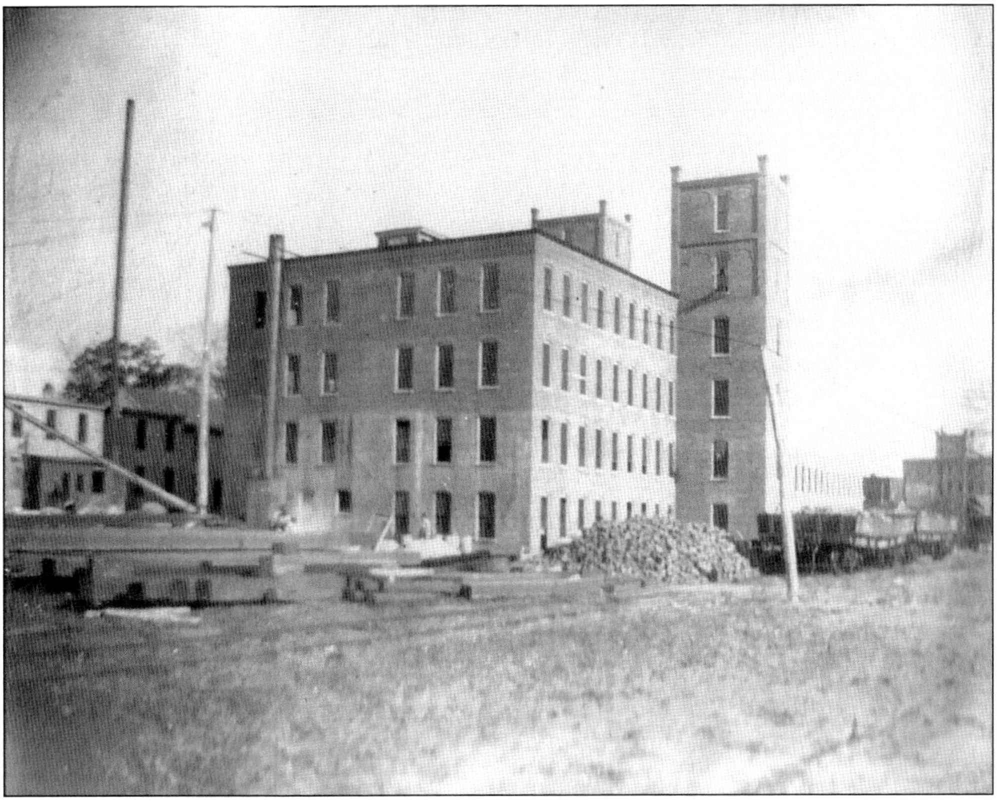

This 1904 view (from the opposite direction of that shown in the photograph at the top of this page) shows a pile of floor joist timbers in front of a gin pole crane and a temporary smokestack. Bricks to be used in the third phase of expansion are piled on the ground, and two flatcars are waiting to be unloaded. The Baldwin Mill is at left, and the five-story storehouse is in the distance at right. (William Johnston Jr.)

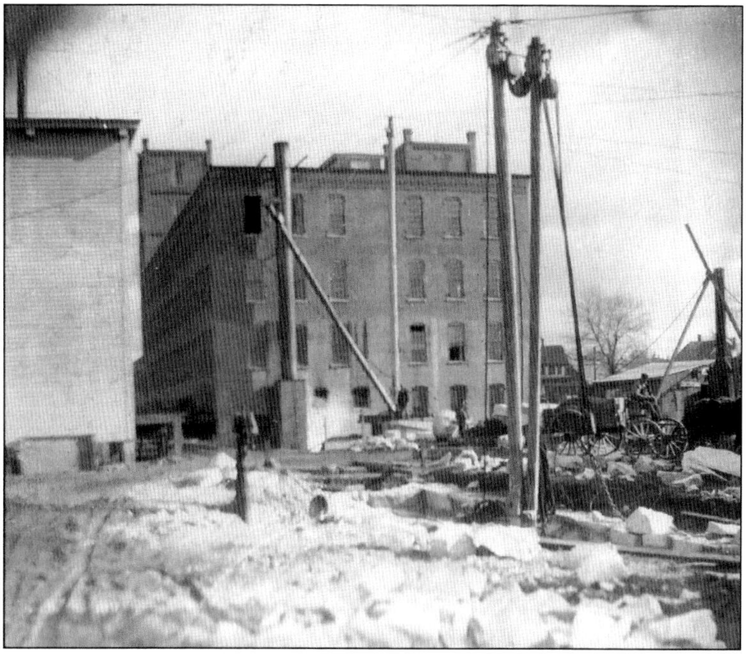

The early stages of a granite block foundation are visible in the foreground, and the man on the wagon may be teamster James Rice, who worked for George C. Moore in 1904. These gin pole cranes involved simple technology used for centuries wherever heavy lifting was needed. The boiler and shack at right likely generated power for electric winches at the base of the cranes. (William Johnston Jr.)

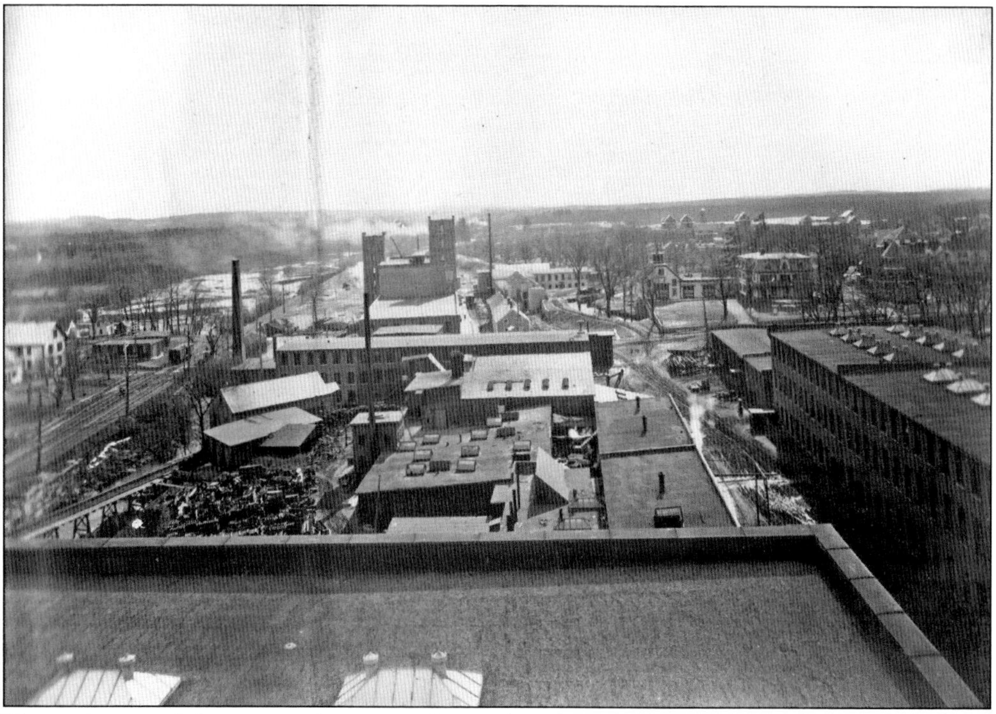

This wide view of the new wool scouring plant, taken from the five-story storehouse tower, shows its relationship with the Chelmsford Foundry Company (in the middle foreground), the Machine & Supply Company (parallel to Princeton Street), and the remaining Baldwin Mill buildings. The mill canal flows past the right side of the Baldwin Mill buildings, under the lawn of the George T. Sheldon estate, and under Princeton Street. (William Johnston Jr.)

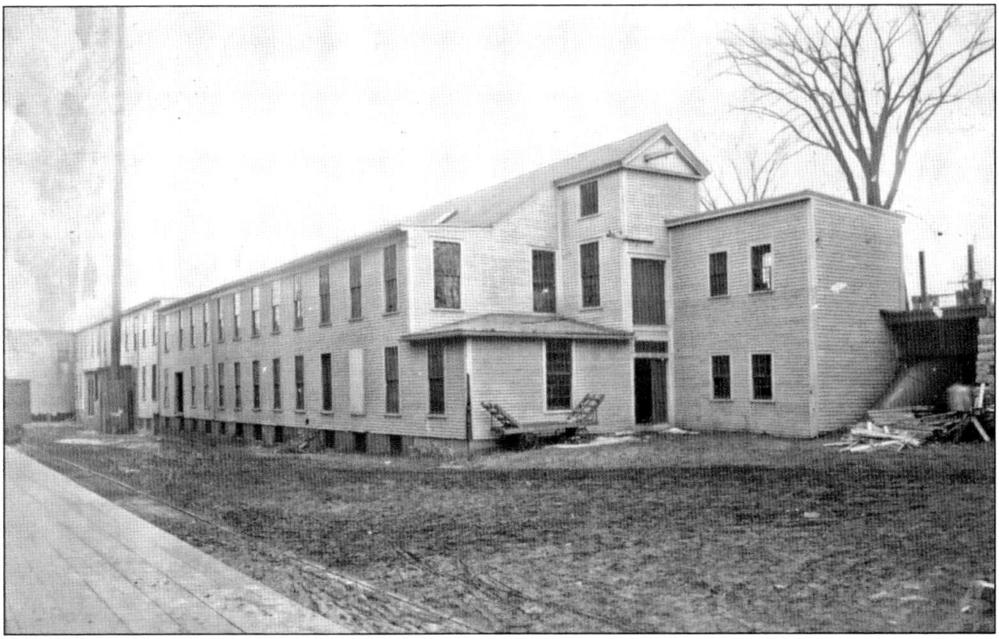

The Baldwin Mill bell tower was removed before this 1906 photograph was taken. Early water power control gates are visible at far right, with the one on the left controlling water going to a large pipe leading to Stony Brook, and the other to a turbine. Some of these wooden buildings were later reconstructed in brick and, in 1986, converted into condominiums. (William Johnston Jr.)

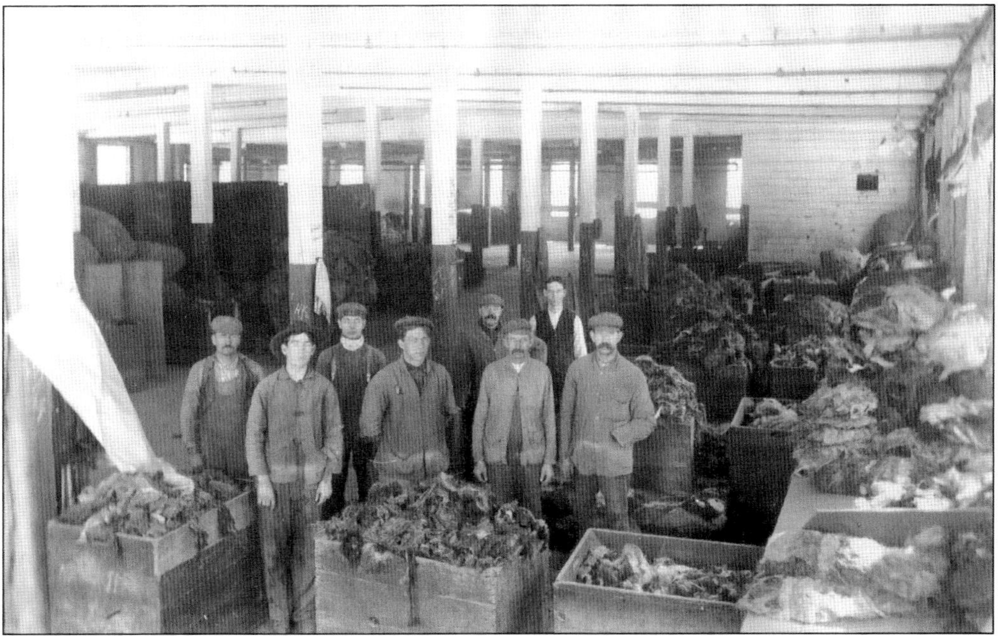

This is the only known photograph taken inside the Baldwin Mill, and it shows wool sorters posing with their work in progress around 1906. The room in the background appears to be the second floor of the 1902 rebuild of the old one-story section. The extensive sprinkler system visible between the roof rafters was installed by George C. Moore in 1903, according to the 1909 *Insurance Engineering Vol. XVII.* (William Johnston Jr.)

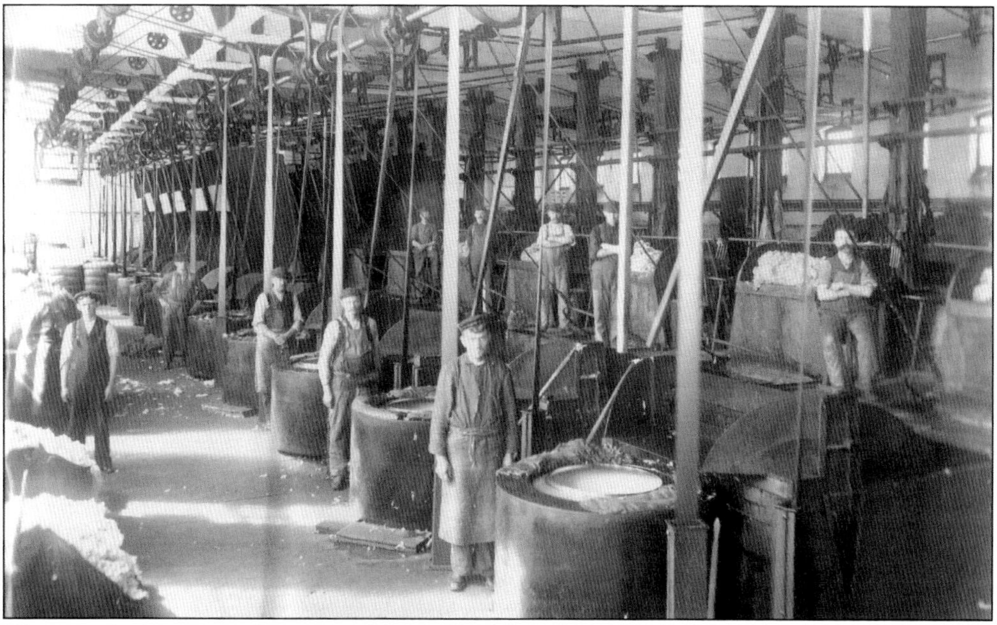

The next five photographs were taken inside the Geo. C. Moore Wool Scouring Company in 1906. Here, the scouring room crew is posing by their machines on the first floor. Washed wool is pushed up in hoppers waiting to be dried, and the spin dryers are loaded and running at full speed. Note the belts that connect pulleys on the ceiling with the dryer pulleys under the floor. (William Johnston Jr.)

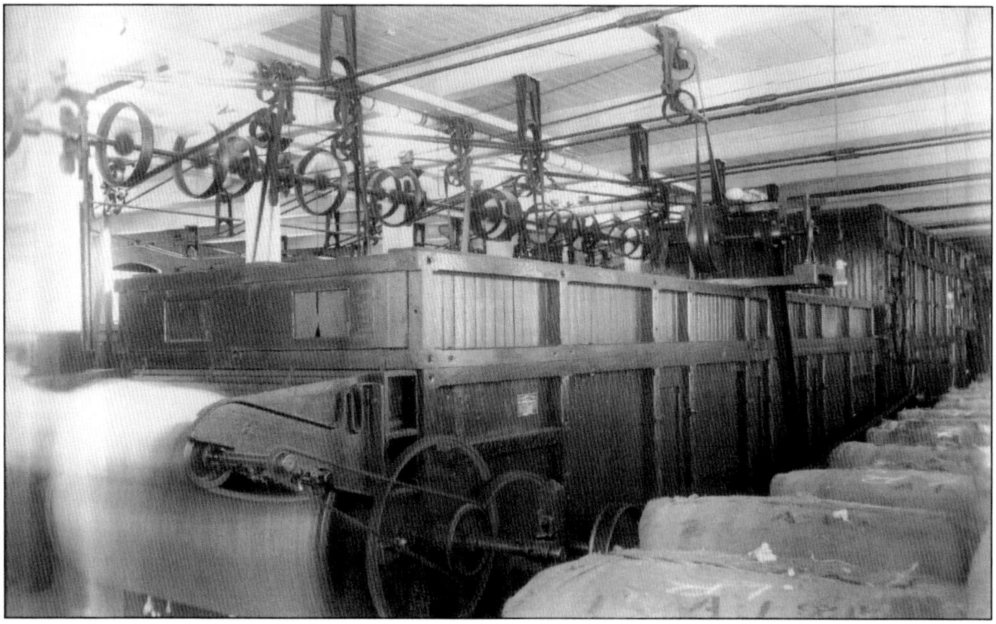

The belts and pulleys shown here moved a conveyor belt system inside the dryer box. Moore did not design this dryer. Instead, he purchased it from Charles G. Sargent & Son in Westford. Sargent co-founded the Abbot Worsted Company in 1855, but sold his interest to Allen Cameron after two years to concentrate on the manufacturing of machinery for cotton and woolen mills. (William Johnston Jr.)

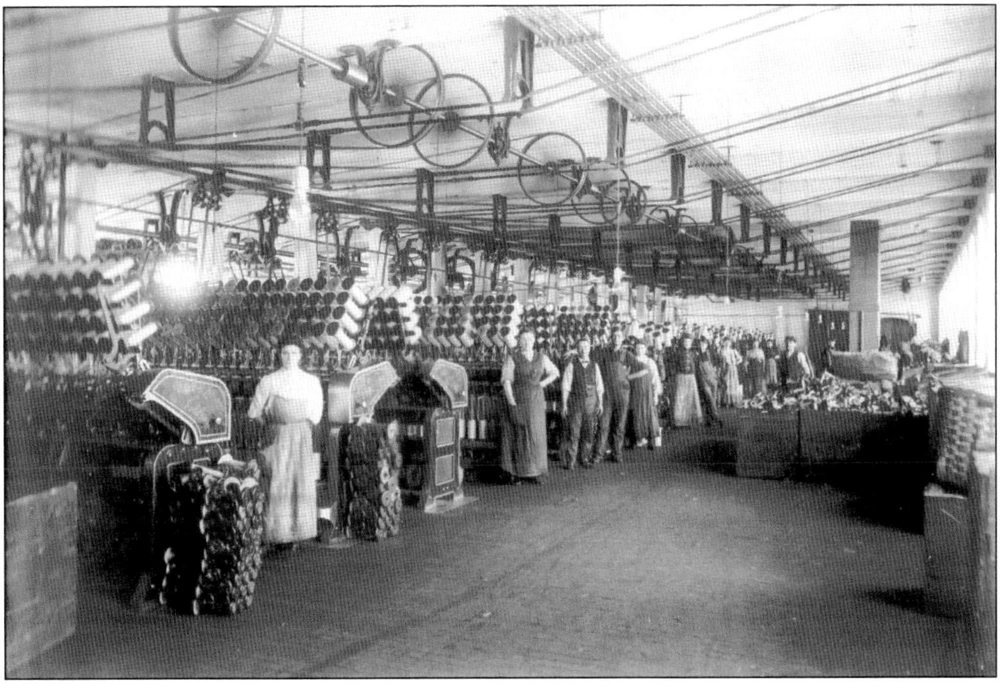

In this drawing room, roving from multiple large spools was combined, stretched, and lightly twisted onto the smaller spools near the floor. The smaller spools were sent on to the spinning room, where twist density and thickness were controlled to meet customer requirements. These workers could have come from Lowell, Tyngsboro, West Chelmsford, or Westford, as there was trolley service to all four towns in 1906. (William Johnston Jr.)

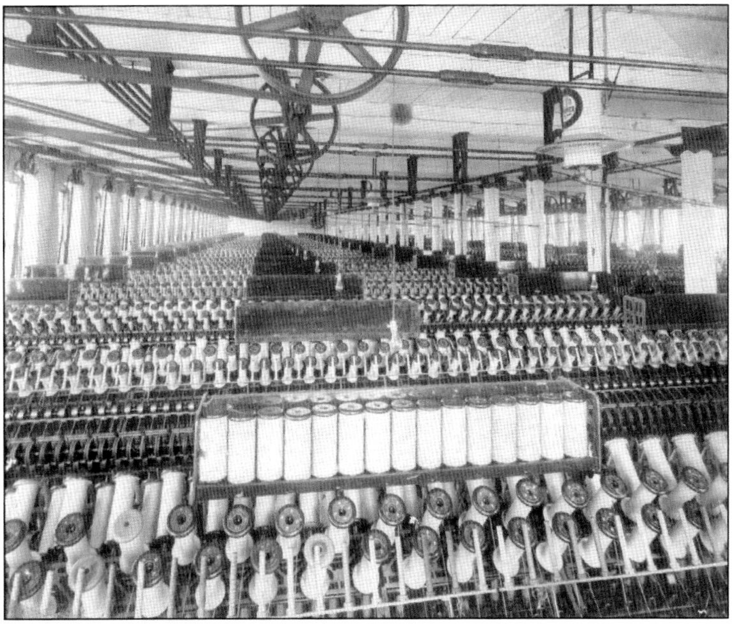

This new spinning room seems to go on forever, with a single line shaft on each side powering thousands of spindles, all in place for this photograph. There are humidifiers plumbed in every few machines, but no sprinkler pipes in sight. At this time, the new mill had capabilities similar to the Moore Spinning Company and Brookside Mill, but in later years, it specialized in wool scouring. (William Johnston Jr.)

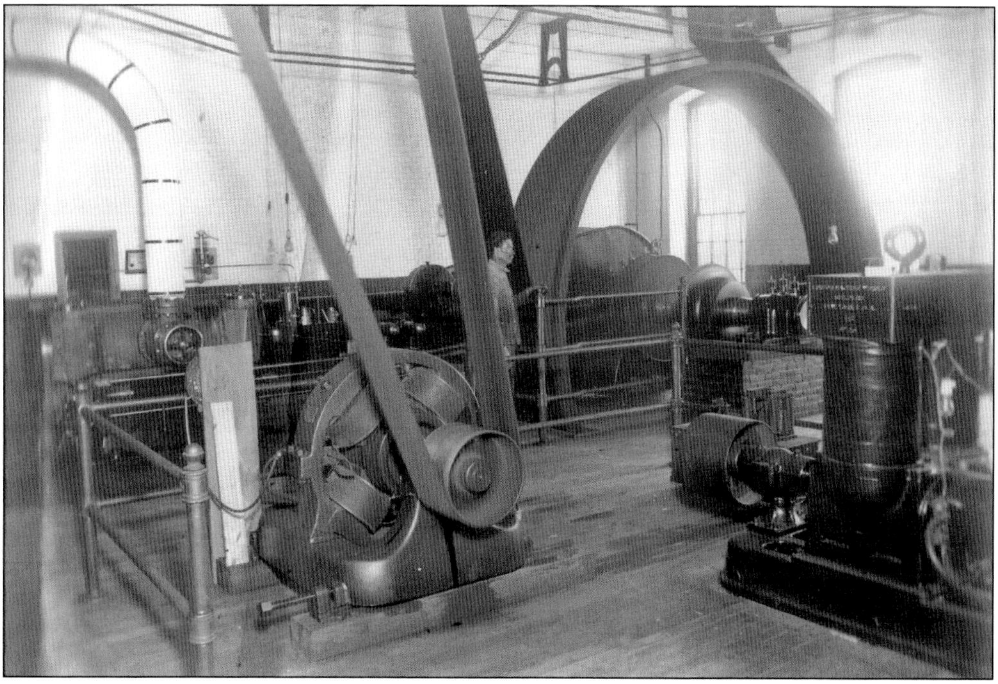

This C.H. Brown horizontal steam engine is shown running line shafts and generating electricity for lighting in 1906. The older generator at right was positioned so it could be belted up if the newer one failed. Several large mill engines like this one survive in the New England Wireless and Steam Museum in North Greenwich, Rhode Island, where enthusiasts get together for an annual Yankee Steam-Up and engine show. (William Johnston Jr.)

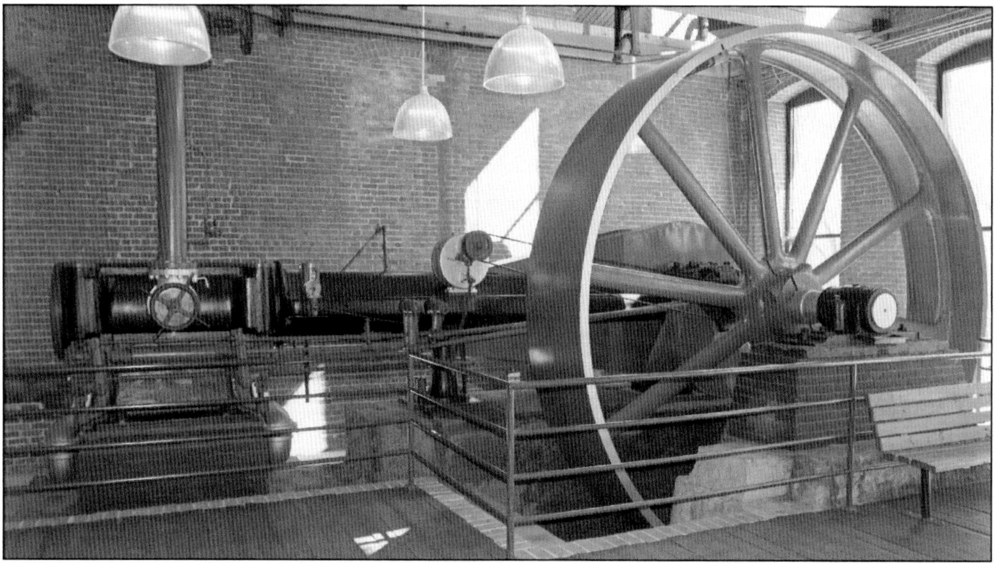

When the mill complex was converted for commercial and residential use in 1986, the C.H. Brown engine was left on display in its original location, as shown here. The floor above was removed to create an atrium with the exposed beams and tie rods left in place. Some of the line shaft and pulley hardware was also mounted on the ceiling to complete the industrial theme. (Photograph by the author.)

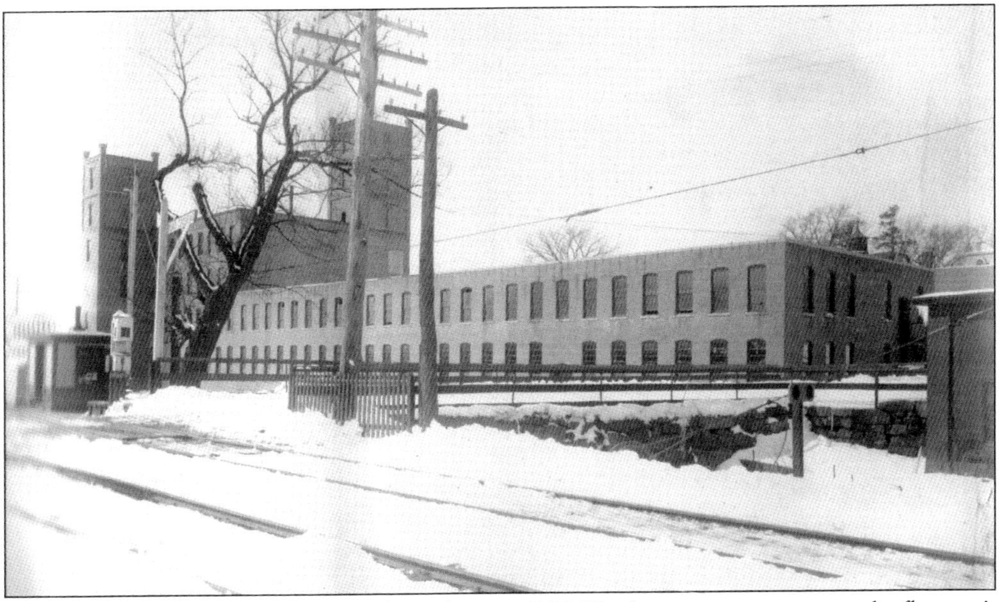

The completed east mill extension is shown here in 1906. The boxes on a post next to the flagman's shack could have been part of a token and ticket system used on single track sections of the Stony Brook branch, to prevent head-on collisions. A train could not enter the track without the token, or, if it was the first of two trains, a ticket for that section. (William Johnston Jr.)

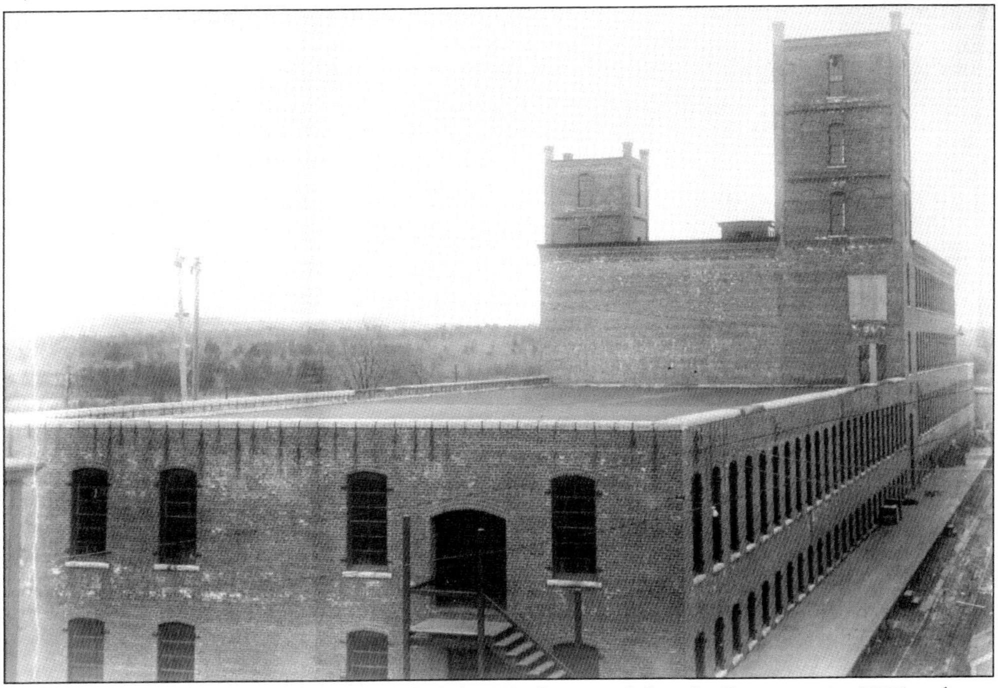

This photograph—taken from the roof of the Machine and Supply Company in 1906—shows the two-story east extension and partially finished west extension with a railroad loading dock extending the full length. This seven-story tower and the tower on top of the five-story storehouse were the tallest buildings ever constructed in Chelmsford. The massive round brick smokestack, which is still in existence, was not built until around 1907. (William Johnston Jr.)

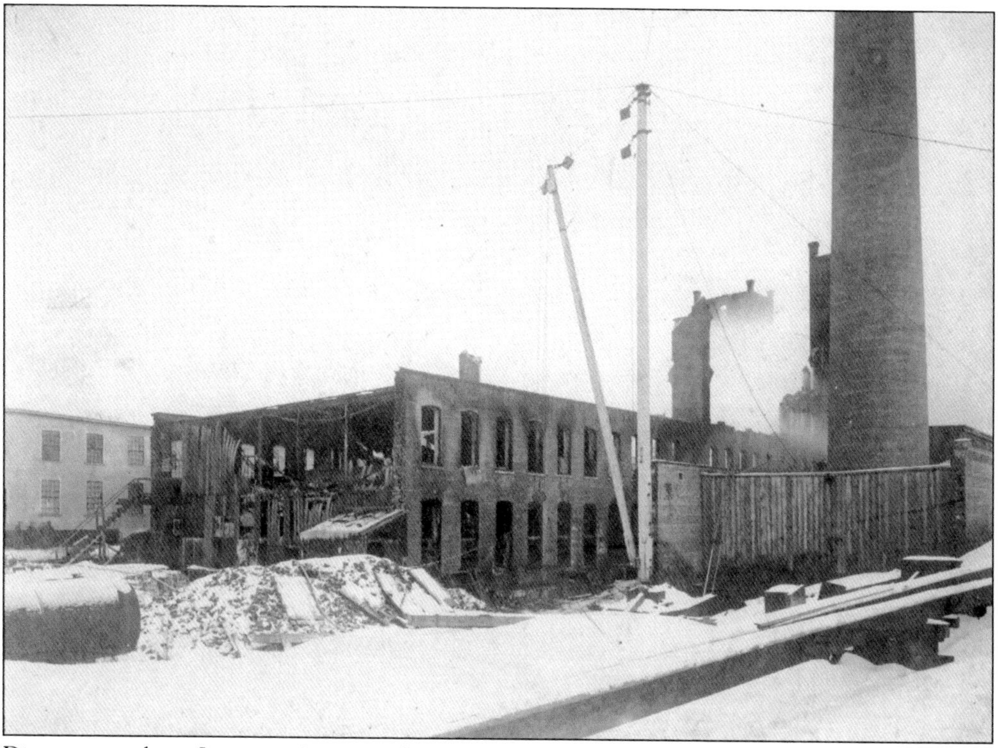

Disaster struck on January 19, 1909, when a first-floor burr-picking machine caught fire in the northeast corner, near Princeton Street, and quickly spread to the gauze-like wool on other machines. Overseer Samuel Ogley, who discovered the fire, managed to get about 100 operatives safely out of the building. This photograph shows temporary wooden walls where further construction was planned for the main and coal storage buildings. (William Johnston Jr.)

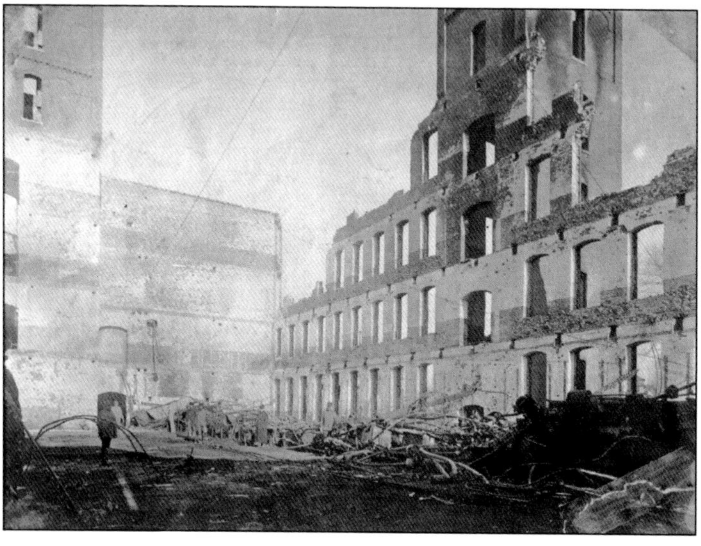

In 1903, George C. Moore had installed a sprinkler system in the relatively undamaged Baldwin Mill, according to *Insurance Engineering*, but he inexplicably did not install sprinklers in this new mill. The seven- and six-story elevator towers were still standing, but everything was destroyed in the four-story and west two-story sections. Moore is standing second from right. (William Johnston Jr.)

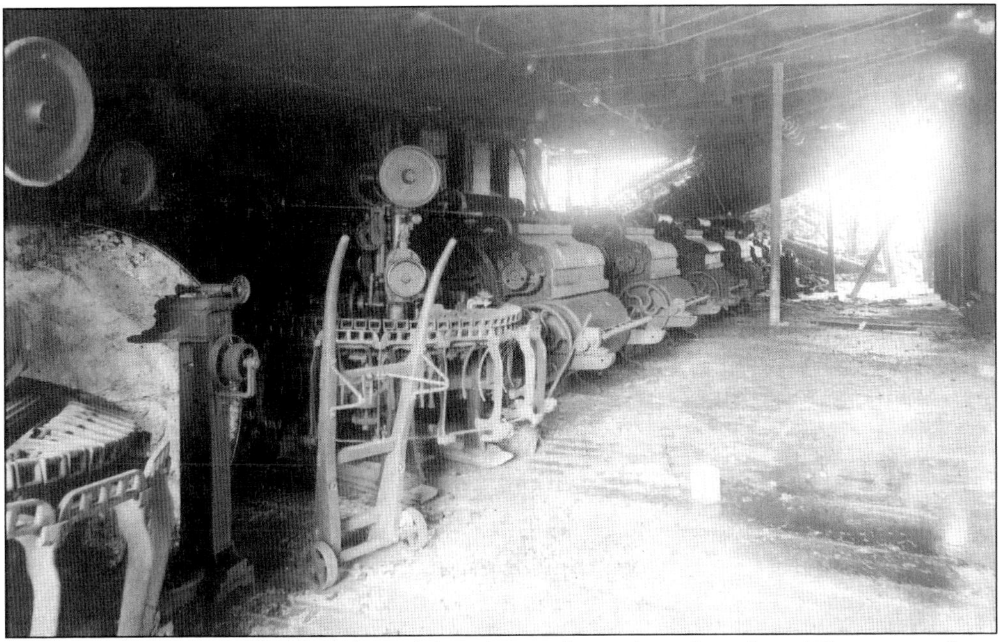

This room where the fire started was left in better shape than the others. The two combing machines and six carding machines at left were being prepared for salvage and rebuilding. Business continued in the undamaged Baldwin Mill while a new building was designed and built. Edgar R. Dixon ran the Baldwin Mill, and one year later, he was also in charge of the new mill. (William Johnston Jr.)

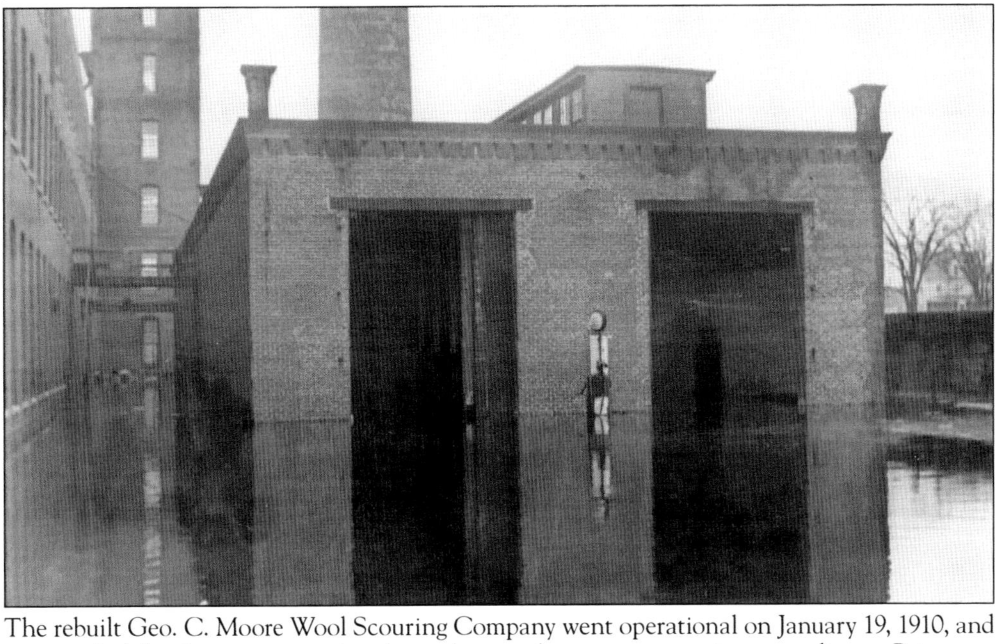

The rebuilt Geo. C. Moore Wool Scouring Company went operational on January 19, 1910, and consisted of the three-story section shown here and a two-story section extending to Princeton Street. This photograph shows the completed coal storage building and round smokestack at the height of the Great Flood Disaster around March 22, 1936, when a sudden thaw and heavy rains created historic flooding across New England. (Chelmsford Historical Society.)

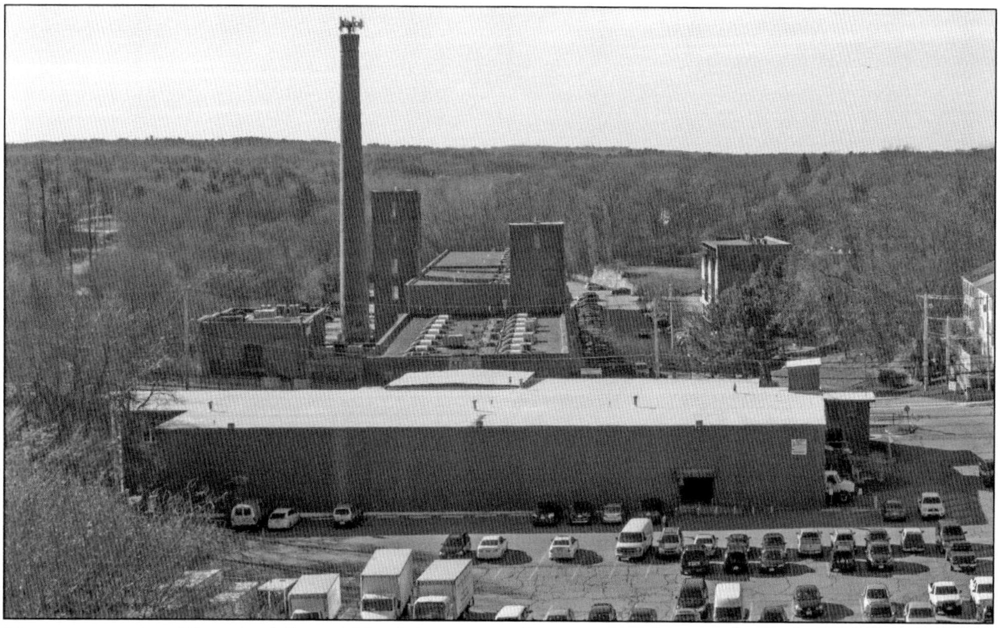

The present-day Geo. C. Moore Wool Scouring Company mill complex is beyond the former North Chelmsford Machine & Supply Company building, with its light colored roof. A three-story office building was added to the left of the smoke stack, the seven-story elevator tower is now five stories, and the Baldwin Mill, upgraded to brick construction, is now a condominium complex. (Photograph by the author.)

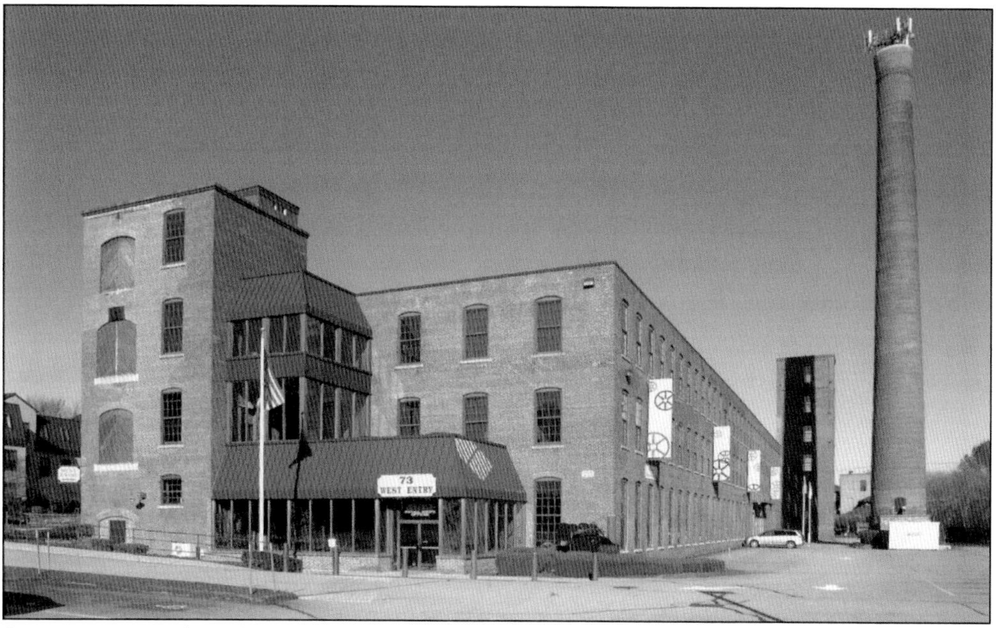


Starting in 1959, the Gilet family ran the complex as the Gilet Wool Scouring Company. In 1985, the Gilets sold it to Northview Realty Trust, which, with the Braeburn Development Corporation, converted the complex for commercial and residential use as shown here. In 1990, the mortgage was foreclosed upon, and in 1991, Gilet Bros. repurchased the complex; the company continues to run it as The Mill. (Photograph by the author.)

# *Four*

# Freeman Lake

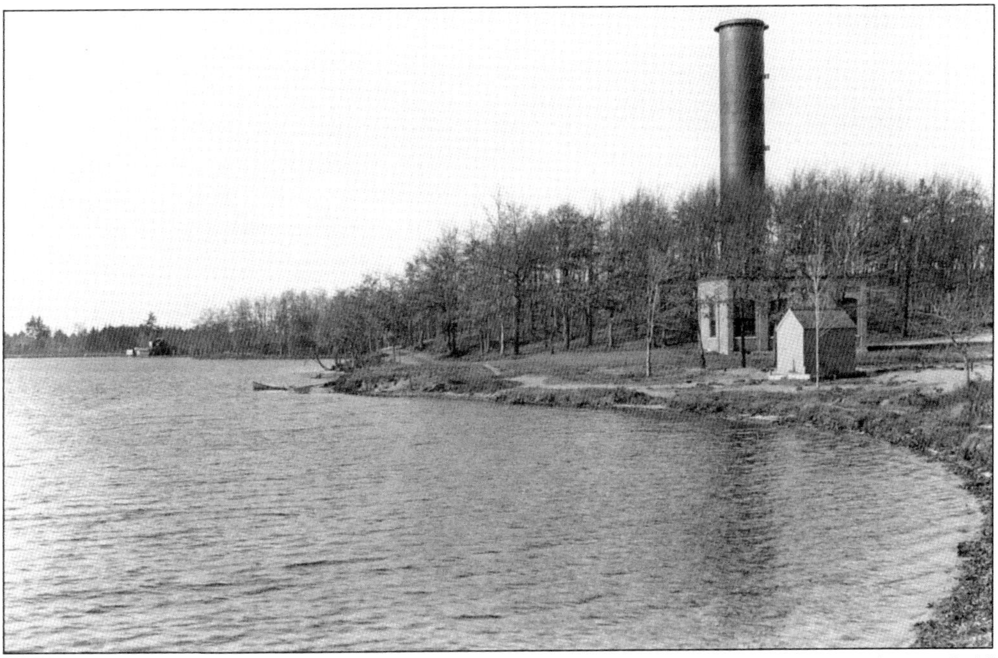

Freeman Lake was formerly called Annanniesumsick (its Native American name), Newfield Pond (Newfield was the original name of North Chelmsford), Leach's Pond, and Crystal Lake. George C. Moore had provided pressurized water for firefighting at his mills since 1876, and he was on the committee of five who selected the site of Chelmsford's first municipal water supply in 1906, which consisted of the pump house, two wells, and 354,000-gallon standpipe shown here. (Chelmsford Historical Society.)

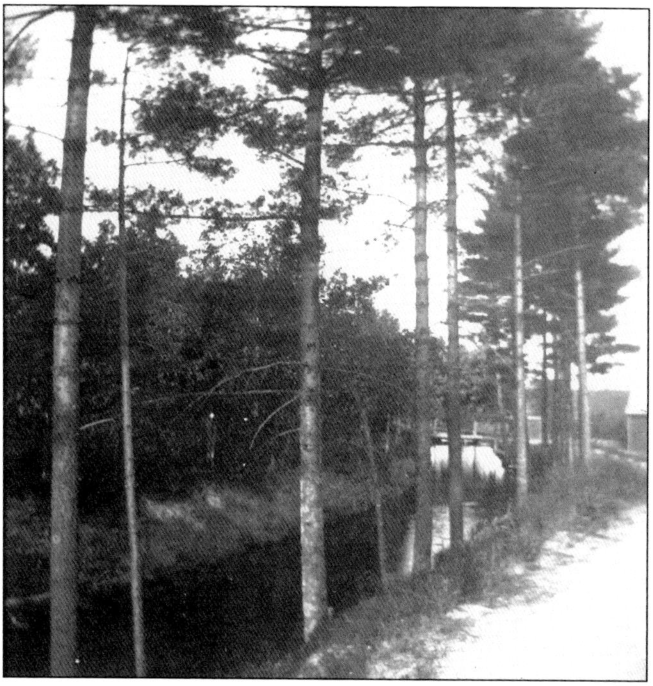

In 1707, John Richardson, in cutting a channel from Freeman Lake to supplement Stony Brook water power for a new ironworks, accidentally drained the 100-acre pond. In 1824, William Adams sold the pond to Gen. Shepherd Leach with land for a canal to fill the pond from Stony Brook and another, shown here, to direct its water toward a new foundry between Princeton and Middlesex Streets. The Spring Street bridge crosses the canal, and the Boston Ice Company barn is at far right. (Chelmsford Public Library.)

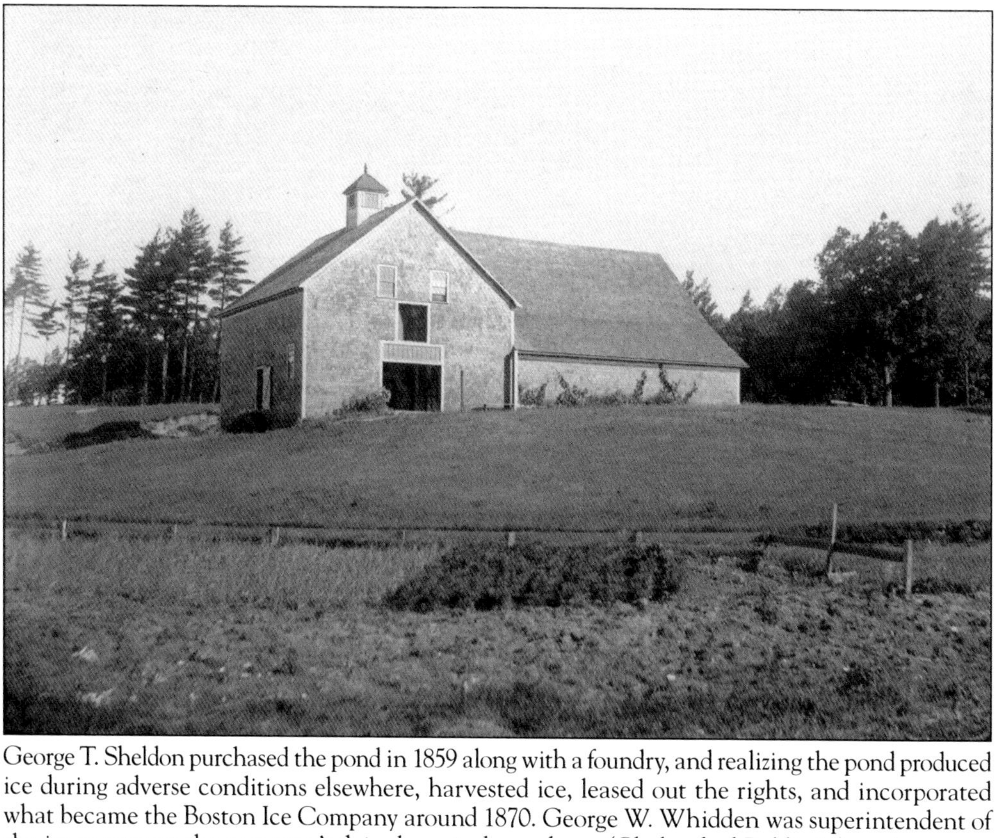

George T. Sheldon purchased the pond in 1859 along with a foundry, and realizing the pond produced ice during adverse conditions elsewhere, harvested ice, leased out the rights, and incorporated what became the Boston Ice Company around 1870. George W. Whidden was superintendent of the ice company; the company's dairy barn is shown here. (Chelmsford Public Library.)

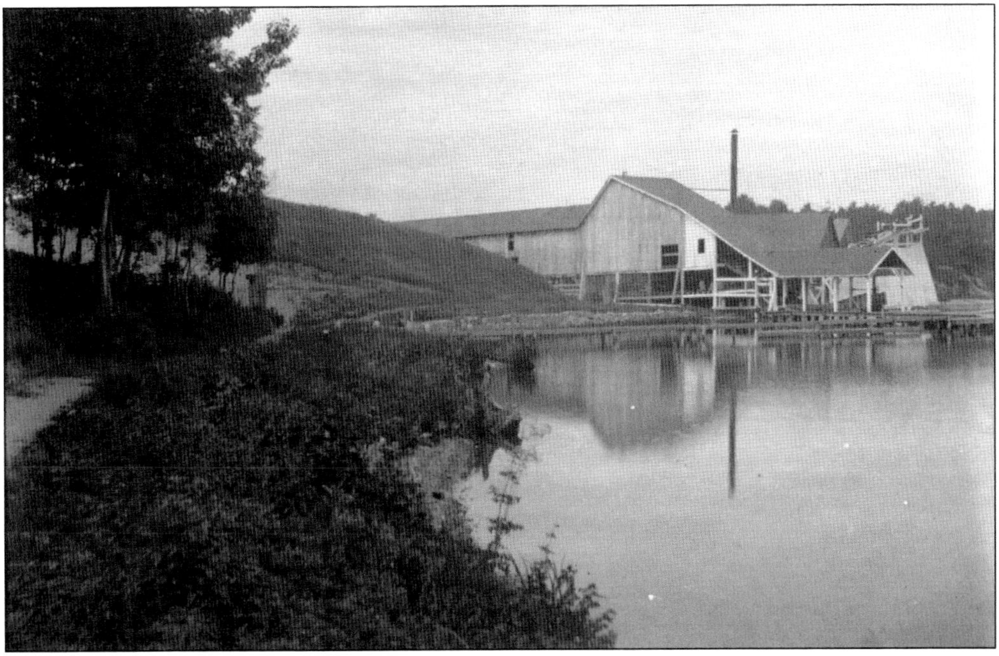

According to the *Lowell Daily Courier*, on January 22, 1901, the icehouses were filled with 50,000 tons of ice by a team of 300 men hired for a two-week period to cut the ice into large blocks, float them over to the two steam engine–driven conveyors shown above, and pack them in sawdust and hay. The men were paid a total of $5,000 and discharged. A smaller group of men stayed on and loaded several hundred tons of ice per day into boxcars—for shipment to Boston icehouses—using the wooden runway, loading platform, and railroad siding shown below. Small crews stayed on through the summer to move ice from storage to railcars (at $1 per ton) for delivery to Boston, where it sold for $3 per ton wholesale and $5 per ton retail. (Both, Chelmsford Public Library.)

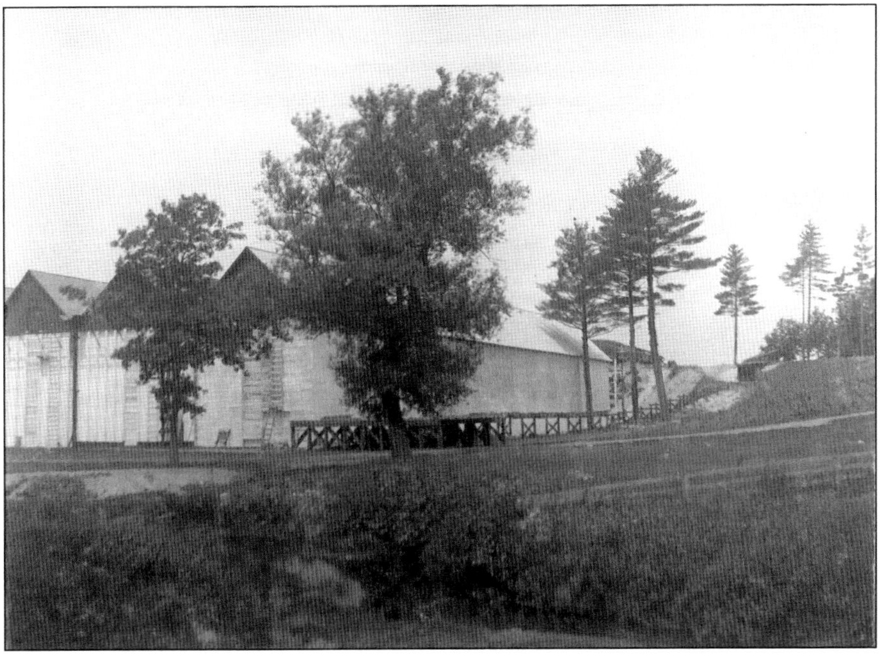

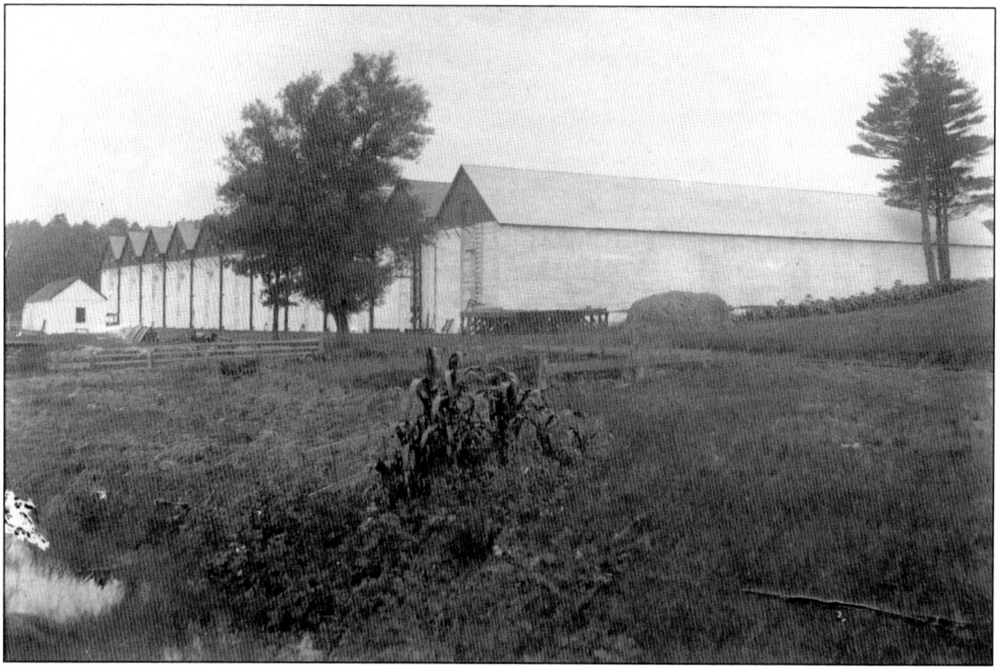

Boston Ice Company superintendent George W. Whidden was at work on Sunday, May 26, 1901, with two of his employees and two outside contractors doing repairs on the roof of one of the icehouses. A fire broke out, and a breeze quickly spread the flames from roof to roof, destroying all the icehouses, the engine and boiler houses near the pond, and the blacksmith shop. They were later rebuilt. (Chelmsford Public Library.)

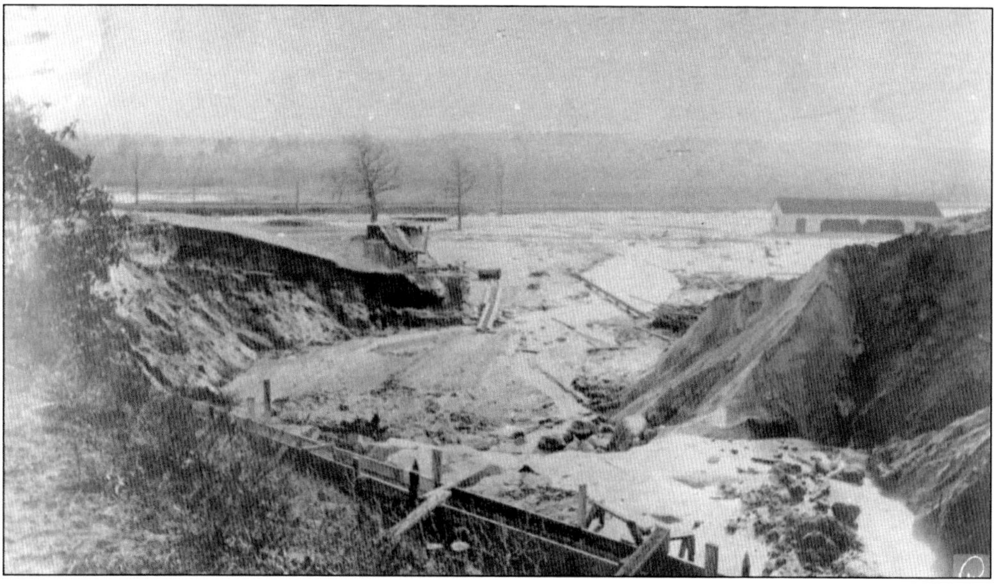

On December 26, 1905, another disaster occurred near the Boston Ice Company. Heavy rains, combined with the closing of the mills for Christmas, caused water to spill over and break through the earth-and-sand canal bank just downstream of the control gate. The hoisting engine used to lift ice from the canal onto the wooden runway was washed away, and the stable was surrounded by mud. (Chelmsford Historical Society.)

The Moore Spinning Company night watchman noticed the lack of water flow in the canal at daylight and alerted George C. Moore of the problem. With 600 mill operatives idled and no water for the fire protection pumps, a high priority was placed on repairing the breach and rebuilding the canal. The spectators shown here are viewing the damage. (Chelmsford Historical Society.)

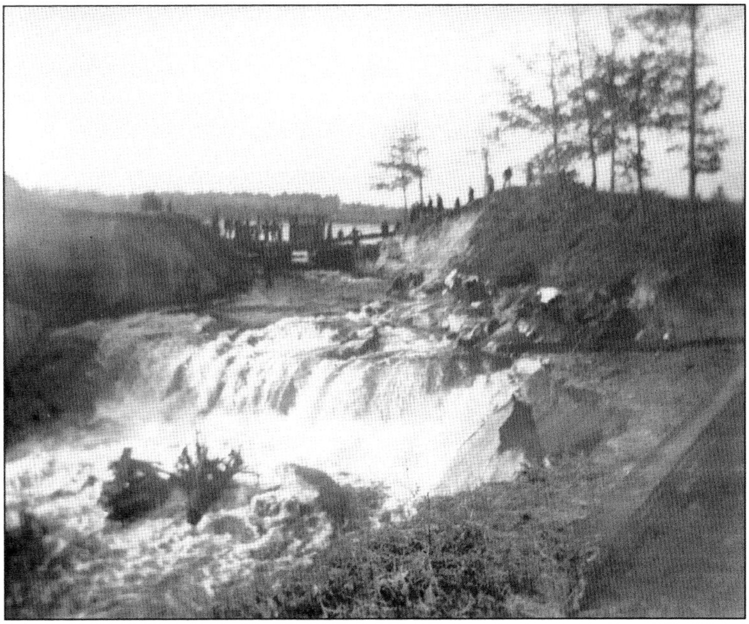

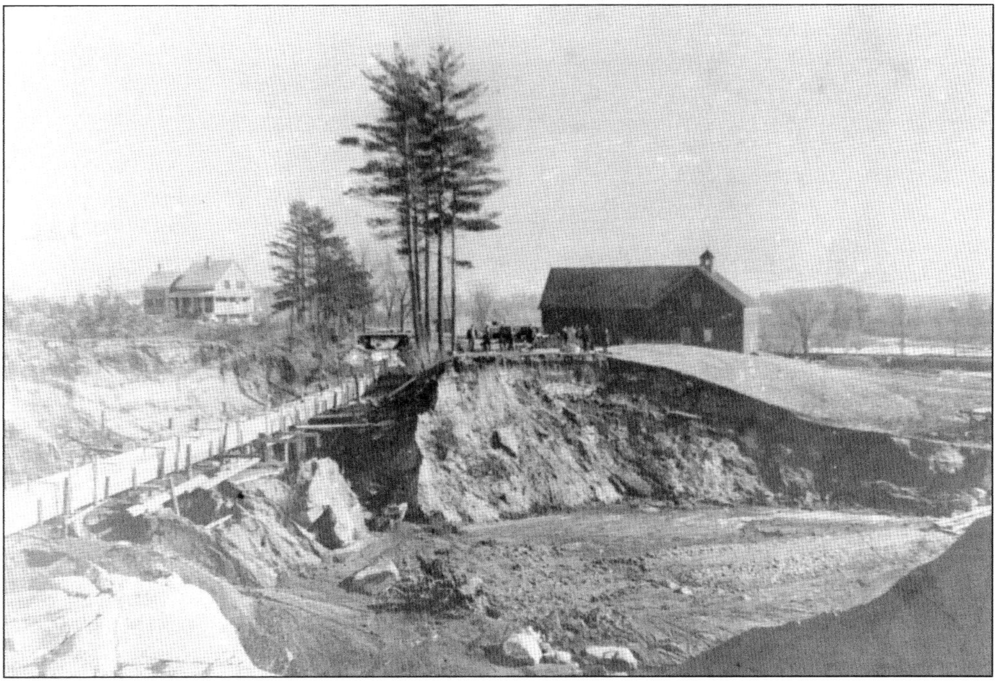

This view shows a temporary wooden sluiceway intended to direct water into the canal for fire protection. In the background are, from left to right, the house at 12 Spring Street, the Spring Street bridge, and the Boston Ice Company barn. George W. Whidden remained superintendent until the Boston Ice Company went out of business after another massive fire around 1927. By 1932, refrigerators were rendering icehouses obsolete. (Chelmsford Historical Society.)

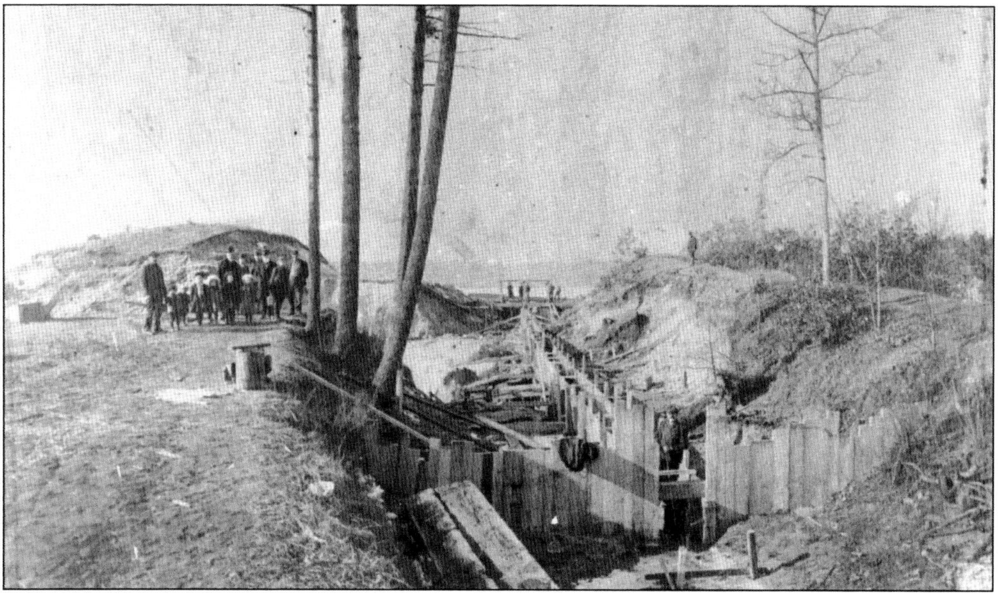

Some of the workers brought their children to see the temporary dam repairs. This view shows the location of the break in the canal bank at left, the canal entrance at center, and the lake beyond not yet high enough to fill the sluiceway. Today, the mill canal is dry and overgrown with brush. (Chelmsford Historical Society.)

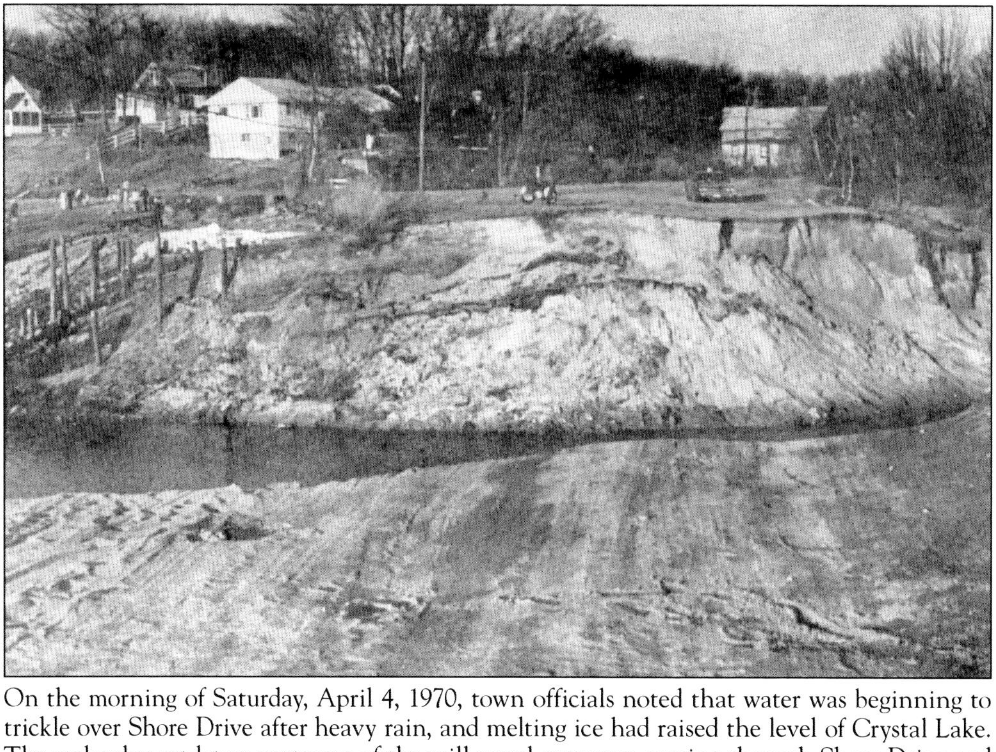

On the morning of Saturday, April 4, 1970, town officials noted that water was beginning to trickle over Shore Drive after heavy rain, and melting ice had raised the level of Crystal Lake. The embankment let go upstream of the mill canal entrance, cutting through Shore Drive and draining the lake in about 30 minutes. The water flowed across Stony Brook, reaching Richardson Road to the southeast and Princeton Street to the northeast. (Chelmsford Historical Society.)

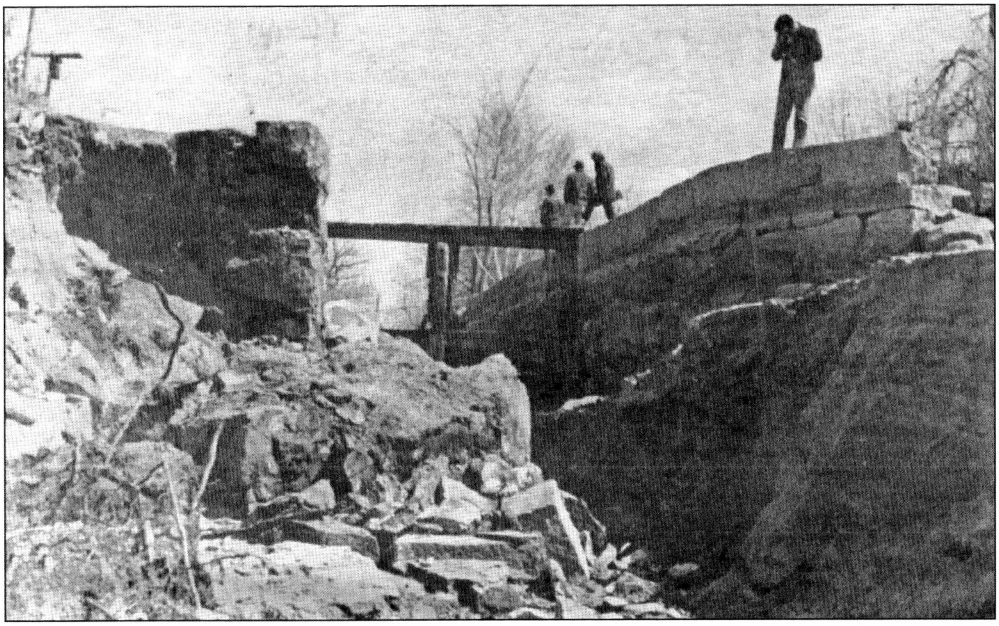

This was the view looking up from the bottom of the lake to the entrance of the mill canal, which had been reinforced with granite walls after the 1905 break. Businesses on Princeton Street were damaged, and about 2,000 feet of Boston & Maine Railroad track was undermined and shifted. Massachusetts governor Francis Sargent flew in by helicopter the Monday after the incident and viewed the scene with other state and local officials. (Chelmsford Historical Society.)

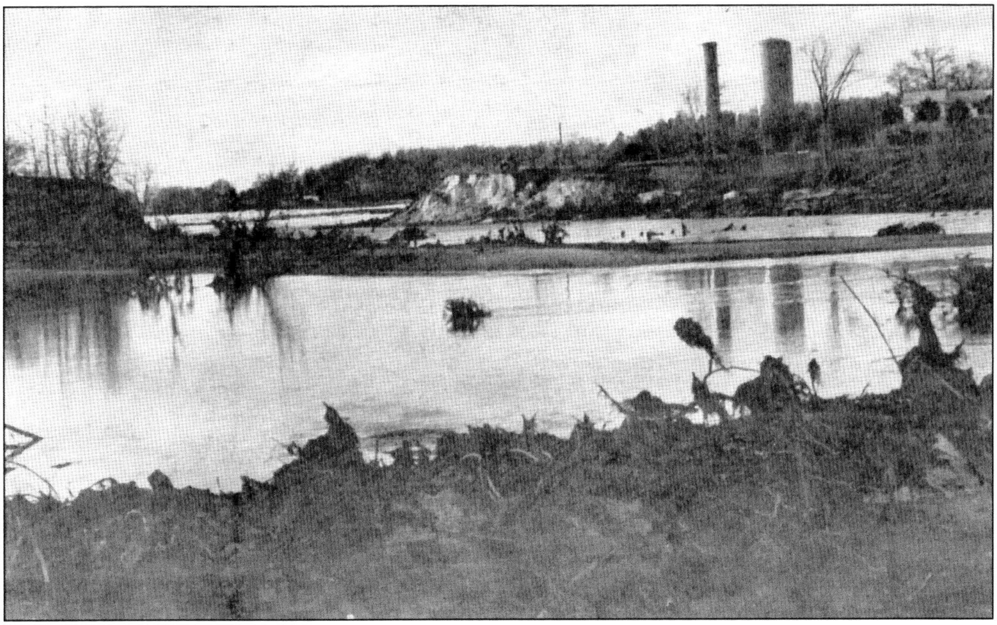

A temporary road was built so that isolated Shore Drive residents could access Route 3, and the Boston & Maine Railroad repaired its tracks in a day and a half. In 1970, the original North Chelmsford Water District standpipe was still in use beside a new 1.8 million–gallon water tank installed in 1968. The old standpipe was removed in 1991 after Hurricane Bob blew off its iron cover. (Chelmsford Historical Society.)

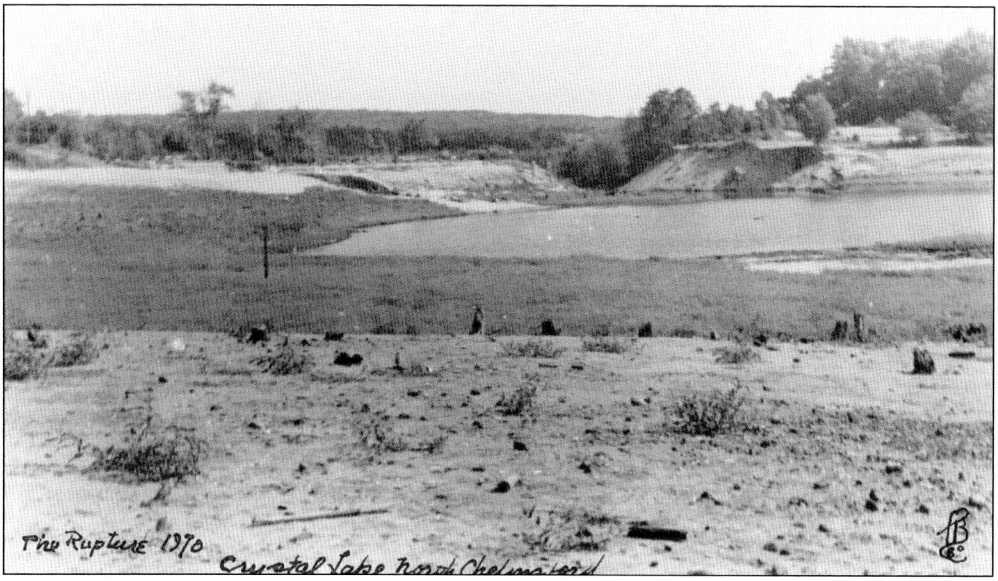


Stumps from trees that could have grown after the accidental draining in 1707 and before 1824, when the canal was built, were exposed as ice melted and the lake bed dried out. The Board of Selectmen received pledges of assistance in rebuilding the lake from Gov. Francis Sargent, the US Army Corps of Engineers, and the Small Business Administration. State representative Bruce Freeman filed a Crystal Lake restoration bill in 1972. (Chelmsford Historical Society.)

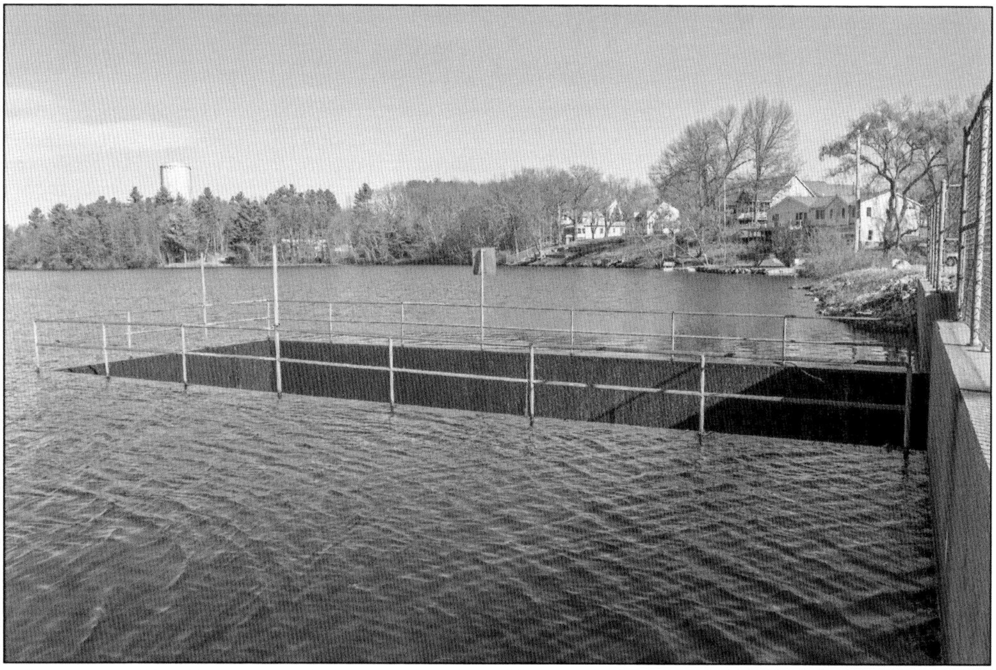

After years of hard work, the lake was finally refilled in March 1977, but some pollution issues had to be resolved before the town beach at Varney Playground could be opened, and there was seepage to repair. After Rep. Bruce Freeman died on June 18, 1986, Crystal Lake was renamed Bruce Freeman Lake in recognition of his work in getting the funds necessary to rebuild the dam. (Photograph by the author.)

# *Five*

# VINAL SQUARE

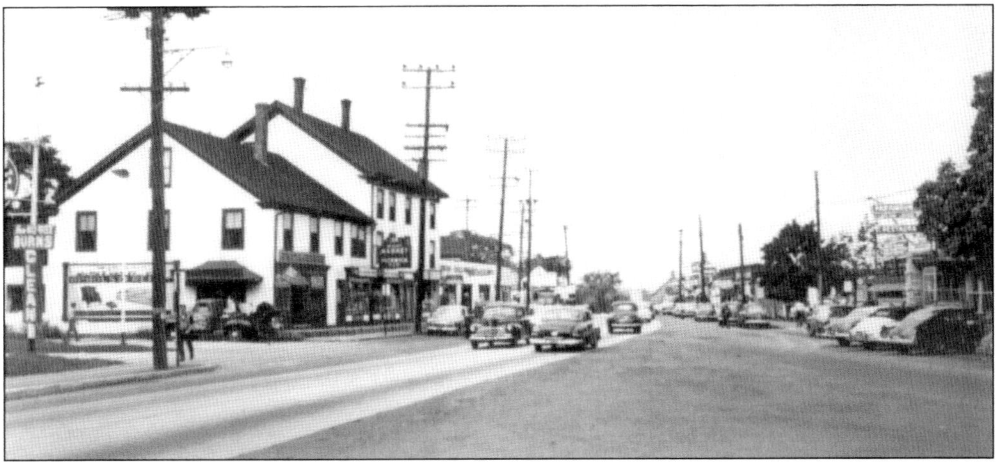

The old Village House at 33 Vinal Square was a commercial and residential center of Vinal Square during its lifetime. Some of the many businesses occupying the lower floors of the building included Vinal Square Drug Store, Anton's Cleaners, Russell's Bakery, Milton E. Hadley Upholstery, North Chelmsford Market, Brookside Farm Store, Arthelem Santerre's barber shop, a meat market, a pool room, a haberdashery, and a beauty salon. (Linda Prescott.)

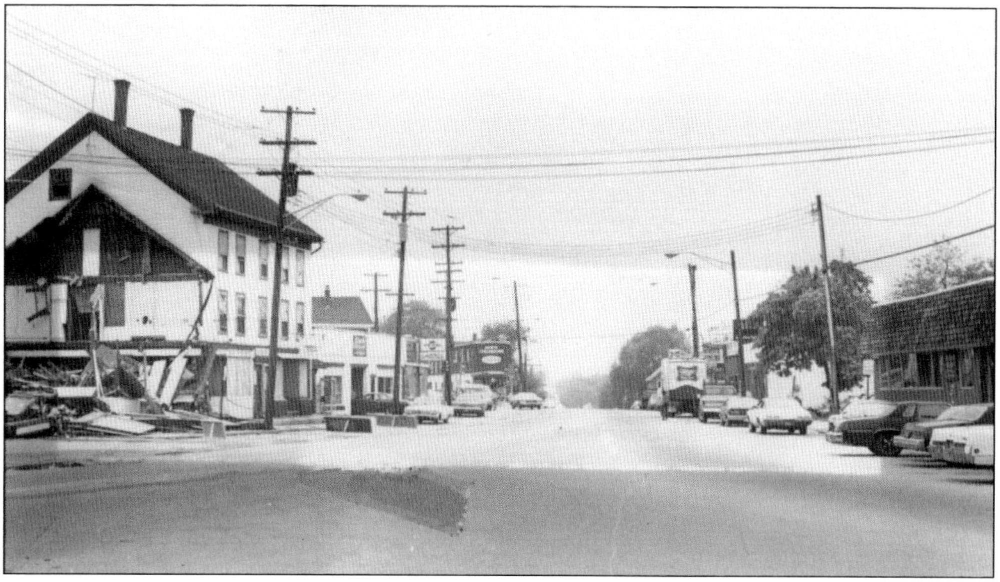

John H. Valentine Sr. was a North Chelmsford postmaster, lawyer, town counsel, town moderator, state representative, judge in Lowell District Court, and the owner of the Village House until his death in 1969. Its demolition took place on May 22, 1979, as part of a Vinal Square cleanup effort, with the site becoming a parking lot for the businesses next door and eventually being enlarged and paved. (Linda Prescott.)

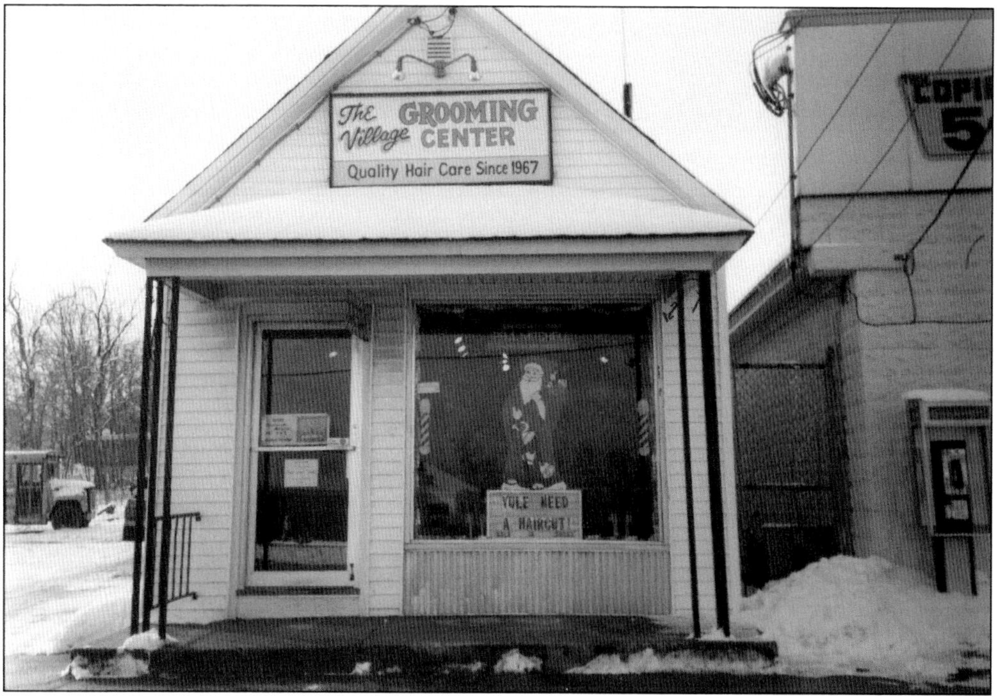


George S. Elliott ran a small variety store here at 29 Vinal Square until 1936, when his son Henry S. "Cap" Elliott, a gasoline station mechanic, took over. Cap was legendary with neighborhood kids and ran the variety store until his death in 1954. Pete Ricciardi and Bob Scharn started the Village Grooming Center here in 1967, and Ricciardi still owned the business in 2016. (Peter Ricciardi.)

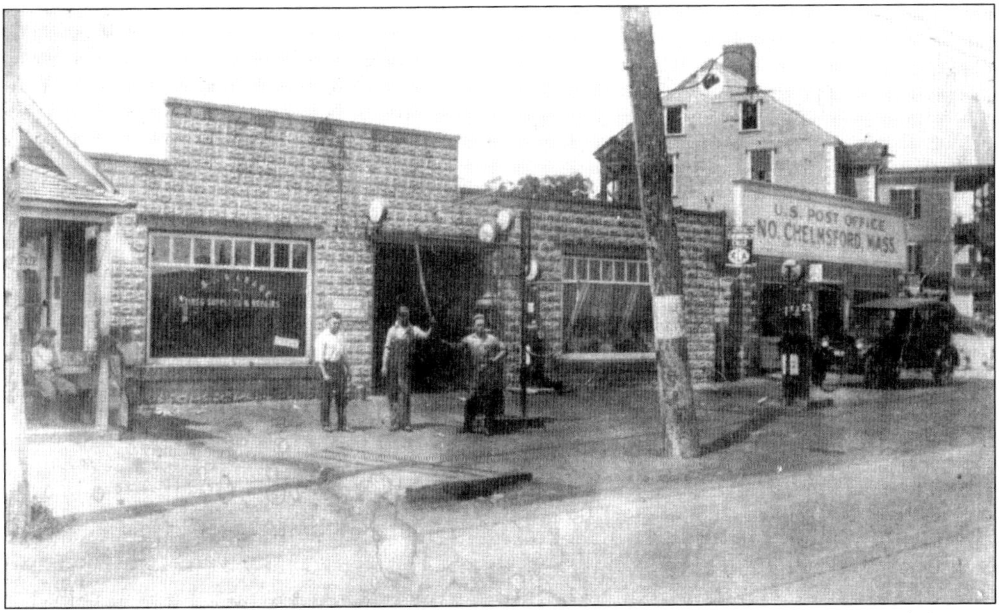


Elliott's variety store is at far left, and the service station next door at 25–27 Vinal Square later became the Cushman Bakery and is now home to Rosie's Diner. John H. Valentine's post office at 21 Vinal Square is at right, and the Adams Tavern looms above it at 15 Vinal Square. (Peter Ricciardi.)

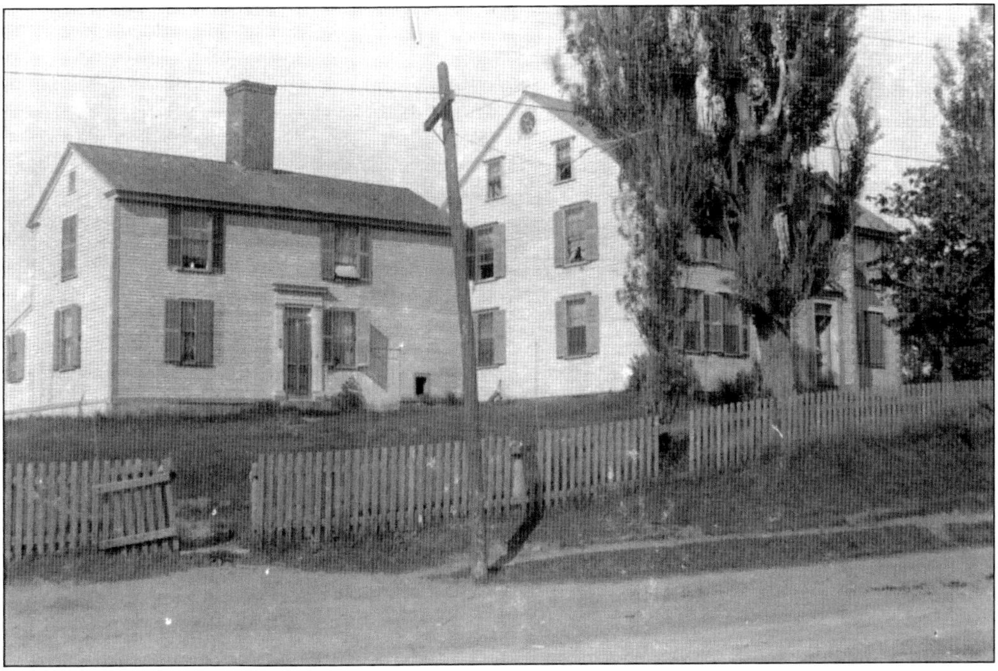

The smaller building at left was constructed in 1770 between Groton and Dunstable Roads as a tavern and residence for William Adams, the grandfather of T.J. and B.F. Adams. The selectmen declared it too small and threatened to take away his tavern license, so the larger structure was built in 1781. The smaller house was later moved across Groton Road and positioned as shown here. (Chelmsford Public Library.)

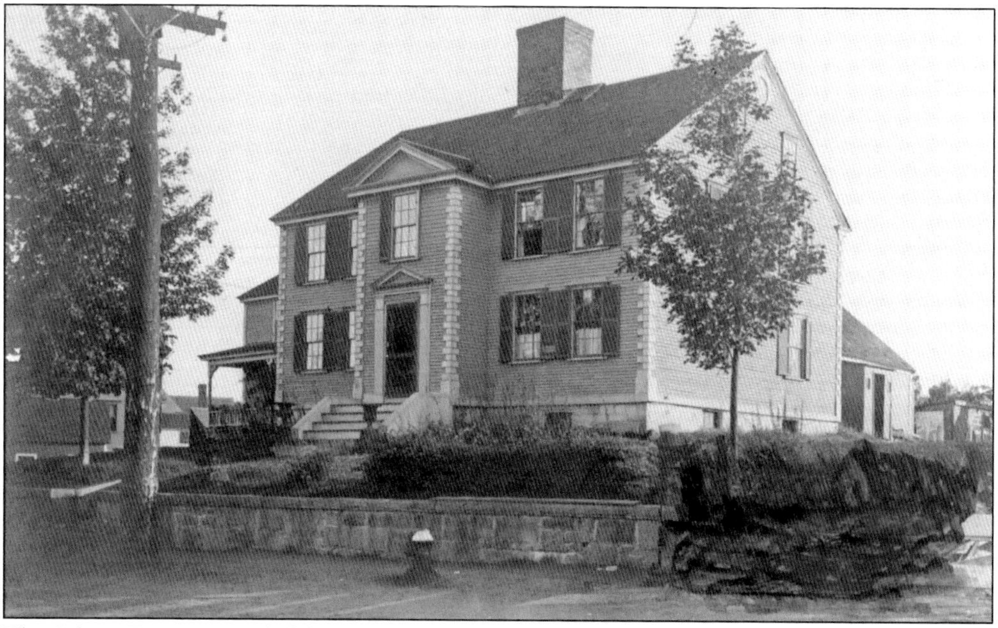

The Adams Tavern preceded the Adams Hotel by 50 years and served stage and horse traffic going from Boston to New Hampshire. William Adams's son, a well-respected military officer and town official also named William, was instrumental in attracting industry to his massive land holdings, which included much of North Chelmsford. His grandsons T.J. and B.F. Adams, also military officers, continued to develop the family's land inheritance. (Chelmsford Historical Society.)

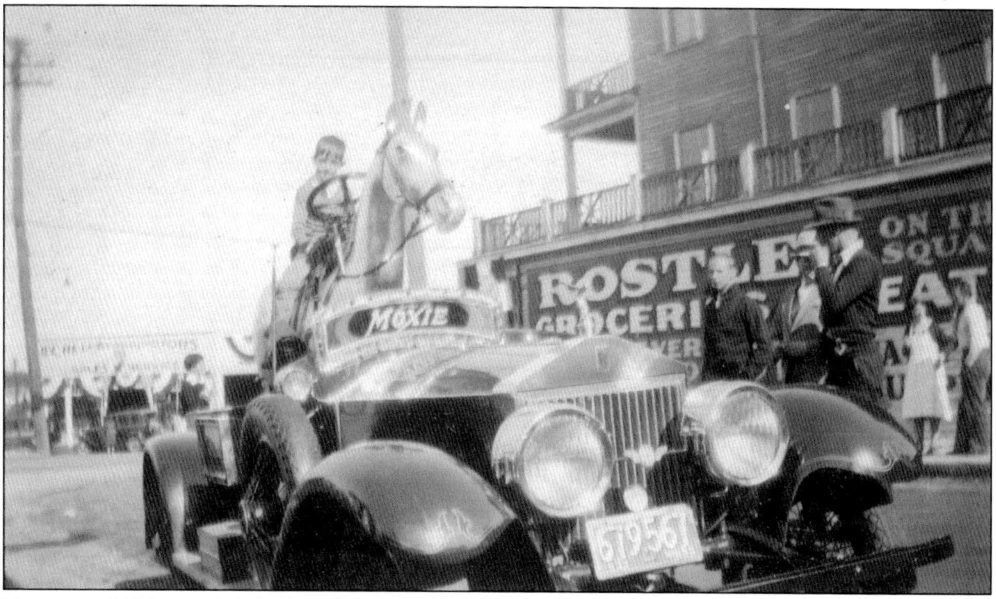


Ten-year-old Francis Miskell had the thrill of sitting atop the driver's saddle on a Moxie Rolls-Royce in 1932. During the late 1920s, when these promotional vehicles were built, Moxie outsold Coca-Cola in the United States. During the 1930s, the Great Depression and an attempt to substitute cheaper ingredients hurt business. Percy T. Robinson's North Chelmsford Motors is at left, and the Adams Street side of Sigmund E. Rostler's grocery and provision store is at right. (Francis Miskell.)

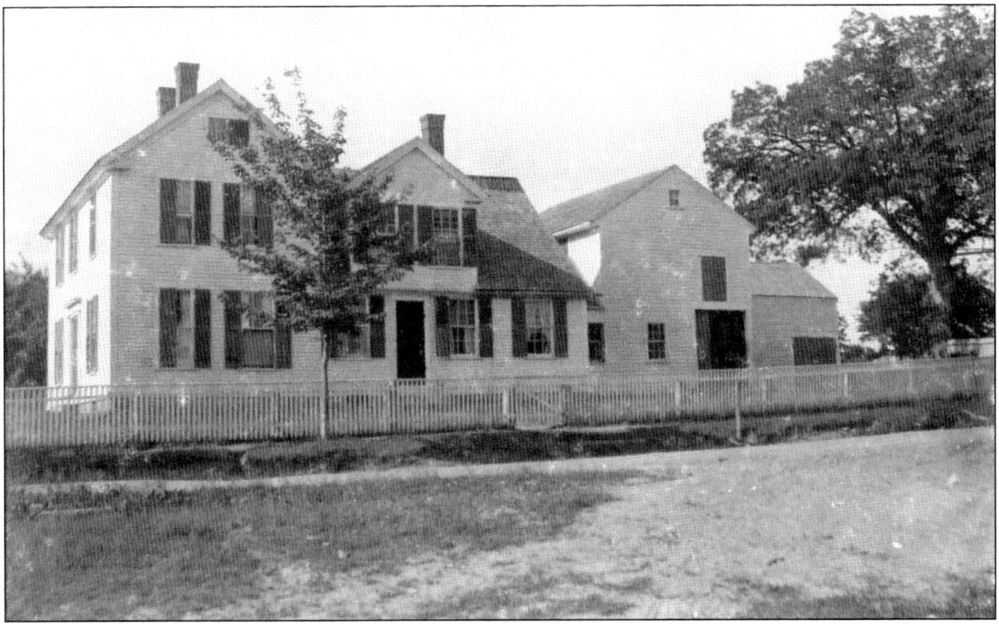

When this c. 1900 photograph was taken, teacher Mary Howard, widow of Calvin Howard, who died at age 48 in 1870, lived here at 4–8 Groton Road. Other residents included her son Henry E., daughter-in-law Ora C., and granddaughters Mary B. and Cara E. Howard. Henry was a moulder at one of the local iron foundries. The house and outbuildings have been converted into four apartment units. (Chelmsford Public Library.)

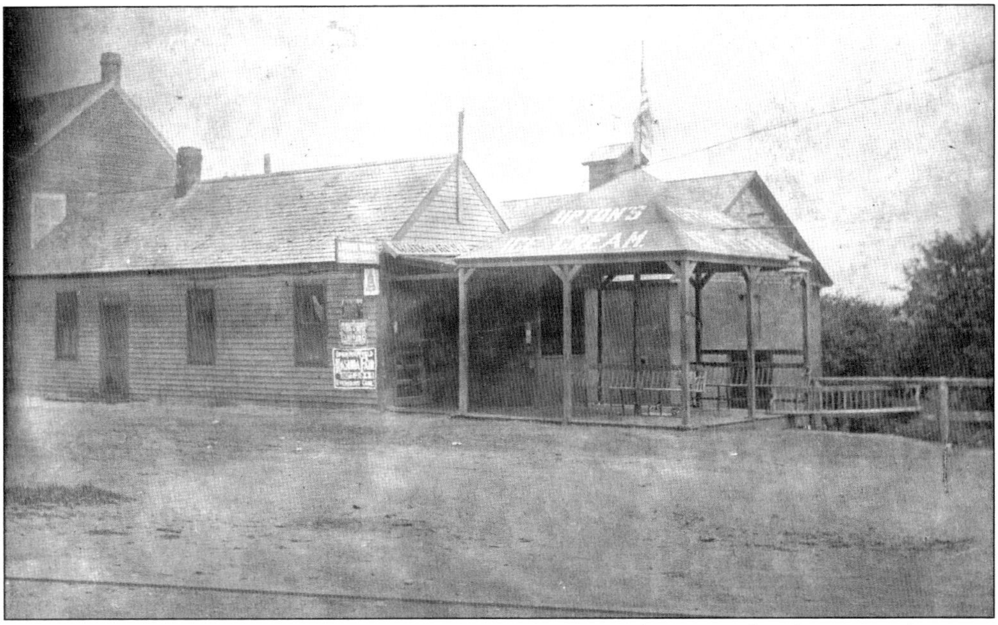


For a few years around 1905, teamster John P. Upton ran a confectionary, lunchroom, and waiting room for trolley patrons here at the junction of Dunstable and Tyngsboro Roads. The two-story building at far left is still standing today, incorporated into the North Chelmsford Hardware block, but the large barn on the other side of Tyngsboro Road was removed sometime before 1917. (Chelmsford Historical Society.)

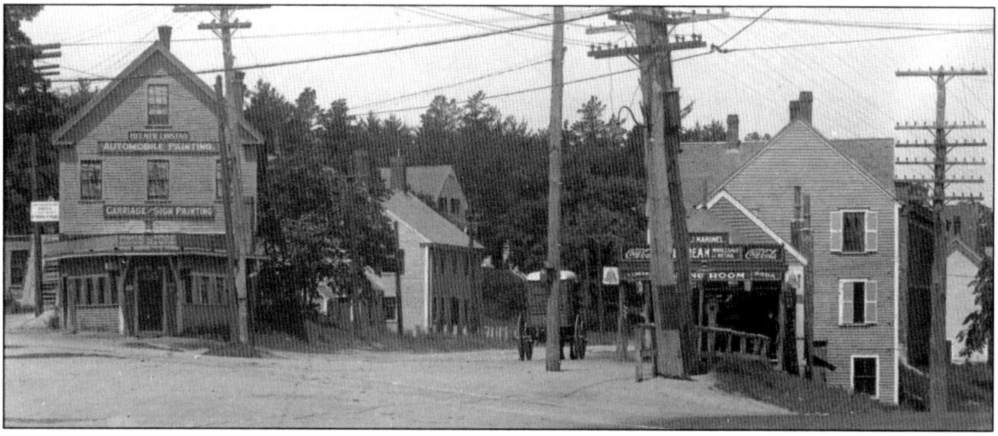


In 1915, painter Helmer Linstad had moved to Lowell, but John S. Westwood ran the drugstore below his paint shop at left. John Marinel Jr. grew up in the large house to the left of the wagon at 20 Groton Road, and his wife, Alice, ran the trolley waiting room and store, advertising "Ice Cream, Fruit and Confectionary, Cigars and Tobacco, Dry Goods and Notions." (Chelmsford Historical Commission)

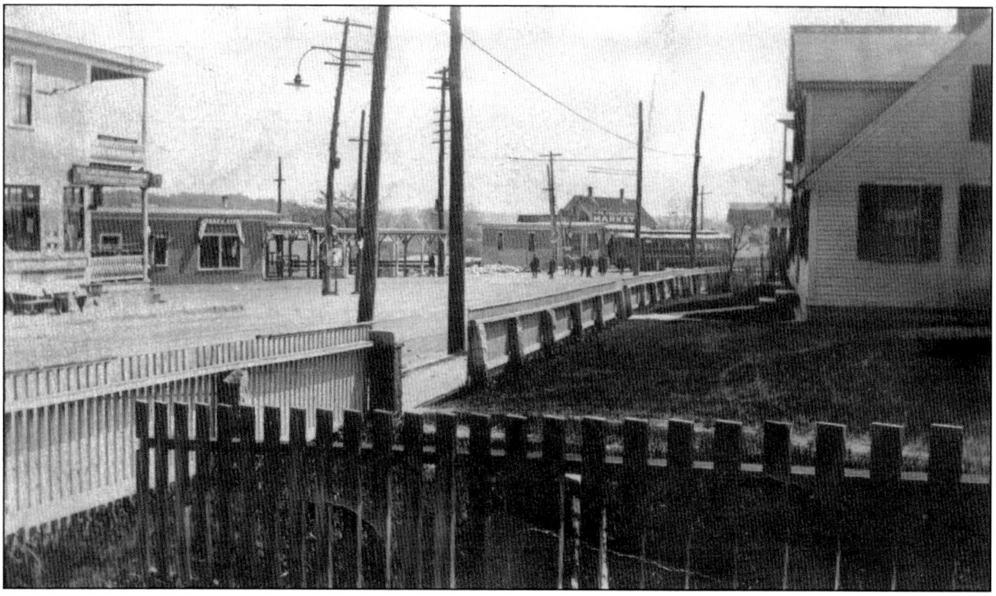


In 1917, John S. Westwood's drugstore was still located between Groton and Dunstable Roads. David F. Small, brother-in-law of John Marinel Jr., and Joseph A. Stone ran a wholesale ice cream and party supplies business next to the waiting room, and Alice Marinel continued to operate the store. Edward F. Anderson's North Chelmsford Market is behind the Tyngsboro-bound trolley, and Mary Howard's house is at right. (George Merrill.)

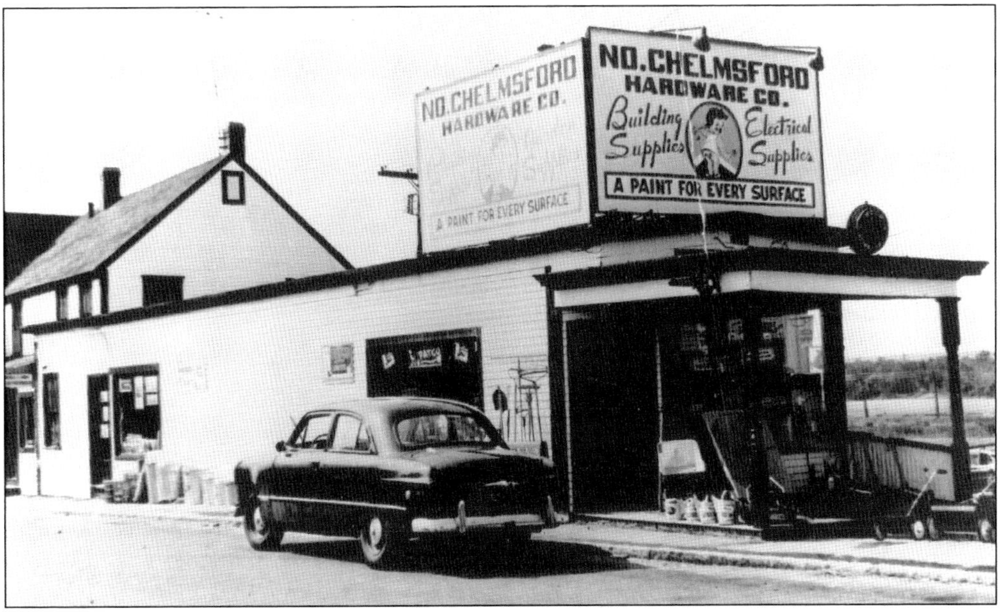


In 1946, James K. Quinn Sr. and John Cafiso purchased the former waiting room and nearby buildings at the junction of Dunstable and Tyngsboro Roads, which, by that time, consisted of a variety store, a secondhand shop, and two apartments. Quinn bought out Cafiso's share of the North Chelmsford Hardware Company in 1948 and later added offices above the one-story section shown here in 1950. (James K. Quinn Jr.)

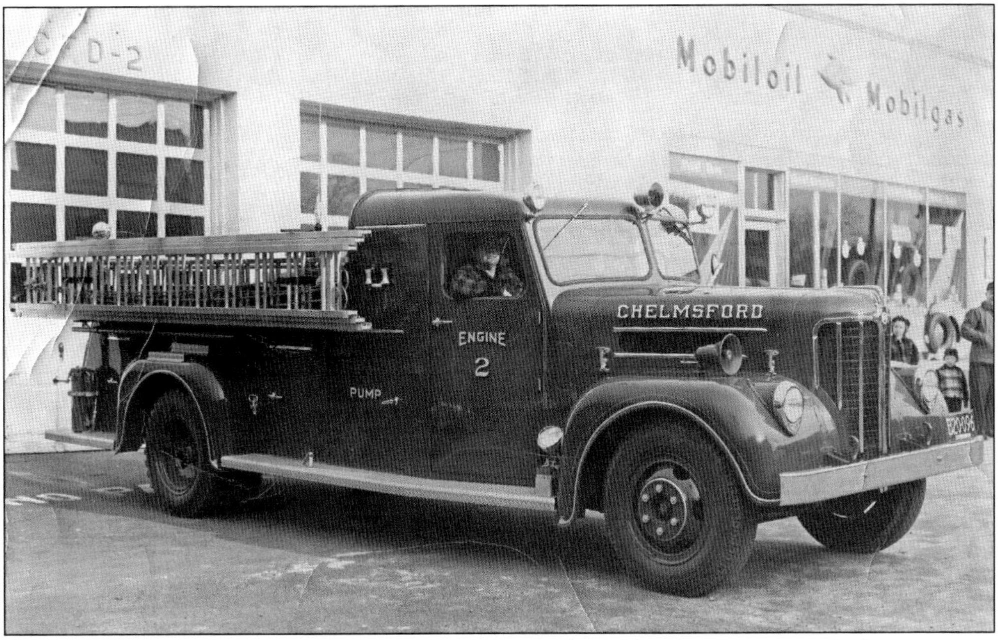


This Maxim 750-gallon-per-minute pumper was purchased by the town in 1951 for service as Engine No. 2 in North Chelmsford and housed in a rented service bay at the Vinal Square Mobil Station. A long-needed, town-owned fire station was constructed in 1956 on the vacant site of North Chelmsford High School, next door to North Town Hall on Princeton Street, and opened in December of that year. (Chelmsford Fire Department.)

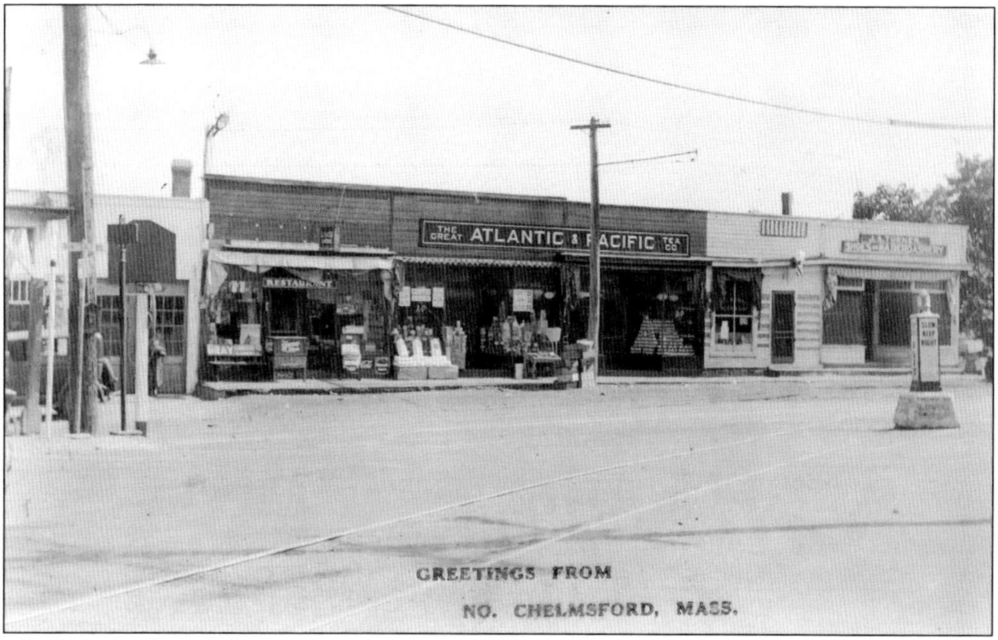


The Great Atlantic & Pacific Tea Co. occupied this storefront from around 1925 until 1949. Alphonse Gilbert's barbershop (next door) and James A. Turner's men's furnishing and shoe store (next to Wotton Street) were gone by 1932. Other stores came and went until December 1984, when Charlie Parlee's J & C Management purchased the entire block and rebuilt it to modern standards. (Chelmsford Historical Society.)

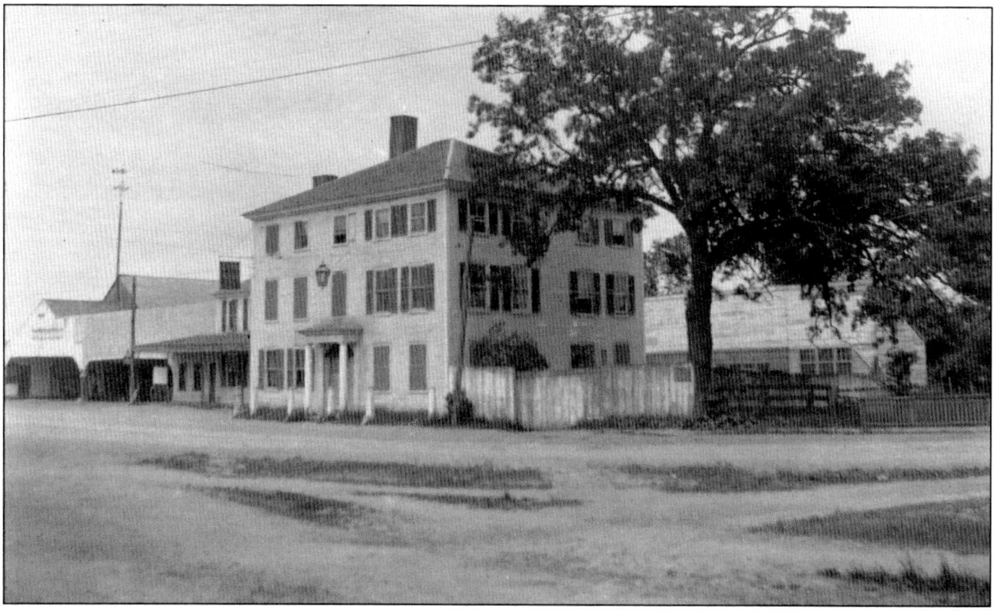

The Adams House hotel was managed by about 40 different men after it was constructed by the Adams family in 1820. Around 1900, when this photograph was taken by Simon Towle, Joseph A. Ryan was the owner-operator, along with his family. One of the earlier hotel operators was Frank H. Harris, who also owned the nearby Wannalancit Park dog and horse racing track in the late 1890s. (Chelmsford Public Library.)

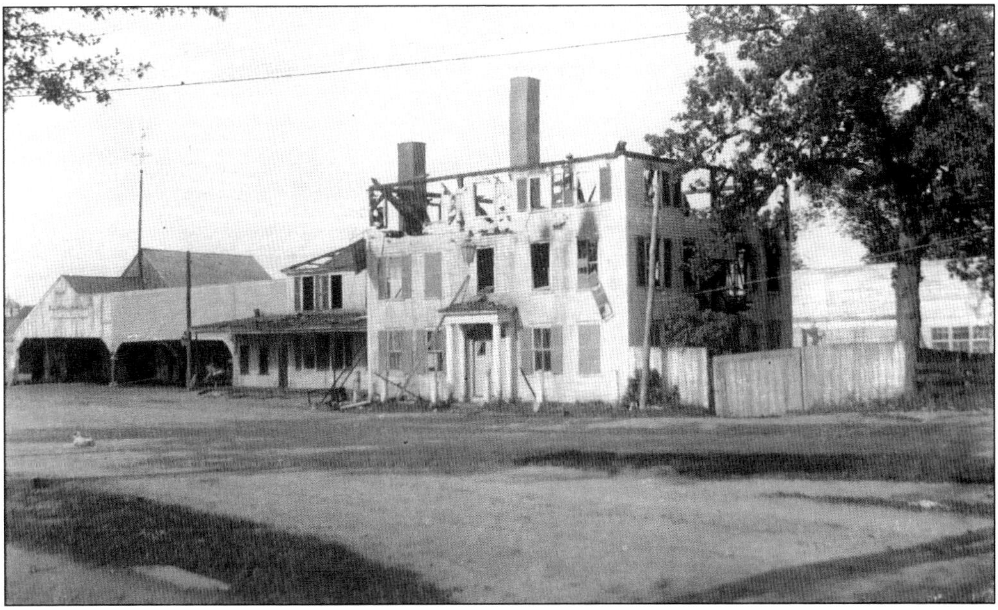

On Sunday, September 16, 1900, there were about 12 boarders in the 30-room Adams House. Around 4:00 p.m., boarder Albert Stevens left his third-floor room for a few minutes, and when he returned, he discovered his kerosene lamp had exploded and the room was ablaze. Nobody was injured, but the blaze could not be stopped before it destroyed the main house and part of the ell. (Chelmsford Public Library.)

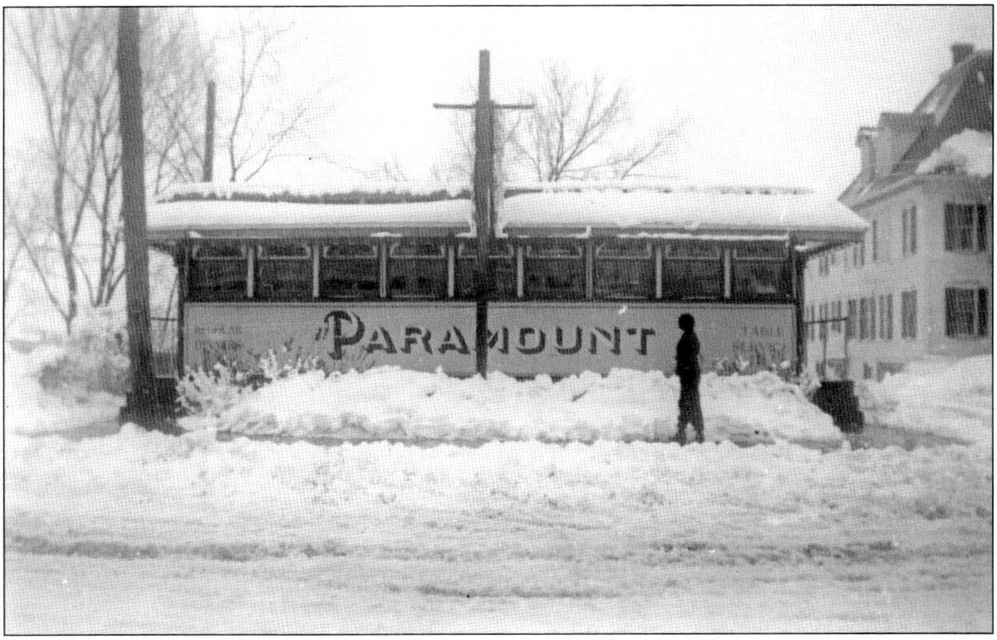

In 1931, diner No. 686 was constructed by the Worcester Lunch Car Co. and installed on the site of the Adams House livery stable as the Paramount. Former quarryman Frank DeAmicis operated the diner, and in 1948, it became the Paramount Lounge when a brick structure was added on the rear with function rooms, a lounge, and a popular bar in the back. The new Adams House is visible in the background at right. (Francis Miskell.)

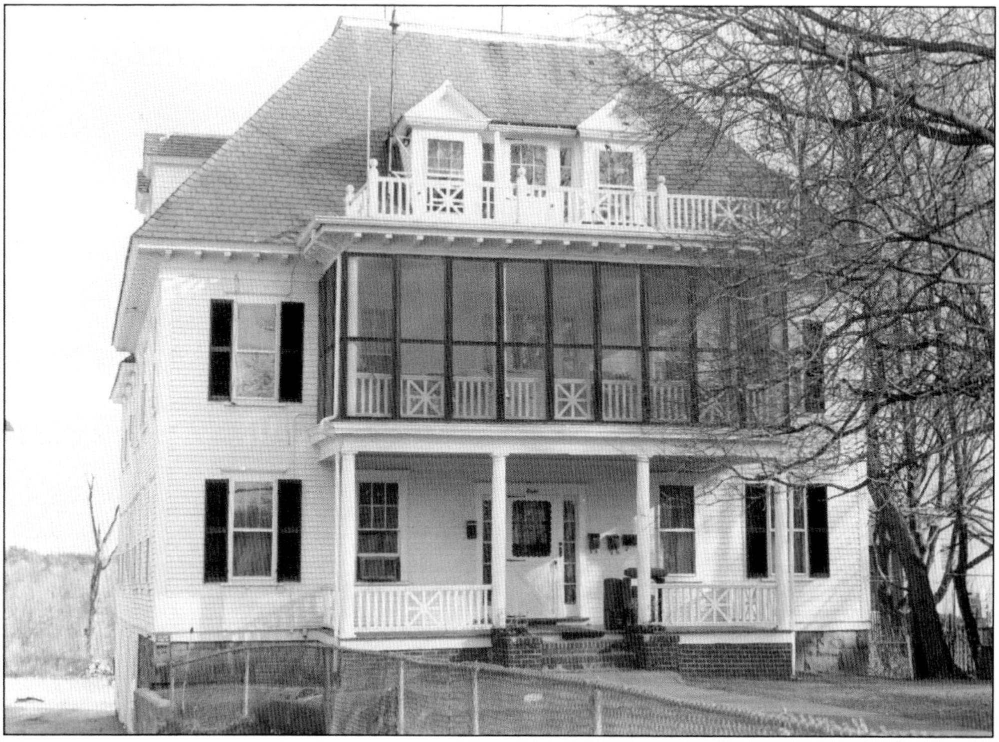

The new Adams House Hotel, located at 8 Middlesex Street, opened in March 1901 with a lunchroom in the basement and 20 rooms in the three other stories. The new building was situated exactly 300 feet away from the Second Congregational Church to avoid denial of a liquor license. This December 1973 photograph shows the hotel as converted to apartments around 1950 and owned by the DeAmicis family. (Chelmsford Historical Commission.)

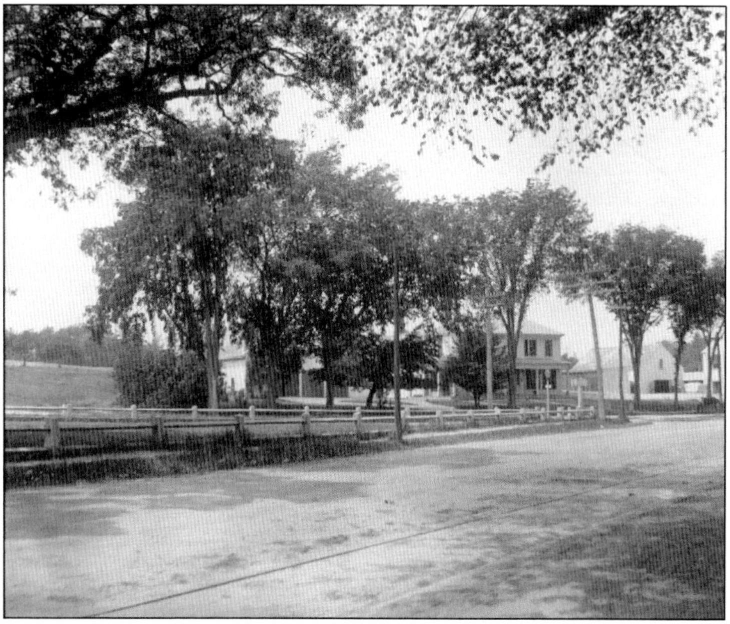

The outbuildings and house behind the elm trees at 9 Princeton Street were formerly owned by Benjamin Franklin Adams and, at this time (around 1900), by the estate of Elisha H. Shaw. The public triangle in the foreground was donated to the town in two equal halves by Adams's estate and Clara, the widow of Thomas Jefferson Adams, in 1884. Note the large barns behind the Village House at right. (Chelmsford Public Library.)

# *Six*

# Middlesex Street

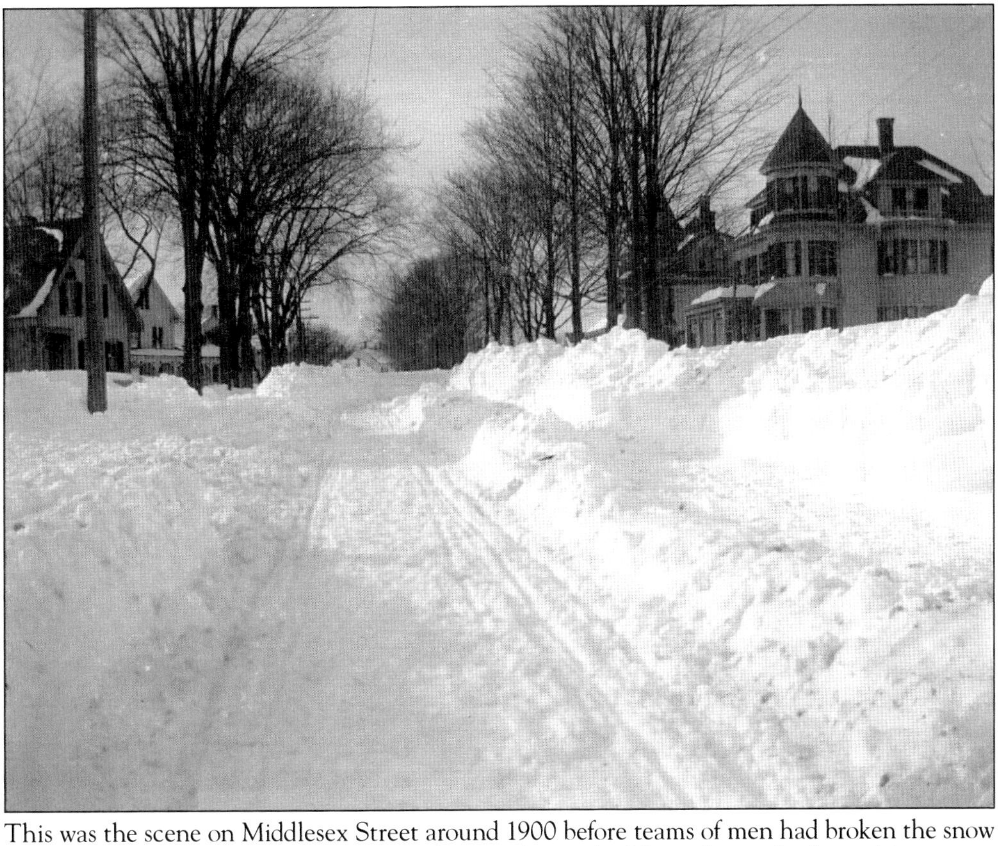

This was the scene on Middlesex Street around 1900 before teams of men had broken the snow drifts enough for a trolley plow to finish clearing the tracks. Horse-drawn sleighs and foot power were the only ways to get around on this day. The Village House is straight ahead, 41–43 Middlesex Street is on the left, and 42 Middlesex Street is on the right. (Chelmsford Public Library.)

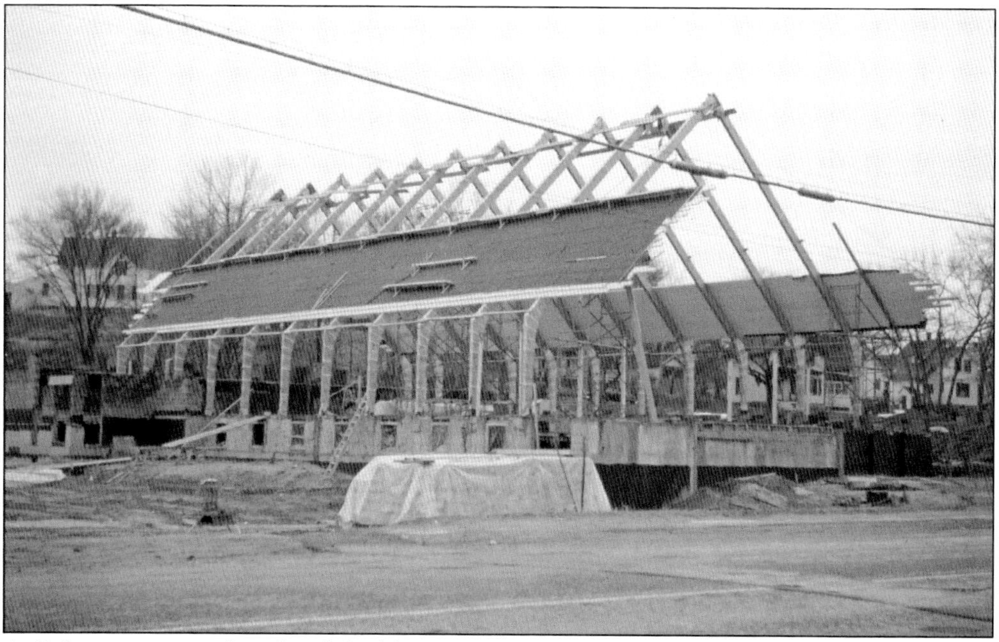

A 42-foot square wooden church building was purchased in 1860 at Middlesex Village for $400, moved two miles to North Chelmsford, and enlarged in 1893. This building at 51 Church Street served St. John the Evangelist Parish, but by 1962, there were 1,700 parishioners in need of a new building, adequate parking, and classroom space. The contract for a new brick building at 115 Middlesex Street went to Walsh Construction Company, and the first Mass was celebrated in the new building on October 20, 1963. The building was dedicated on November 13, 1963, by Richard Cardinal Cushing. A parish center and rectory were added in 1980 and a new parish center in 2009. The house on the left in both photographs is 21 James Street, and houses on Highland Avenue are visible above through the framework. (St. John the Evangelist Parish.)

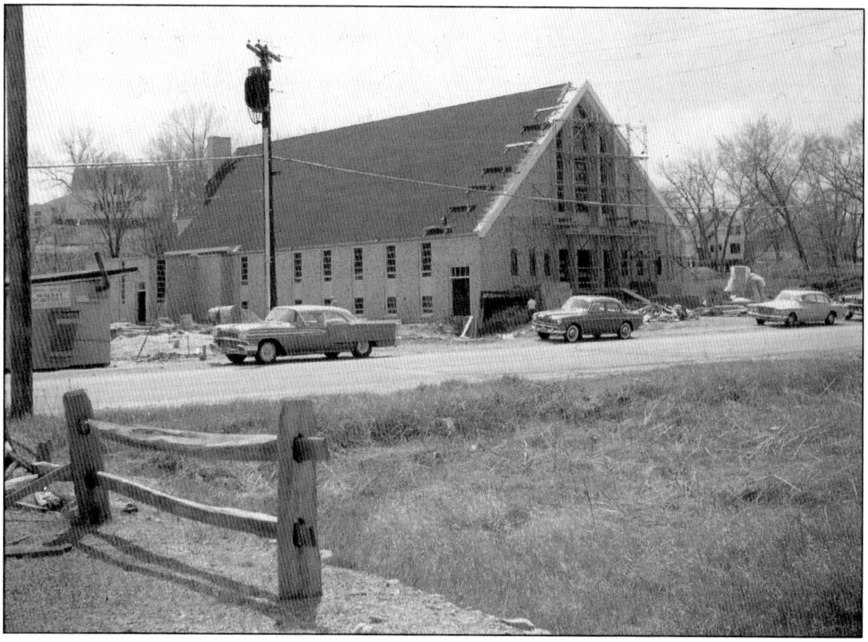

This is the main office of the Wm. P. Proctor Company lumber yard at 106 Middlesex Street around 1942. Although those in the photograph are not identified, employees at that time included clerks Stephanie Allen, Mary Barron, Helen Clark, and Irene Pelletier; hostess Edith Charlton; and secretary Blanche McGlinchey. The building survived a major lumberyard fire in September 1965 and now serves as the Dolan Funeral Home. (Donna Bulka.)

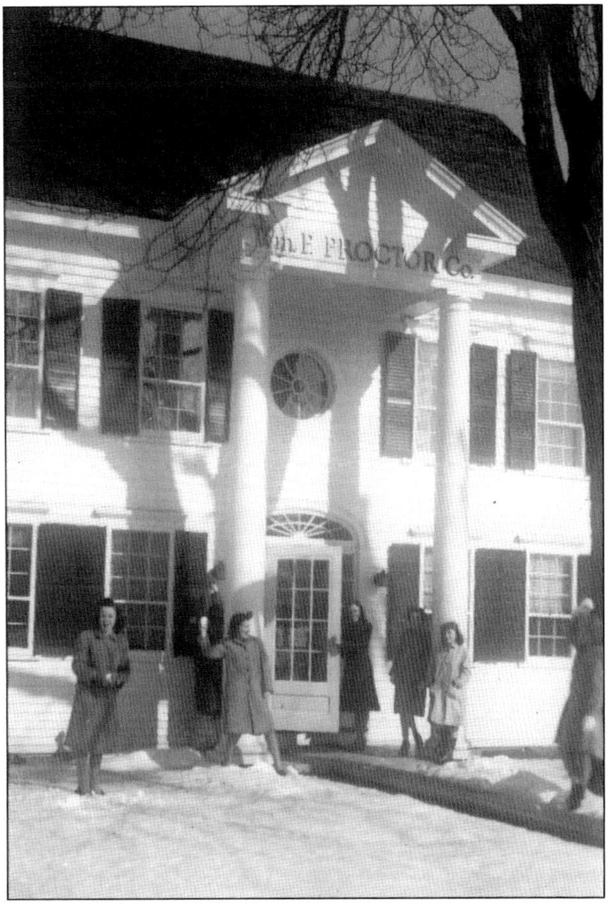

In the 1930s, the Middlesex Canal Toll House was removed from Middlesex Village by Proctor lumber on behalf of its owner, the widow of Judge Samuel P. Hadley. It was placed here, in front of 102 Middlesex Street, a house owned by the lumber company, and restored by salesman Carol Craft and other volunteers. Many of the company's men were serving military duty when these photographs were taken. (Donna Bulka.)

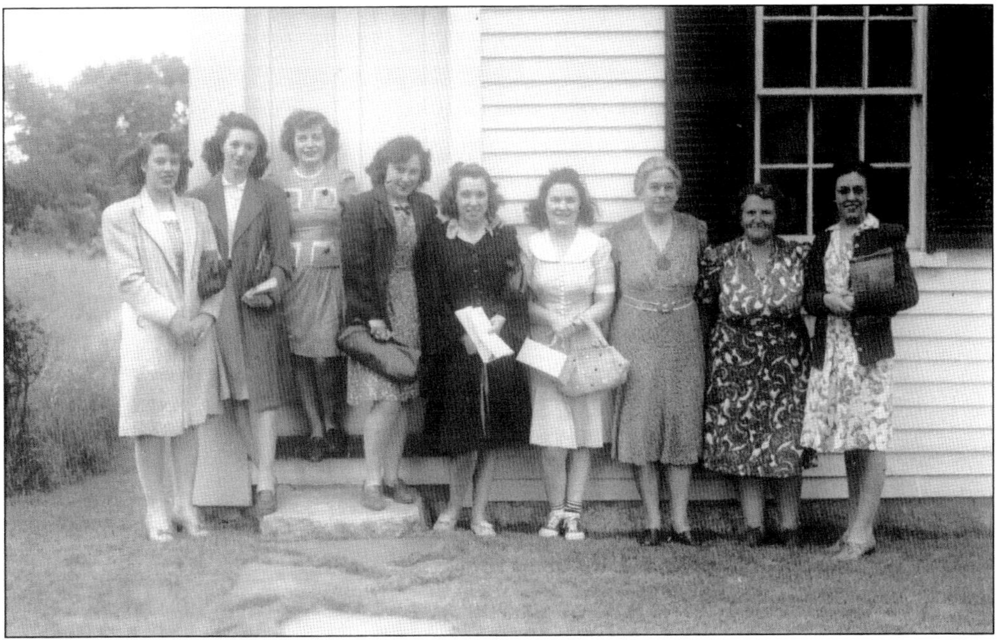

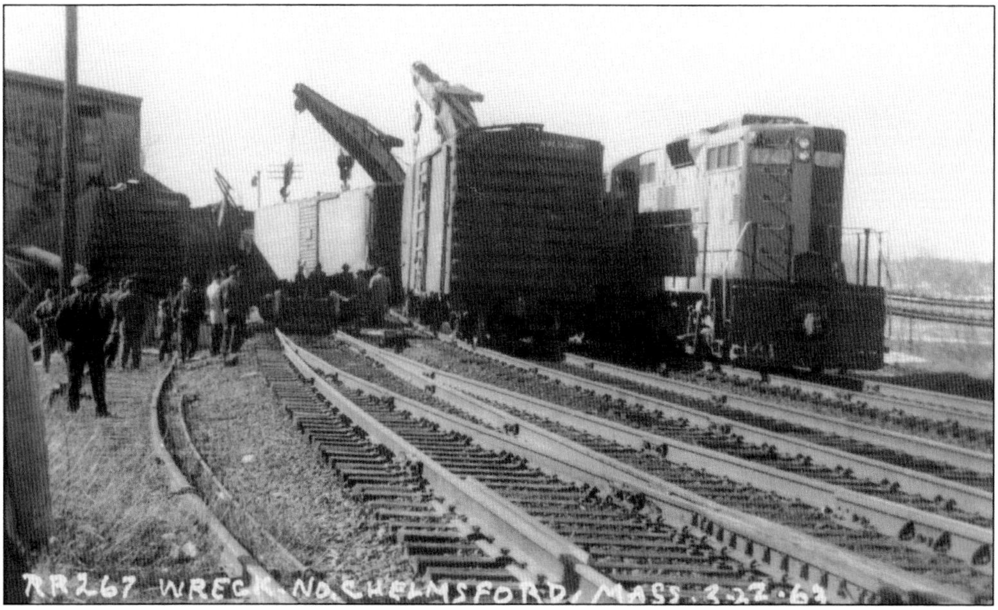


This massive railroad wreck occurred behind the former Wm. P. Proctor Company box factory on March 22, 1963. The damaged buildings were used in the manufacture of wooden boxes from 1905 until the 1930s, when the corrugated cardboard box took over the market. This accident happened the same month that Grossman's opened a home improvement center at the Proctor lumber site, which it had recently purchased. (Bradford Emerson.)

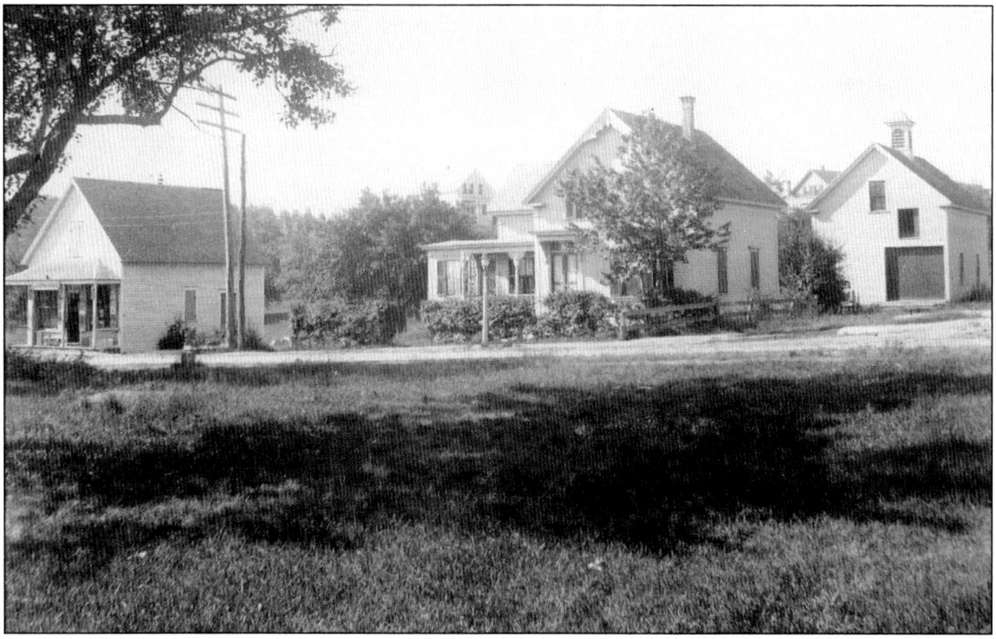

Grocer John F. McManomin lived here at 105 Middlesex Street at the intersection with Highland Avenue. He was sexton and later renter of pews for St. John's Catholic Church on Church Street and was postmaster from 1916 until he died in 1919. The McManomin store and home site is now a lawn on the right side of St. John the Evangelist Parish at 115 Middlesex Street. (Chelmsford Public Library.)

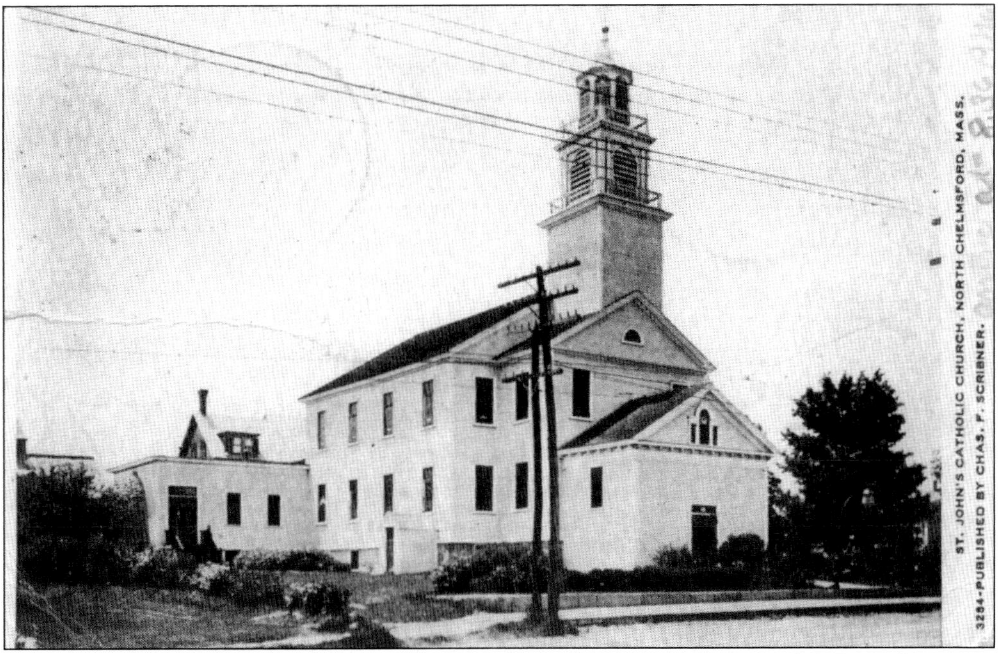


A Congregational church was authorized for Middlesex Village in 1821 and dedicated in 1822. Unitarian parishioners took it over in 1830, but disbanded in 1836 leaving the building vacant. In 1860, Roman Catholic families from several towns saved it from demolition. Volunteers moved it on rollers with armed guards, under arson threat from an anti-immigration group called "Know Nothings," to the corner of Middlesex and Church Streets. (Chelmsford Historical Society.)

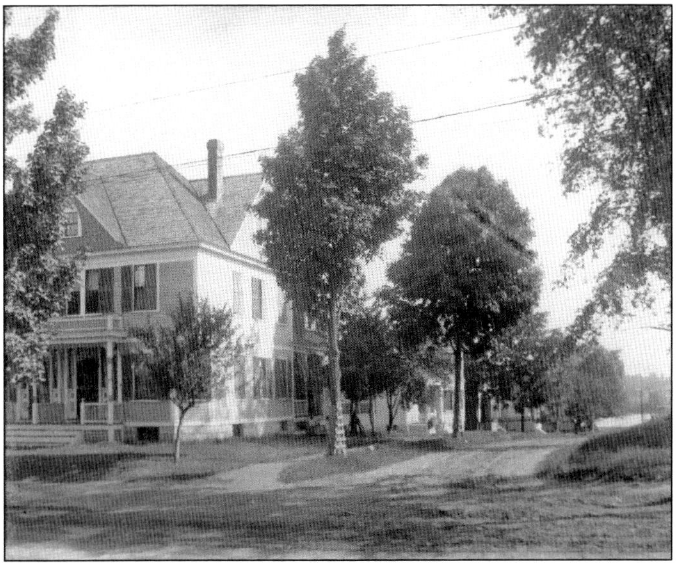

Augustus F. Whidden of 94–96 Middlesex Street was station agent at Bleachery Station in Lowell. When his brother John H. was accidentally killed at his job as station agent in West Chelmsford on August 8, 1894, Augustus took over John's positions there as station agent, constable, and cemetery commissioner. Brother George H. was superintendent of the Boston Ice Company and Charles E. a station agent in Westford. (Chelmsford Public Library.)

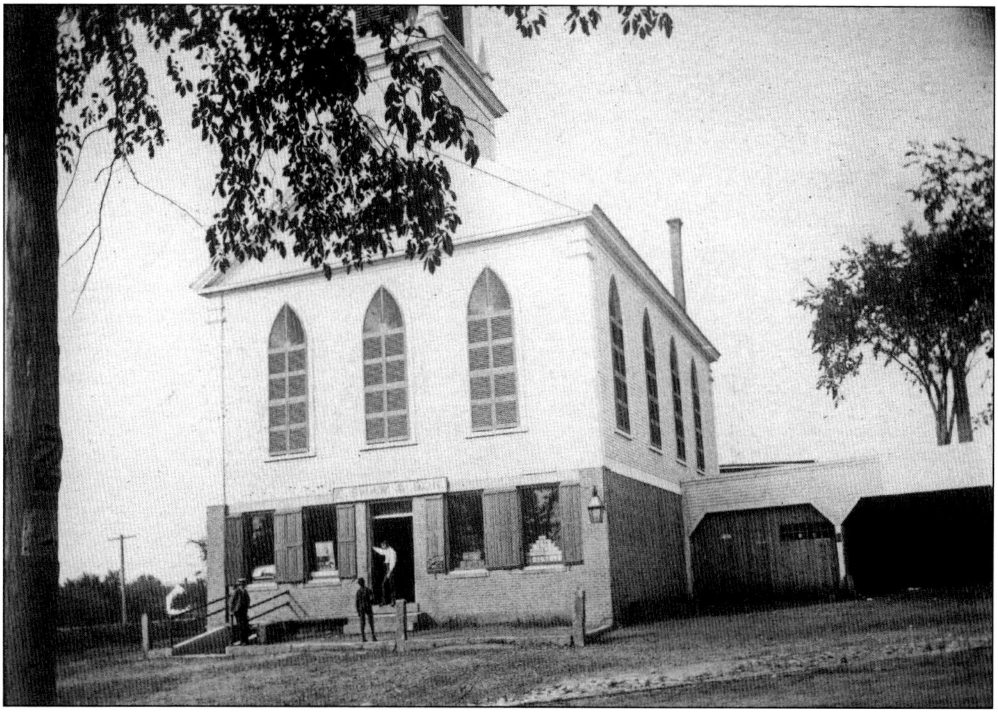

Elisha H. Shaw owned the E. Shaw & Son store under the Second Congregational Church and was North Chelmsford postmaster from 1869 to 1893 and from 1897 to 1899. The church and store burned on January 20, 1893, when a dog accidentally bumped a kerosene lamp set on the floor to provide heat. The glass broke, flames spread across the floor, and the fire could not be stopped. (Chelmsford Historical Society.)

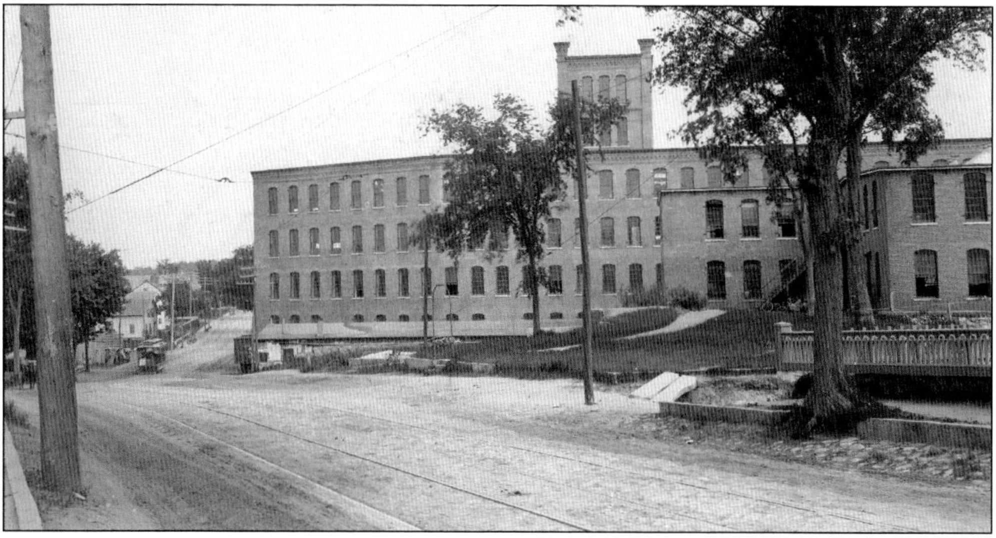

From left to right in this scene are a northbound trolley on Middlesex Street, George C. Moore's storehouse, vacant church and store property, No. 1 Mill, and the Josselyn house lot fence. Shaw acquired the church property after the 1893 fire, and provided land for a new church next door to his home on Princeton Street, but was unwilling to sell this vacant property to Moore. (Chelmsford Public Library.)

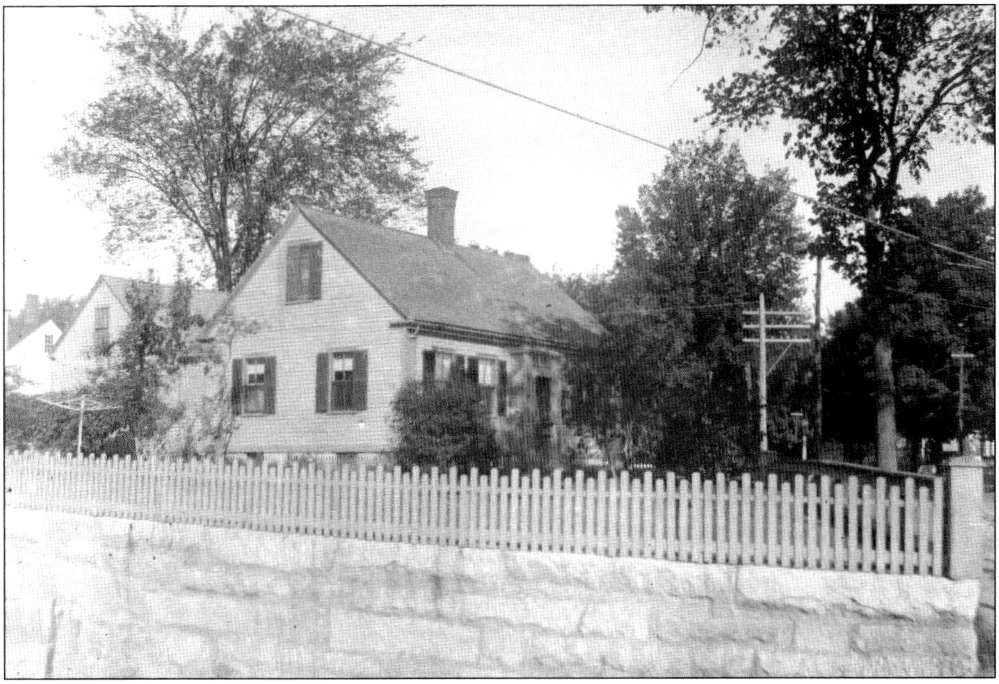

Wallace A Josselyn, a carriage and sign painter in Vinal Square, lived here on the corner of Middlesex and Gay Streets with his wife Carrie, a director of the nearby North Chelmsford Library Association. George C. Moore was building his No. 2 Mill next door in 1898 and purchased the property the same year. The site is now a parking lot, but the stone wall still exists. (Chelmsford Public Library.)

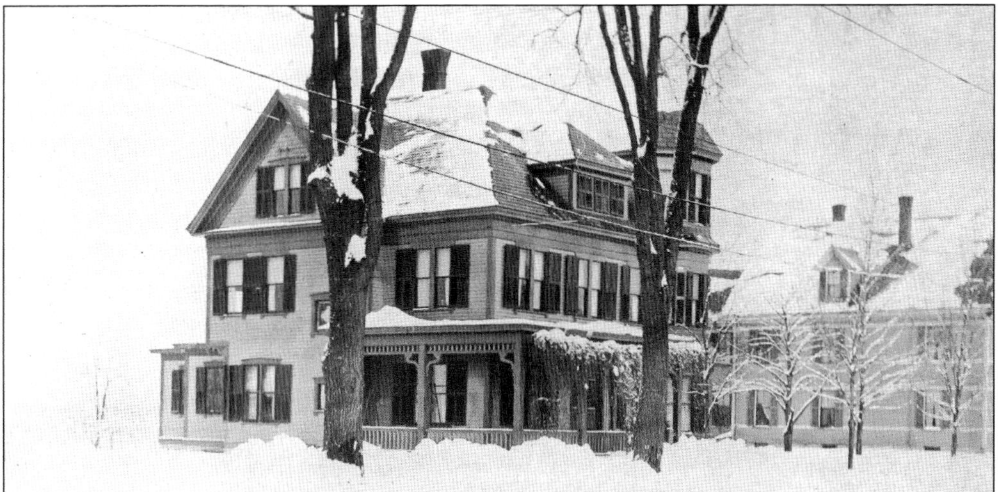

Luther H. Sargent, paymaster for the Silver & Gay Company, built 42 Middlesex Street in 1893 on land purchased from Clara Adams. He was an avid reader and long-time supporter of the North Chelmsford Library Association and Free Public Library, renamed Adams Library in 1896, but died in 1903 at only 61. Pattern maker Oliver M. Greene built the house beyond, at 48 Middlesex Street, around 1888. (Chelmsford Public Library.)

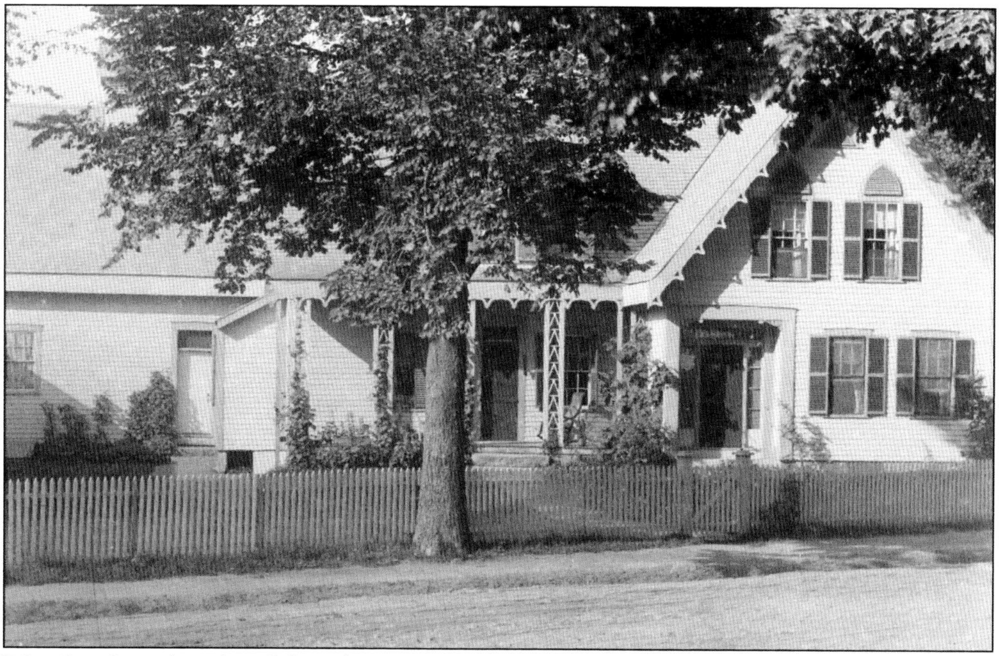

Ziba Gay Sr., a founder of the Silver & Gay Company in 1830, purchased this house at 41–43 Middlesex Street (above) at the corner of Cottage Row (below) in 1848. He made his son Ziba Gay Jr. a partner in the business in 1857, and died in 1864. Ziba Gay Jr. became active in town affairs as a selectman and assessor from 1874 to 1879, as a town auditor from 1880 to 1895, and as president of the North Chelmsford Library Association from 1898 until his death in 1902. His unmarried daughter Emma was North Chelmsford librarian until 1903 and later served as a director for three years. She was also secretary and treasurer of the Adams Library from 1899 to 1901 and a trustee from 1902 to 1910, when she retired. (Above, Chelmsford Public Library; below, Chelmsford Historical Society.)

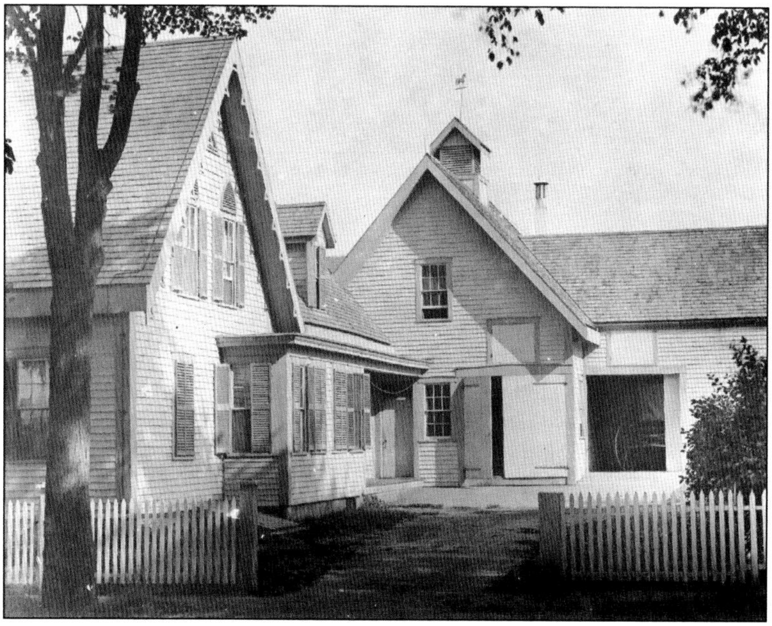

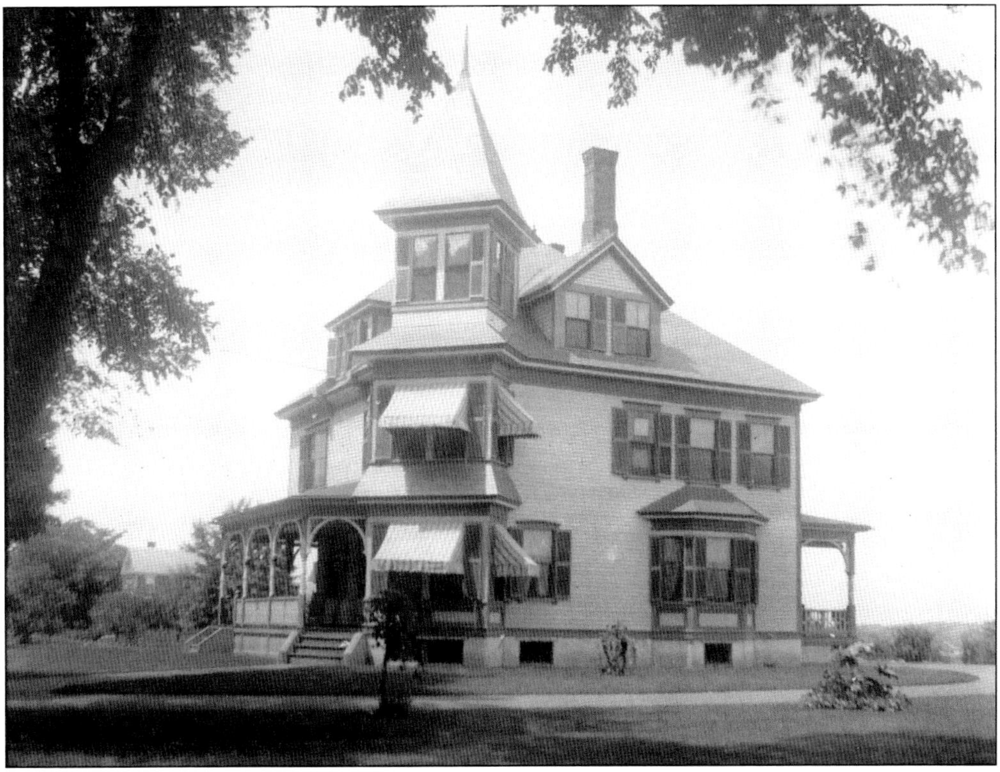

Henry Woods, who built this home at 38 Middlesex Street around 1894, was paymaster and bookkeeper for George C. Moore. His wife, Eliza, died in 1899 and he married Marion, 26 years his junior, in 1900. He later became treasurer and manager of the North Chelmsford Supply Company and secretary, when it became North Chelmsford Machine and Supply Company, until he died in 1915 at age 71. (Chelmsford Public Library.)

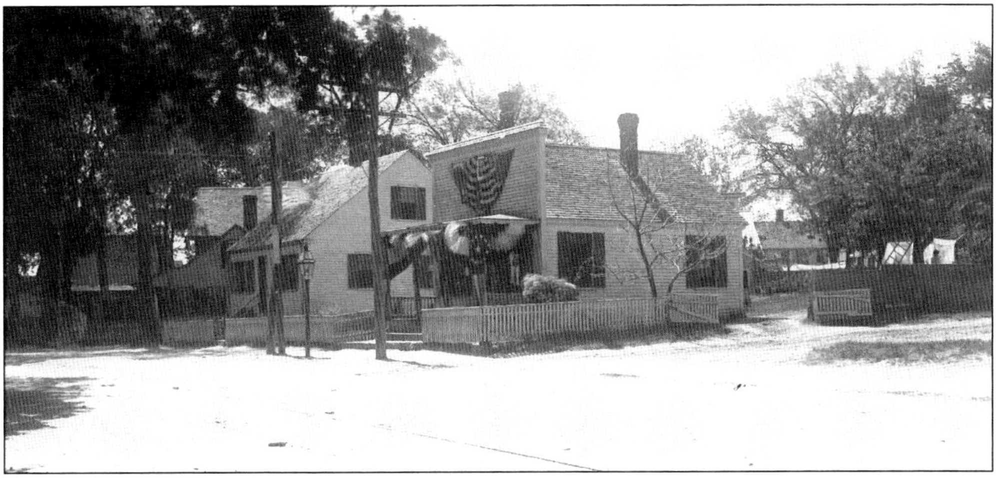

John S. Hall was the railroad crossing tender and ran a shoe repair business on nearby Middlesex Street. On January 22, 1899, he purchased the house at 35 Middlesex Street and building next door, and one month later became North Chelmsford postmaster. The post office, shown here in 1905 with bunting for Chelmsford's 250th anniversary celebration, was later removed and is now the driveway for 29–31 Middlesex Street. (Chelmsford Public Library.)

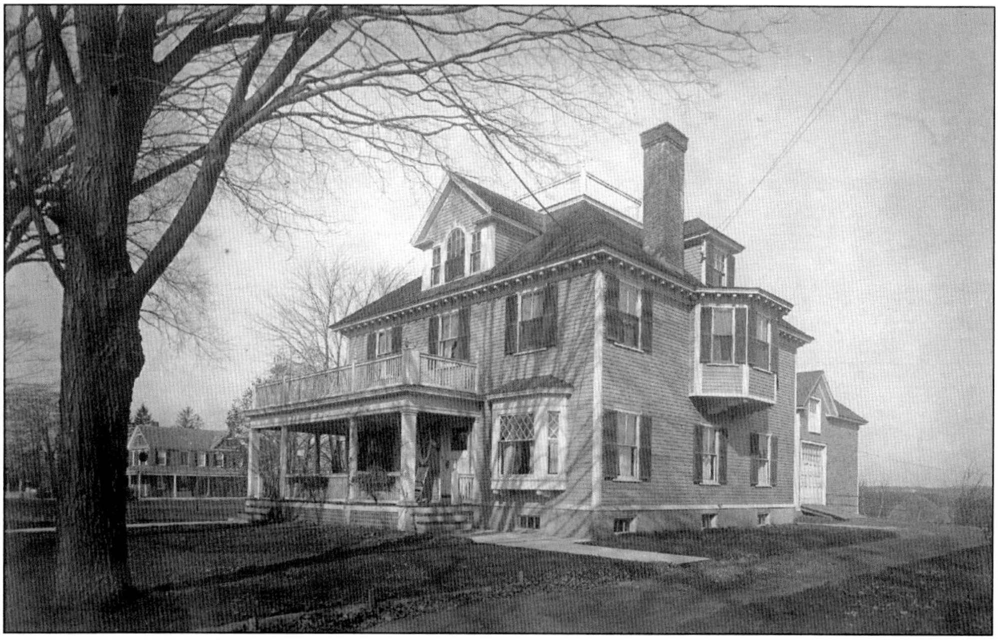

Dr. Fred E. Varney, who transitioned into the medical practice of the late Dr. Nathan B. Edwards in 1894, acquired land from Clara Adams in 1899 and built this home and office at 34 Middlesex Street. As a School Committee member and Board of Health agent, Dr. Varney was an advocate of proper physical fitness for children, and his gift of Varney Playground was accepted in 1931. (Chelmsford Historical Society.)

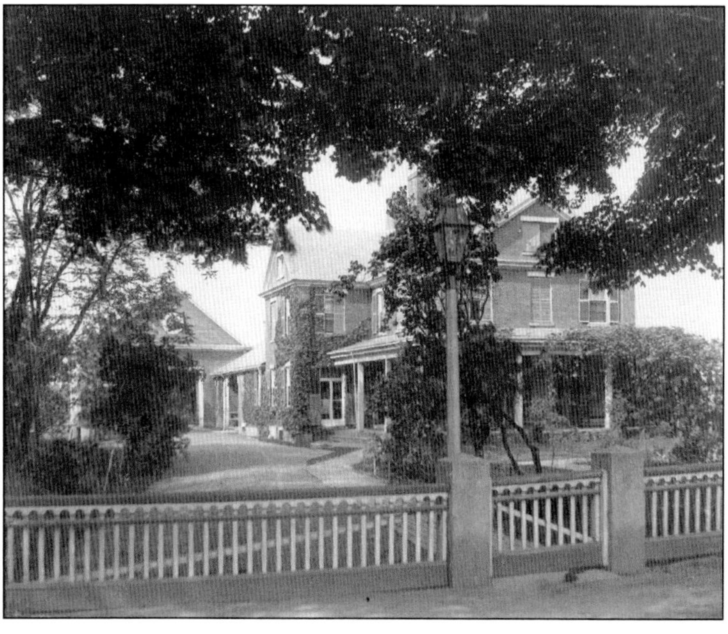

Clara A.H. Adams, 22 years younger than her late husband Thomas J. Adams, lived here at 8 Middlesex Street. She owned the Adams Tavern and future Adams Street in Vinyl Square, and the northeast side of Middlesex Street from Wotton to Gay Streets, with the exception of the Adams Hotel. She sold the lots at 34, 38, 42, and 48 Middlesex Street before she died in 1900. (Chelmsford Public Library.)

# *Seven*

# PRINCETON STREET

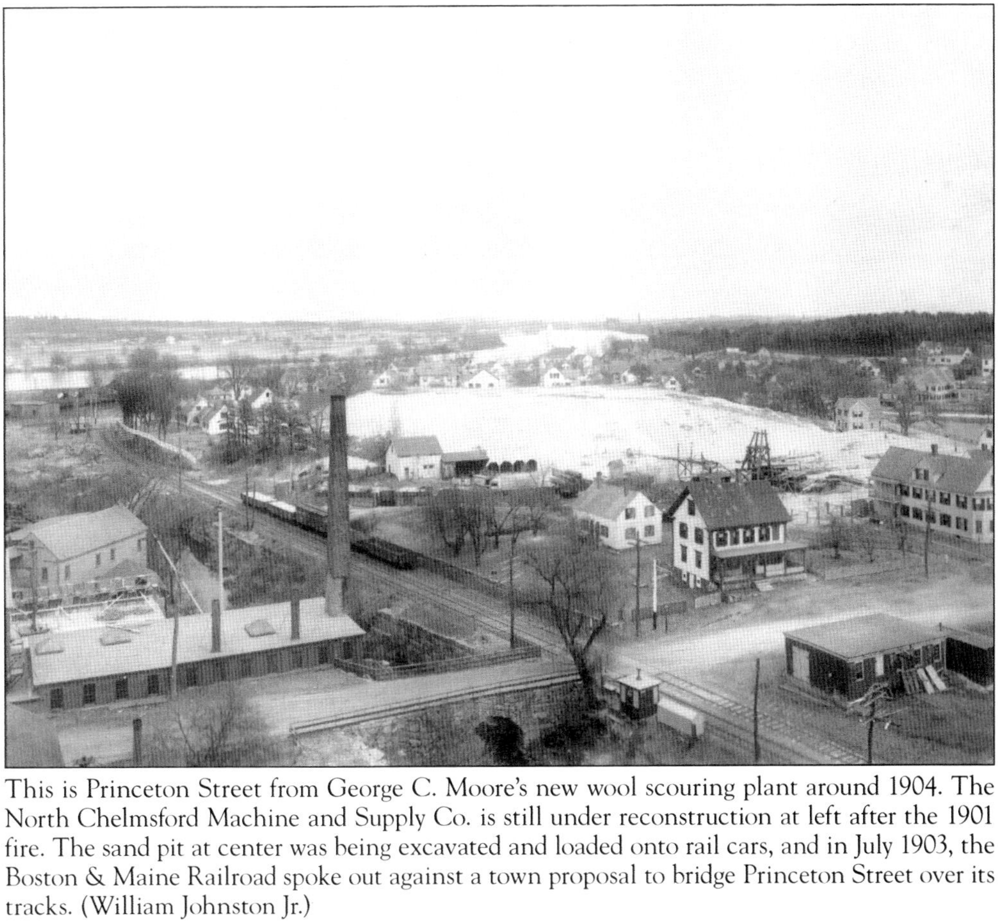

This is Princeton Street from George C. Moore's new wool scouring plant around 1904. The North Chelmsford Machine and Supply Co. is still under reconstruction at left after the 1901 fire. The sand pit at center was being excavated and loaded onto rail cars, and in July 1903, the Boston & Maine Railroad spoke out against a town proposal to bridge Princeton Street over its tracks. (William Johnston Jr.)

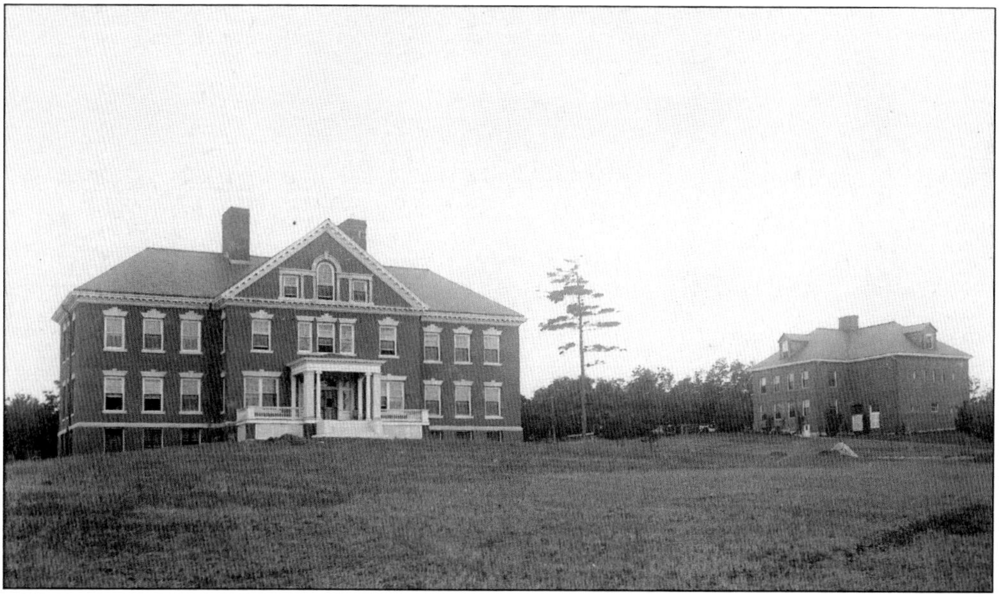

The Middlesex County Truant School was opened in 1894 for the reformation of boys age 7 to 16 who were habitual truants or had committed other minor offenses. The facility was originally built on 64 acres of farmland and is located at 225 Princeton Street near the Lowell city line. The name was changed to Middlesex County Training School in 1908. (Chelmsford Public Library.)

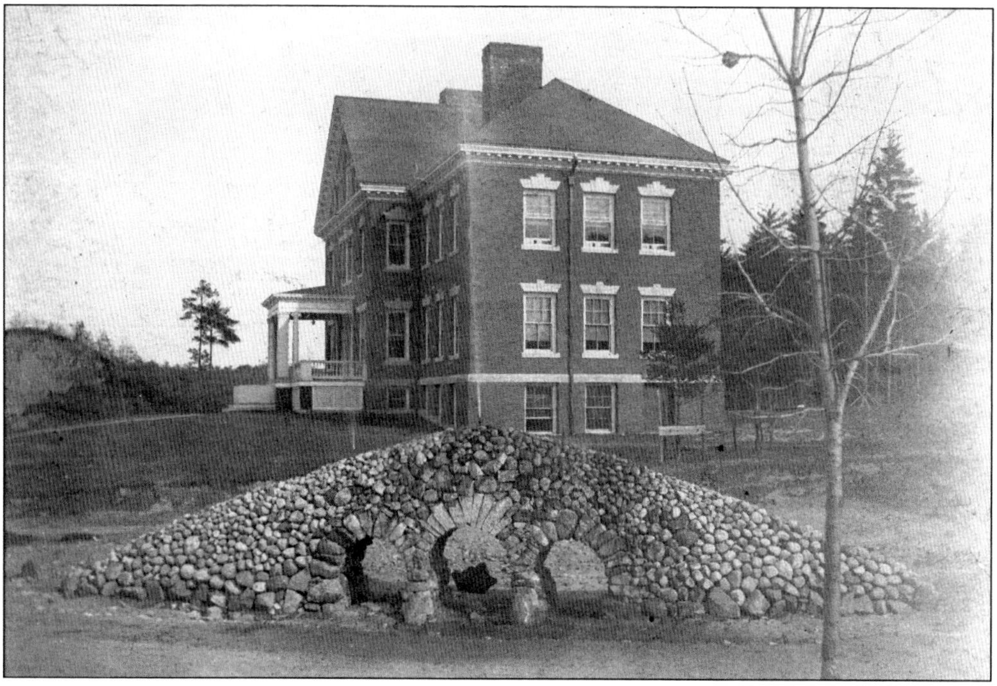

Bigelow Hall, named after County Commissioner Francis Bigelow of Natick, was one of three dormitory buildings and is the only building still in use under U-Mass Lowell ownership. The granite used in construction of the buildings was provided by North Chelmsford granite contractors John Marinel and Charles J. Willsteed. The stonework decoration in the foreground was built by the boys as part of their industrial training. (Matthew Saxton.)

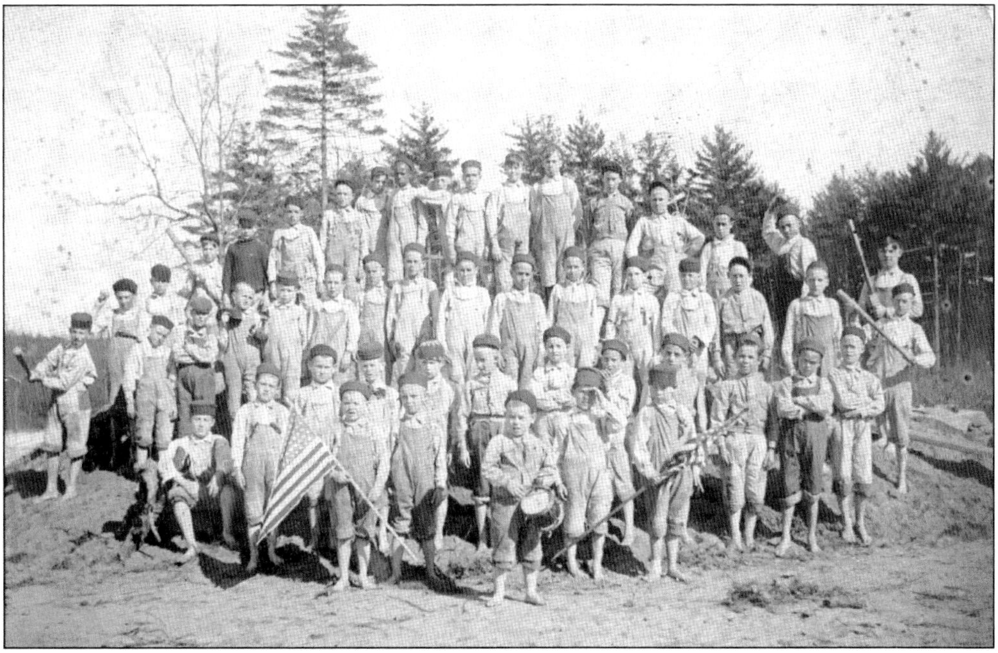

Every day was divided into periods for school, work, and recreation. There was a 30-piece band and baseball teams. This goups of boys is pictured around 1900. The Massachusetts Acts of 1909 forbade any child under 14 who could not read and write from working at any factory, workshop, or mercantile establishment. This drove the need for a third dormitory cottage by 1910. (Matthew Saxton.)

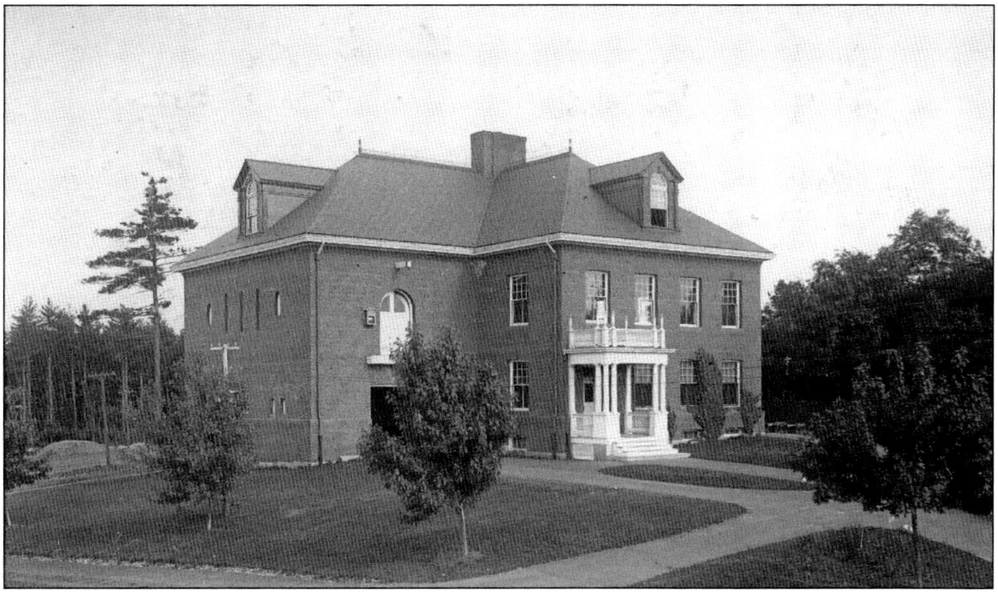

Upham Hall, named after County Commissioner Samuel O. Upham of Waltham, contained a hall, workshop, and laundry. Training included freehand and mechanical drawing, sewing, cooking, gardening, tailoring, carpentry, laundry, and farming. In the early 1970s, there was a movement in Congress toward mandating that public schools could not expel or transfer "exceptional" children without due process of law, driving closure of the Middlesex County Training School in 1973. (Chelmsford Public Library.)

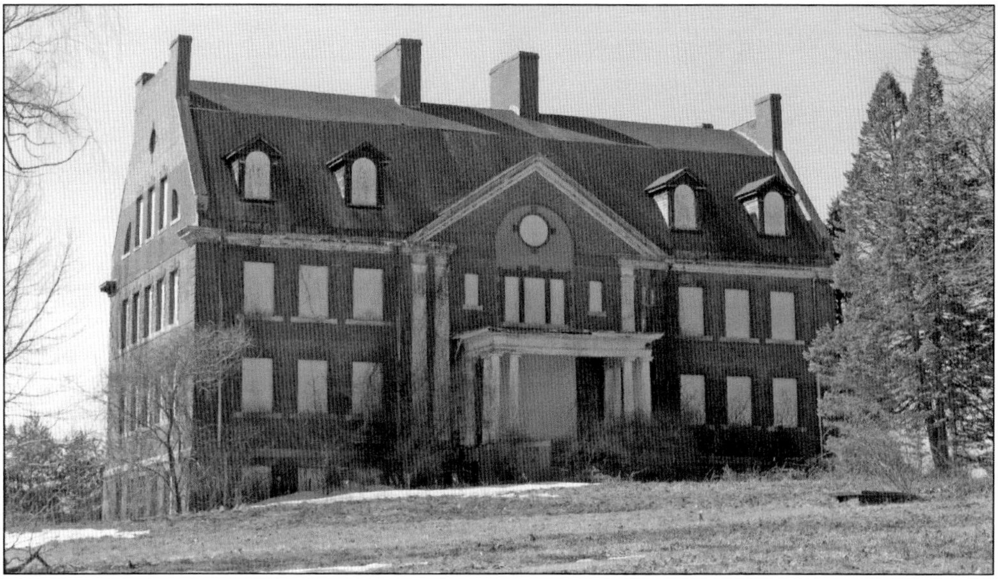

After decommissioning in 1973, the school sat vacant for over 10 years. On May 1, 1984, Wang Laboratories Inc., riding a tidal wave of prosperity in computer development, purchased the 64-acre property for a corporate headquarters. They had a change of plan, gifting 34 acres of the property to U-Mass Lowell on October 22, 1984, and selling the rest. This cottage behind Bigelow Hall was never reused. (Photograph by the author.)

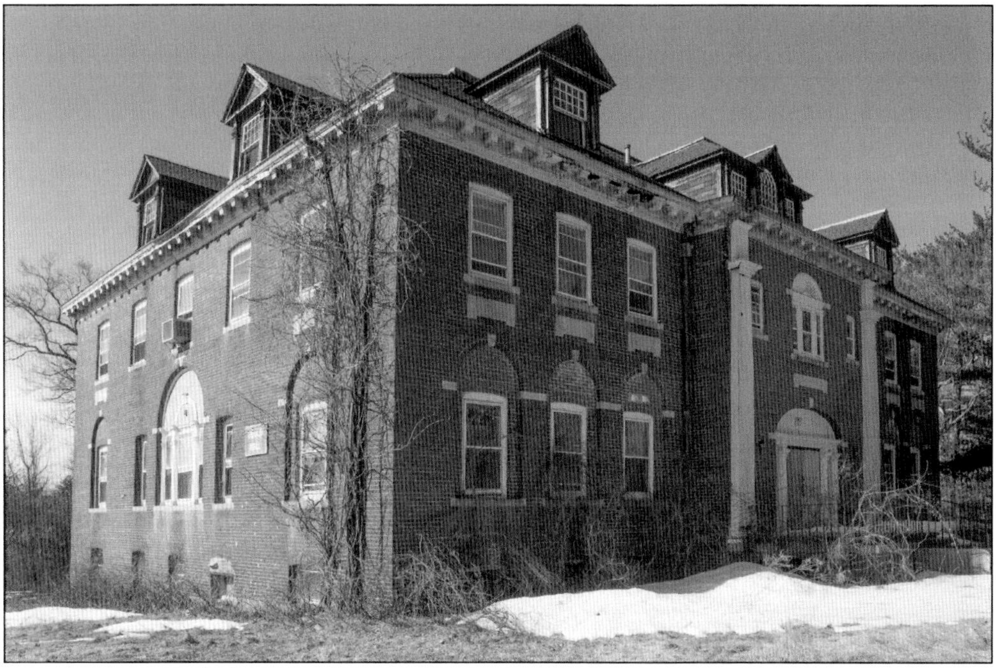

Gould Hall, named after County Commissioner Levi S. Gould of Melrose, was the dormitory cottage built around 1910 to handle an increase in student population. The University of Lowell moved its College of Education to this new West Campus in 1985. The university became part of the University of Massachusetts system in 1991 and the College of Education became the Graduate School of Education in 1998. (Photograph by the author.)

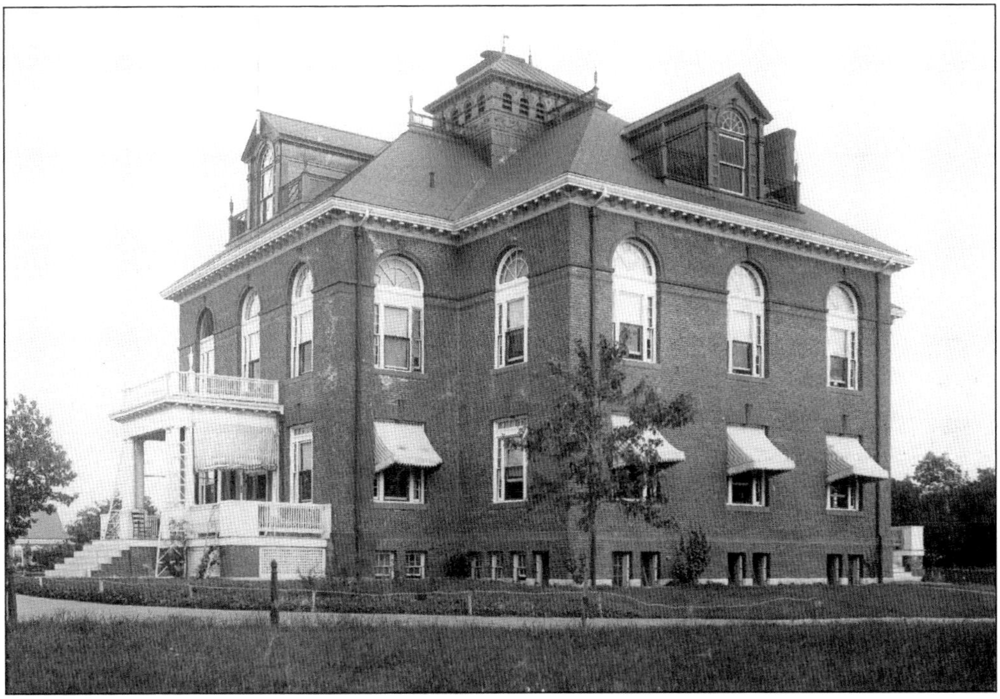

Read Hall, named after County Commissioner J. Henry Read of Westford, was the administrative office building for the school. Most employees lived in the dormitories at the school. In the 1890s, this included instructor Bennett Ward, laundress Lotta Carless, seamstress May Clark, teacher Carrie Erskine, and housekeeper Annie Mason, but superintendent M. Alton Warren and his family were provided a separate house on campus. (Chelmsford Public Library.)

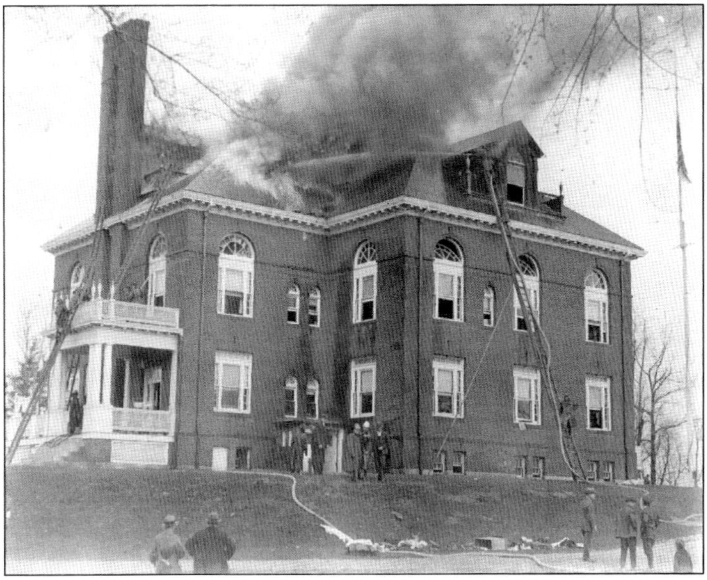

A significant fire broke out in Read Hall in 1925, but the firemen shown here saved the building and it was rebuilt. In the late 1990s, U-Mass Lowell moved the Graduate School of Education to the O'Leary Library on its South Campus. On August 28, 2013, fire broke out again in Read Hall, but this time the vacant building was damaged beyond repair and later demolished. (Chelmsford Historical Society.)

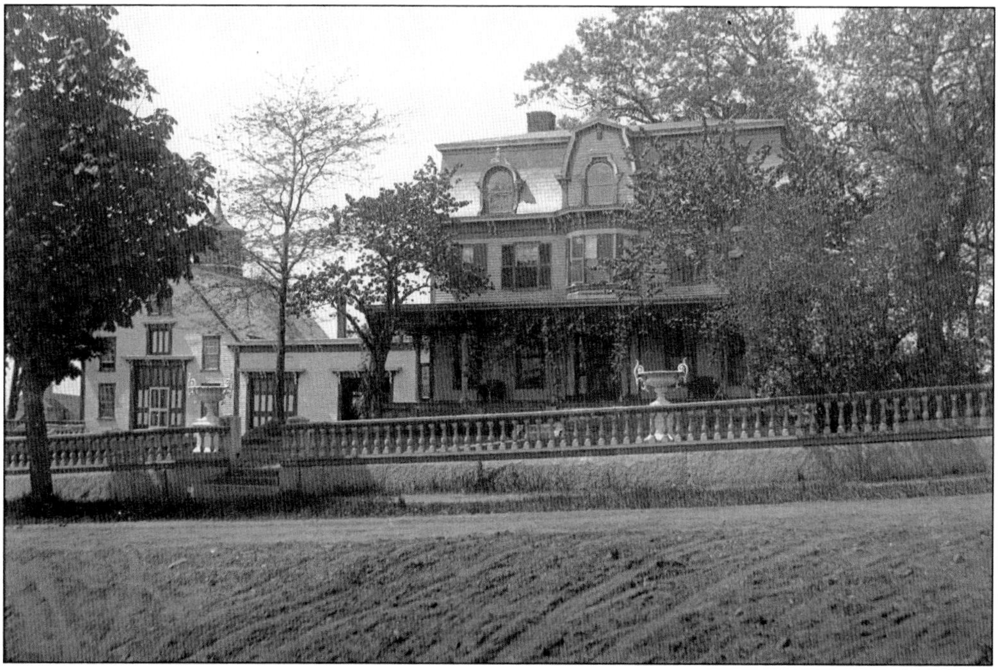

George T. Sheldon was in the ice business on Freeman Lake since 1857, organized the Chelmsford Foundry Company in 1858, and purchased the Baldwin Mill in 1879. He spent all his business hours on Portland Street in Boston but enjoyed riding horses at his 67 Princeton Street homestead shown above. Sheldon's sons, George H. whose house at 53 Princeton Street is shown below, and Royal R. Sheldon, also worked at the Chelmsford Foundry Company. George C. Moore purchased the Baldwin Mill from Sheldon in 1895 and in 1908 purchased these Sheldon homes on Princeton Street. He adapted the first floor of the homestead as the main office of his wool scouring company, used the second floor as his private office, enlarged the barn, and added a concrete floor to the carriage house for his automobiles. (Both, Chelmsford Public Library.)

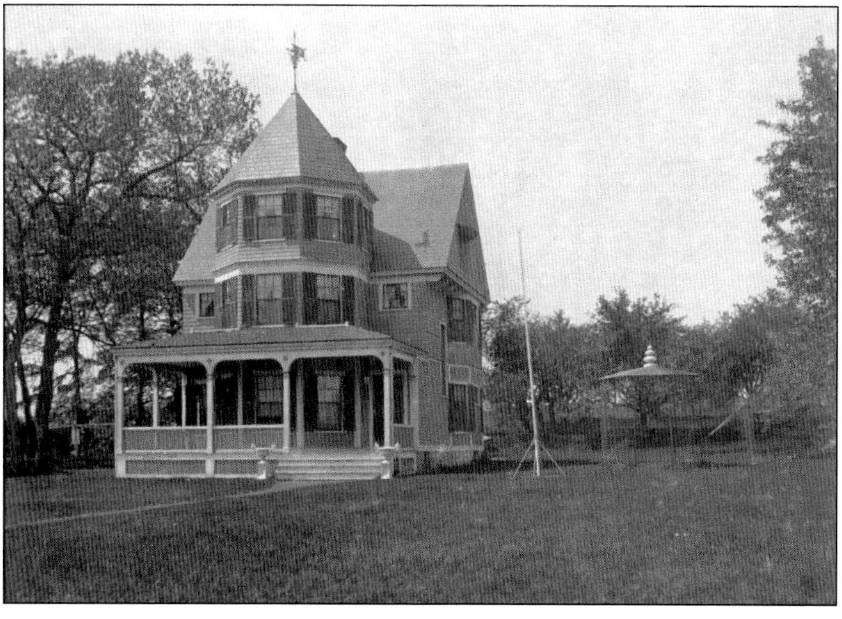

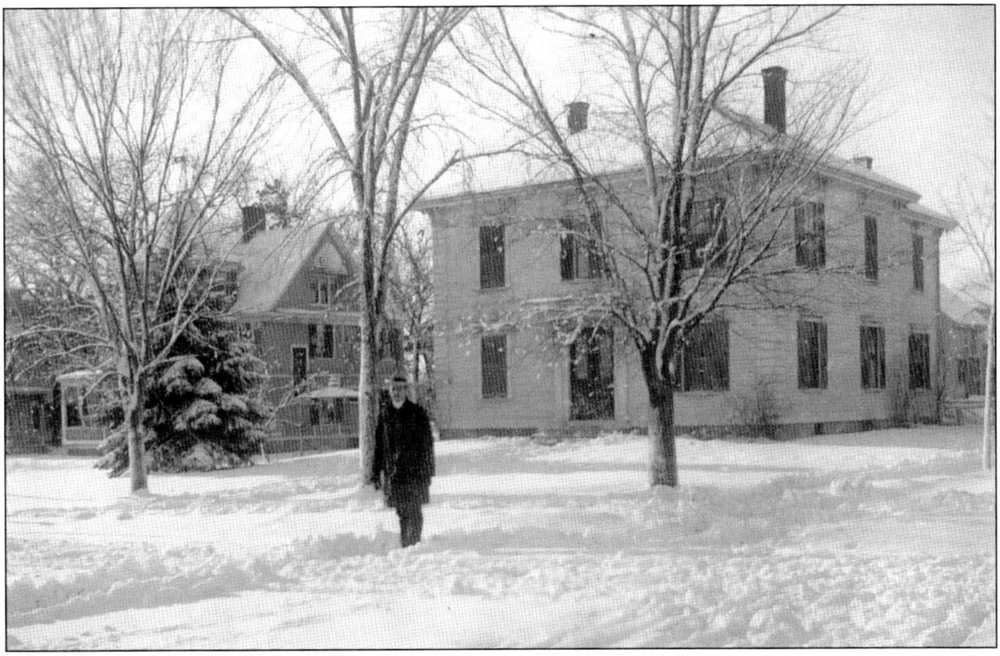

On April 16, 1874, the Proprietors of the North Chelmsford Meeting House, in trust for the Second Congregational Society of Chelmsford, purchased this home at 45 Princeton Street from the estate of Ziba Gay Sr. of Nashua for $300. There were two conditions: it could only be used for the purposes of the Orthodox Congregational denomination, and it could not be encumbered with a mortgage, or ownership would be conveyed to the American Congregational Union. Rev. L. Ingersoll Bryant lived in the parsonage from 1889 to 1997. The George H. Sheldon house is on the left above, and Gay Street is on the right in the spring scene below. In 1962, the American Congregational Union released its 1874 conditional rights, and on November 5, 1965, the Congregational Church in North Chelmsford sold the property to a private party. (Both, Chelmsford Public Library.)

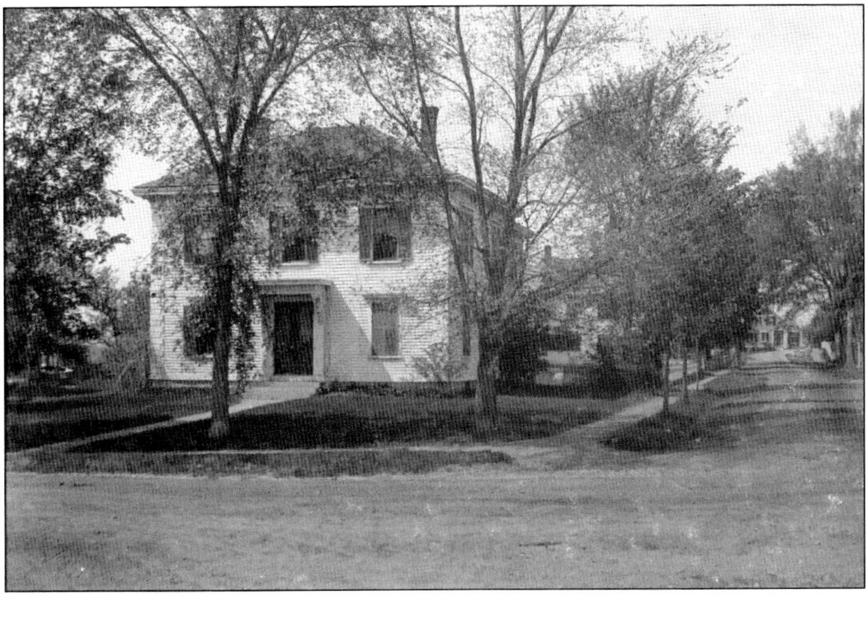

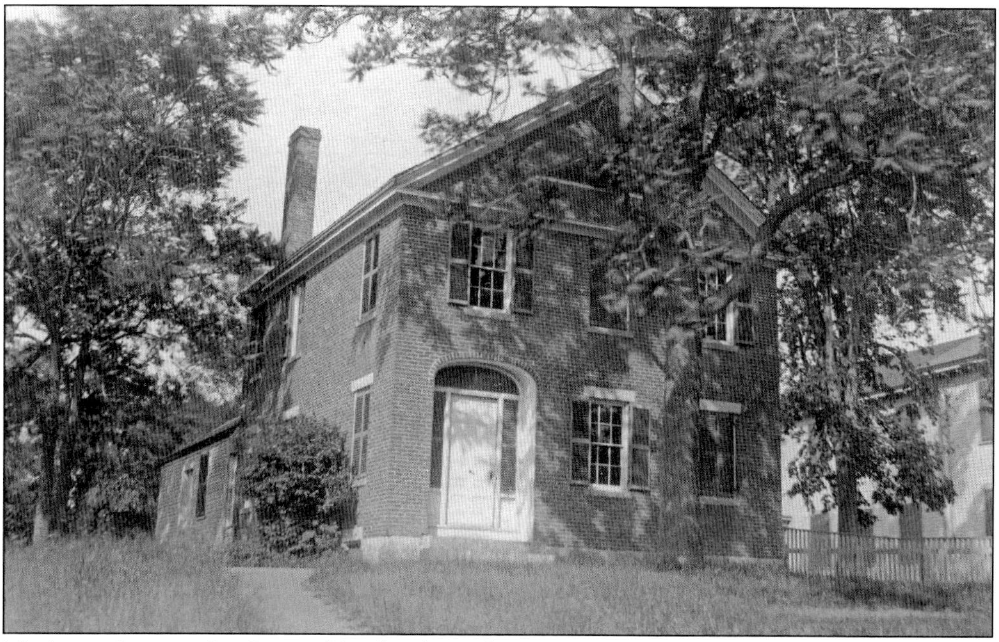

Mechanical genius Ira Gay and his brother Ziba Gay Sr. started a machine shop in 1832 near the foundry started by Gen. Shepherd Leach, who died that year. Ira died in 1837 and Ziba granted Harvey Silver a half interest in 1841, and the rest to his son Ziba Gay Jr. in 1859. Harvey Silver's house, shown here around 1898, was demolished in 1899 for a new school. (Chelmsford Public Library.)

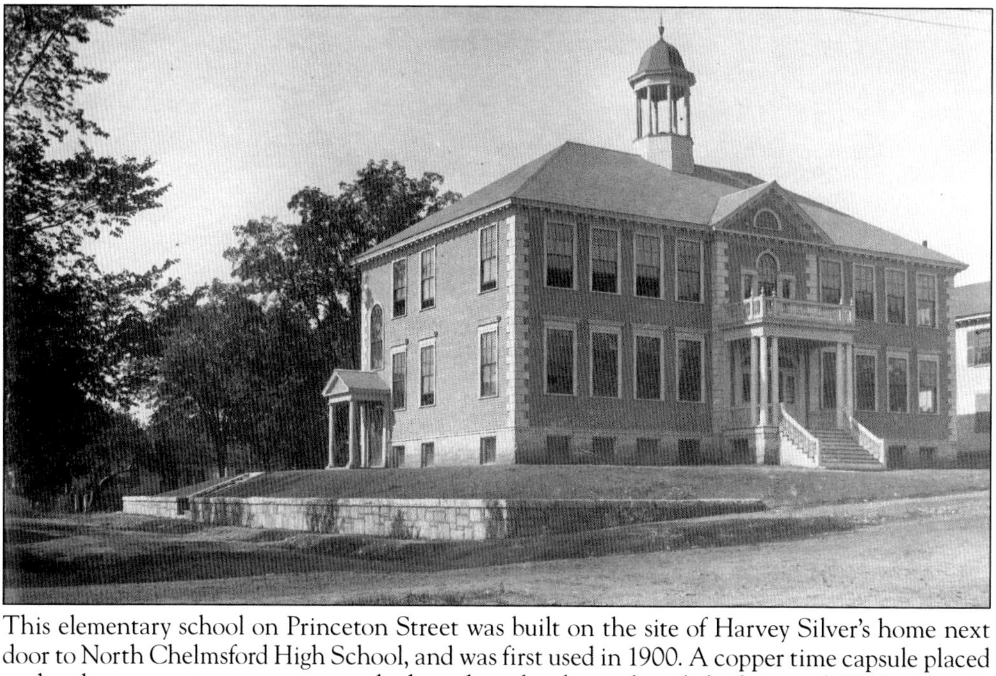

This elementary school on Princeton Street was built on the site of Harvey Silver's home next door to North Chelmsford High School, and was first used in 1900. A copper time capsule placed under the cornerstone was removed when the school was demolished around 1954 and is in the care of the Chelmsford Historical Society. The site is now a parking lot for the Chelmsford Community Center. (Chelmsford Public Library.)

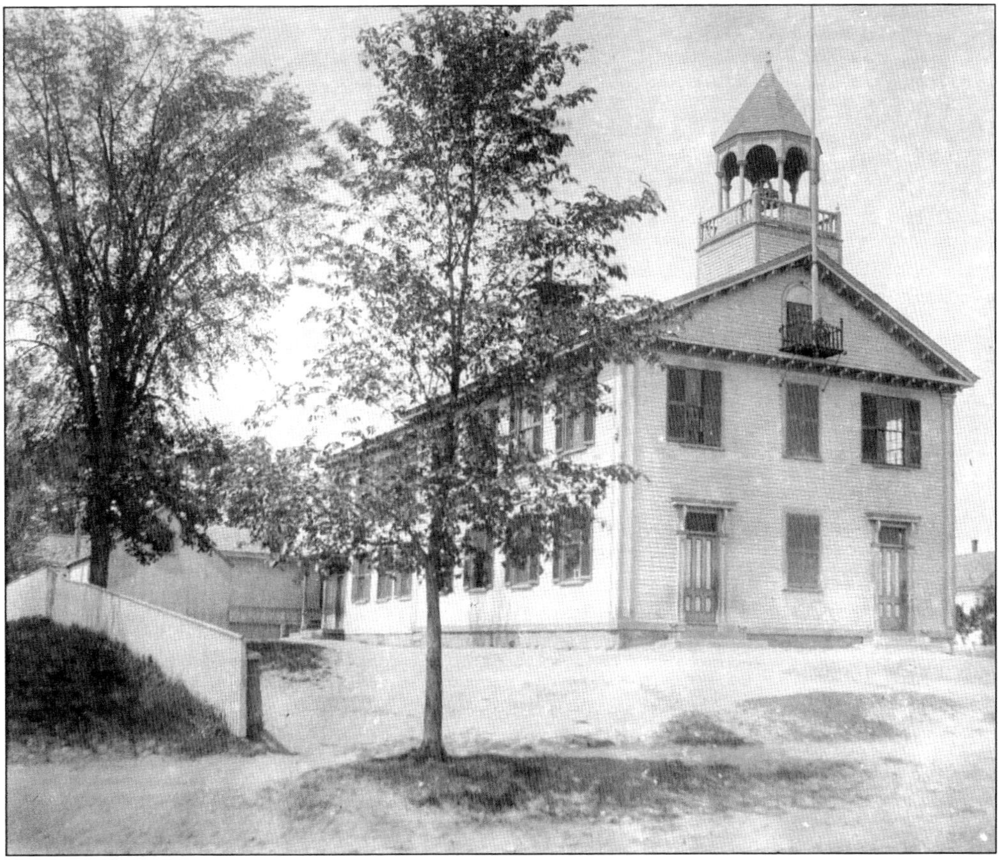

The Princeton Street School was both grammar and high school from 1875 until 1900, when the grammar school moved to the new building next door. It continued as a high school until 1917 when the new high school combining North and Centre was built at 50 Billerica Road and was torn down around 1954. The North Fire Station now occupies this site at 35 Princeton Street. (Chelmsford Public Library.)

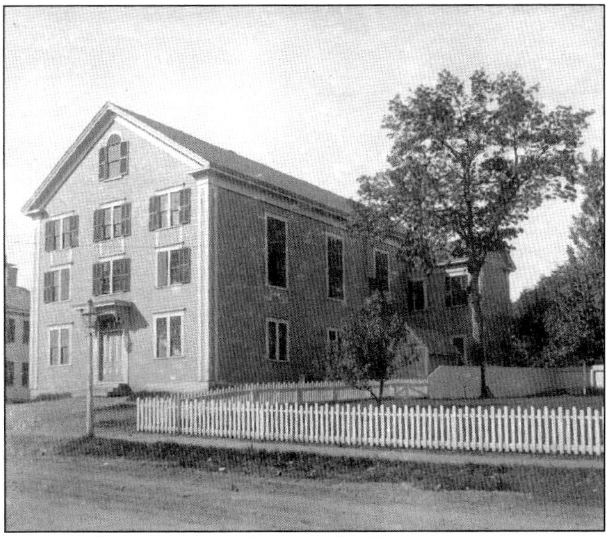

North Town Hall was constructed in 1852 on land donated by brothers Benjamin F. and Thomas J. Adams. In 1886, the building was raised 10 feet to make room for a new story and 20 feet was added to the front under the direction of Ziba Gay Jr., George C. Moore, Christopher Roby, Perley P. Perham, and Jonathan Larcom, who had constructed Centre Town Hall in 1879. (Chelmsford Public Library.)

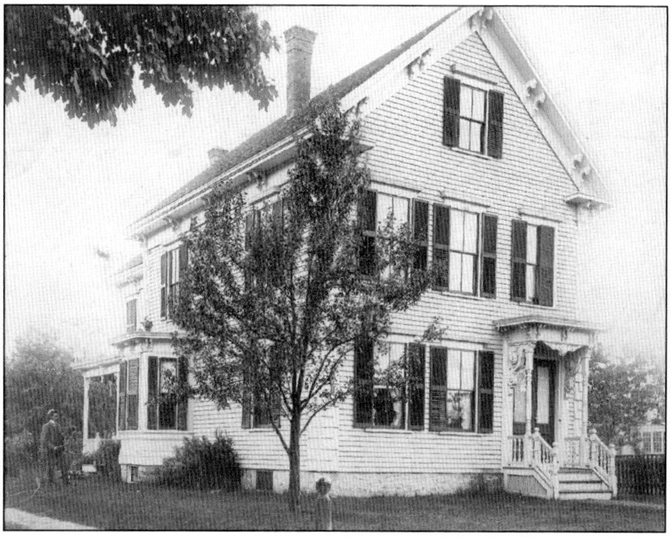

William L. Draper lived here at 17 Princeton Street and operated a carriage manufacturing and repair business at the intersection of Groton and Dunstable Roads. After his wife, Jane, died in 1892, he and his daughter Elizabeth took in Emma L. Towle, a relative of photographer Simon Towle, as a boarder. Both ladies worked for George C. Moore; Elizabeth as a bookkeeper, and Emma as a stenographer. (Chelmsford Public Library.)

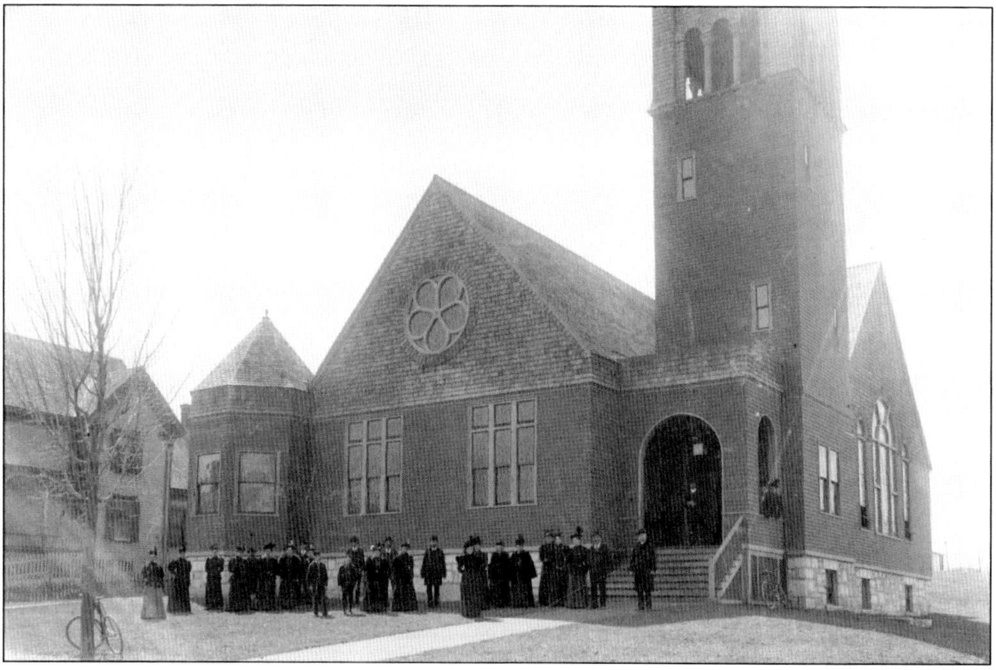

Members of the Second Congregational Church are posing outside the church after a meeting of the building committee in 1898 with Rev. S. Ingersoll Bryant standing in the doorway. After the 1838 church burned on January 20, 1893, Elisha H. Shaw donated land next to his home for this church, dedicated on April 26, 1894. Shaw Street, in between, was accepted in 1926. (George Merrill.)

# *Eight*

# Other North Chelmsford Streets

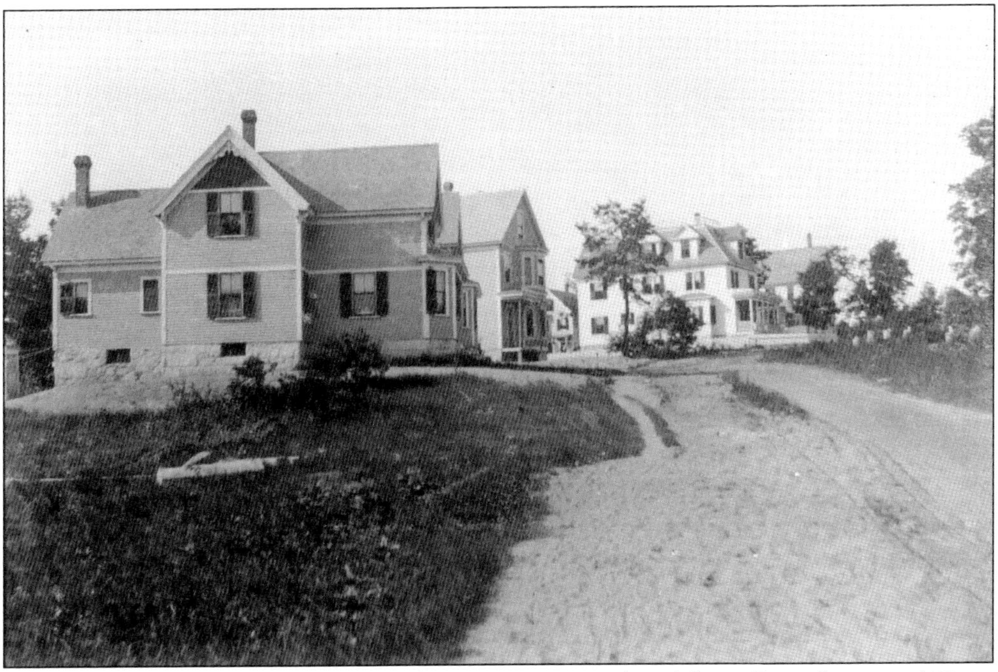

The dirt cart path, shown here around 1895 was accepted as Adams Street by annual Town Meeting in 1903 along with Sherman and Mansur Streets. It runs from Vinal Square, then known as Stevens Corner, to Freeman Lake, where Varney Playground is now located. The Adams Street houses from left to right are Nos. 16, 18 (behind No. 16), 20, and 26–28. Beyond that is 29–31 Newfield Street. (Chelmsford Public Library.)

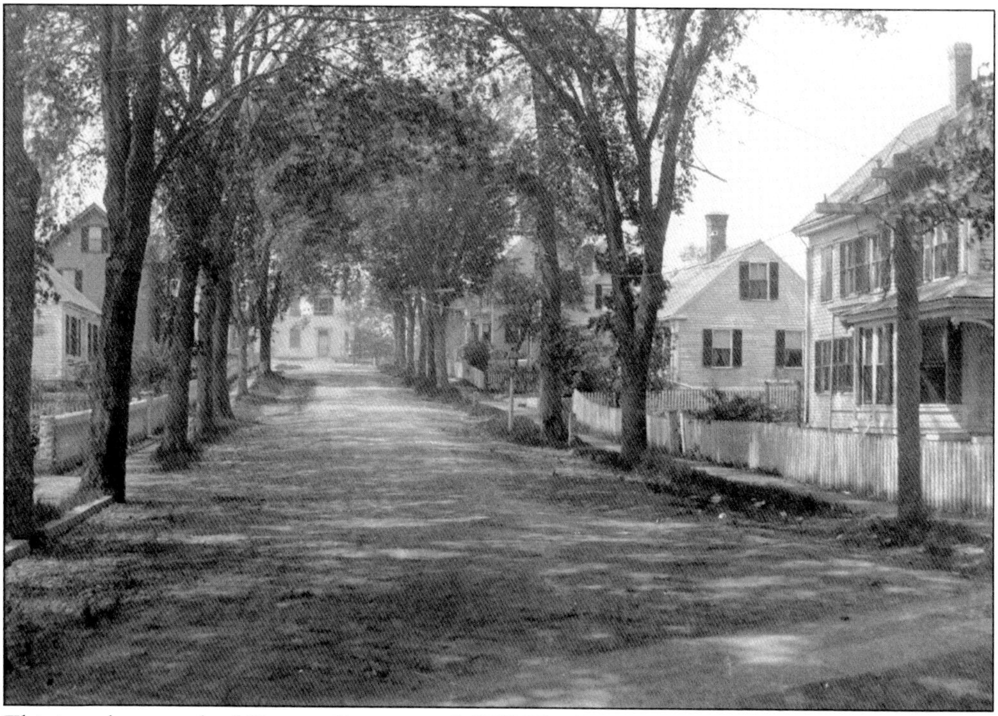

This is a photograph of Cottage Row around 1895. The Princeton Street School in the distance, which later became North High School, has separate entry doors for boys and girls. The houses from left to right are Nos. 10, 14–16, 21–19, 15, 7, and 1B. Captain Lincoln Drake sold land for or built these houses in the mid-1800s for employees of his Chelmsford Foundry Company. (Chelmsford Public Library.)

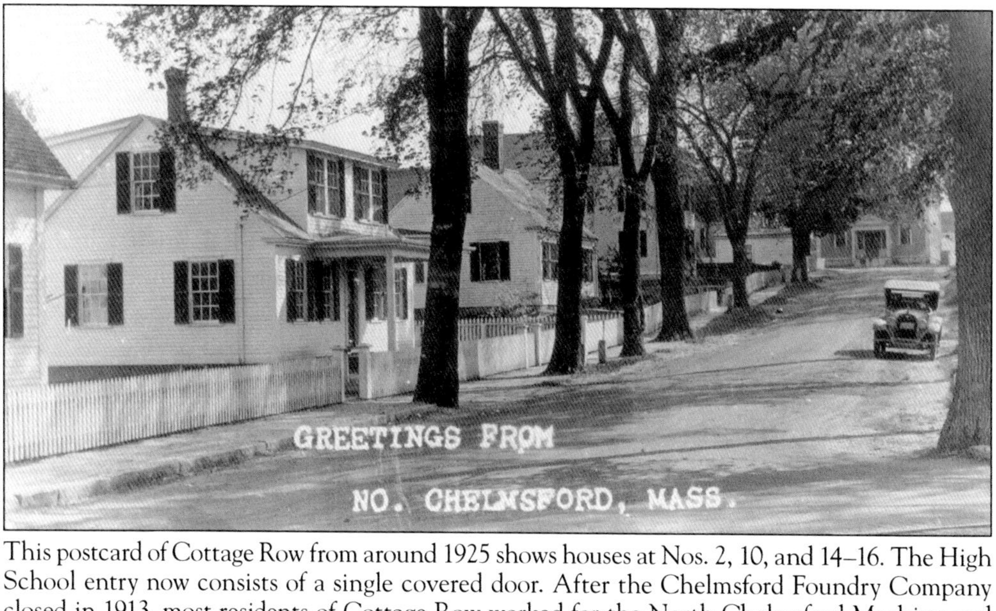


This postcard of Cottage Row from around 1925 shows houses at Nos. 2, 10, and 14–16. The High School entry now consists of a single covered door. After the Chelmsford Foundry Company closed in 1913, most residents of Cottage Row worked for the North Chelmsford Machine and Supply Company (the Crysler Company after 1923), the Silesia Mills (closed in 1931), or the Geo. C. Moore Wool Scouring Company. (Chelmsford Historical Society.)

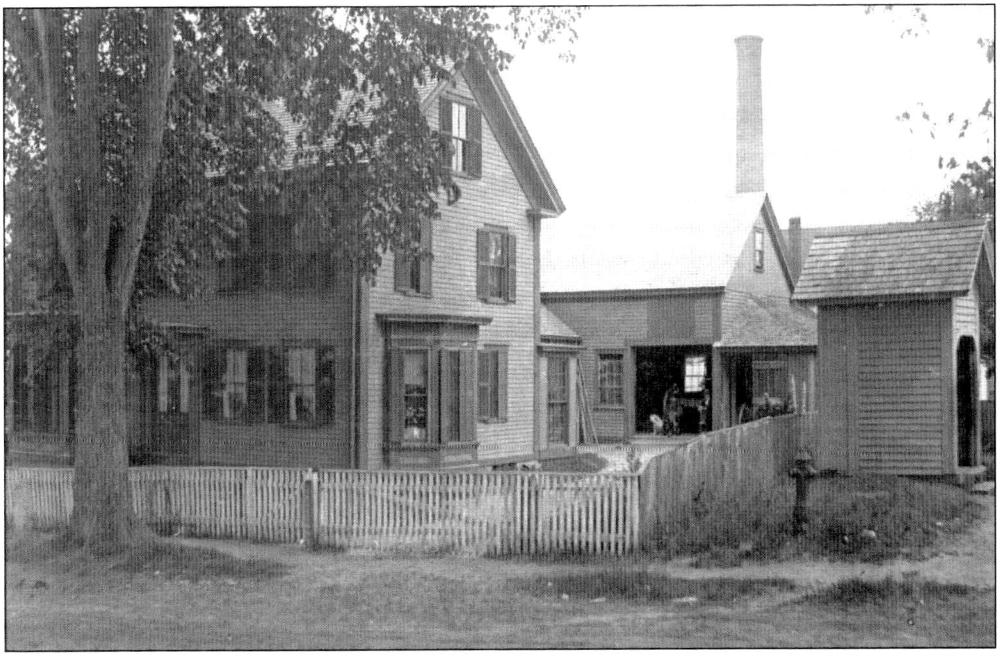

At the time this photograph was taken at 14–16 Cottage Row, machinist James A. Sampson lived here with his wife, Antoinette, daughters Blanch and Florence, and his father, Seth P. Sampson, who was a retired brick mason. James and Seth are likely the two men sitting in the carriage house with the family dog. The Geo. C. Moore Company smokestack stands tall behind the carriage house. (Chelmsford Public Library.)

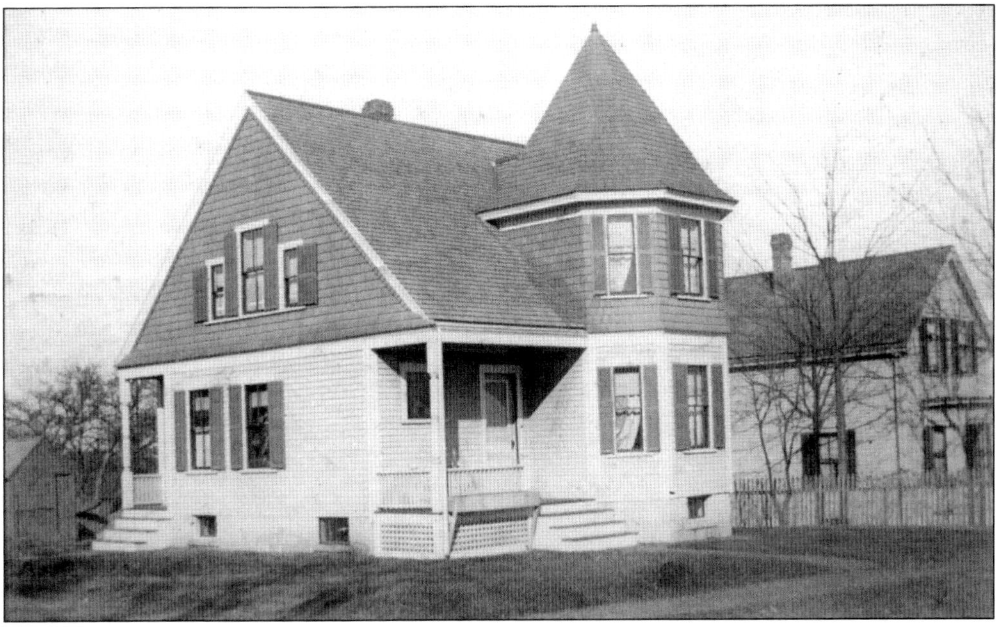

John O. O'Connor was superintendent of Geo. C. Moore Company, which became the Moore Spinning Company in 1902. This house at 58 Depot Street was one of over 40 in North Chelmsford owned at some time by George C. Moore. In 1901, he sold it to superintendent O'Connor, who lived there for 11 years before selling the house and retiring around 1912. (Chelmsford Public Library.)

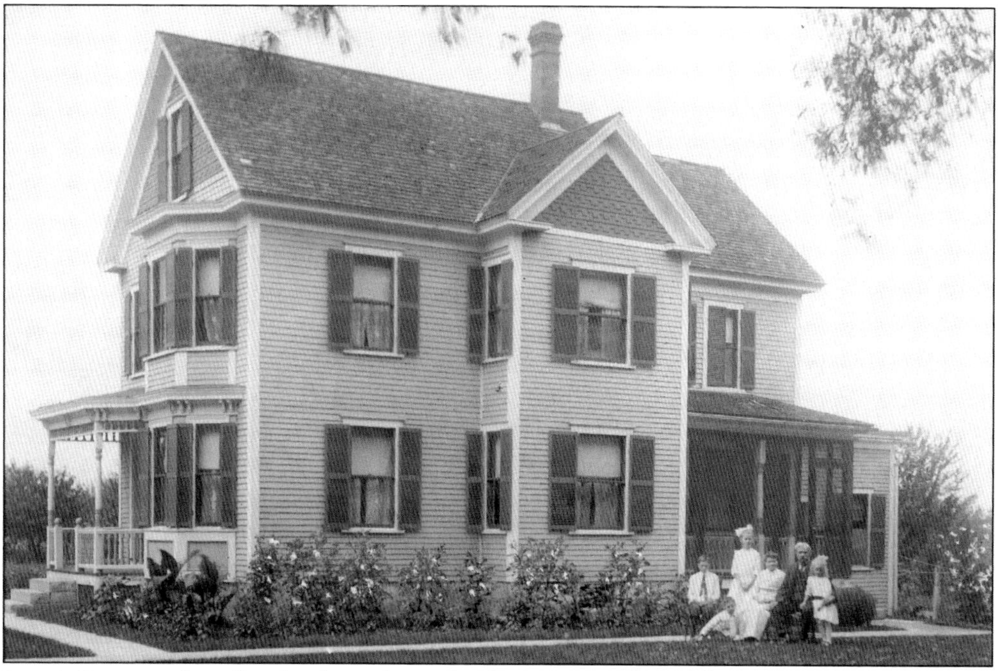

Lars A. Petterson from Sweden, later changed to Peterson, purchased this 61 Dunstable Road home in 1912. Taken around 1920, this photograph shows, from left to right, Carl A., Harry E., Helga C., Augusta, Lars A., and Ebba A. Peterson. Carl became a real estate agent in Central Square and served as a town assessor from 1936 to 1945, selectman from 1948 to 1954, and planning board member from 1954 to 1959. (Chelmsford Historical Society.)

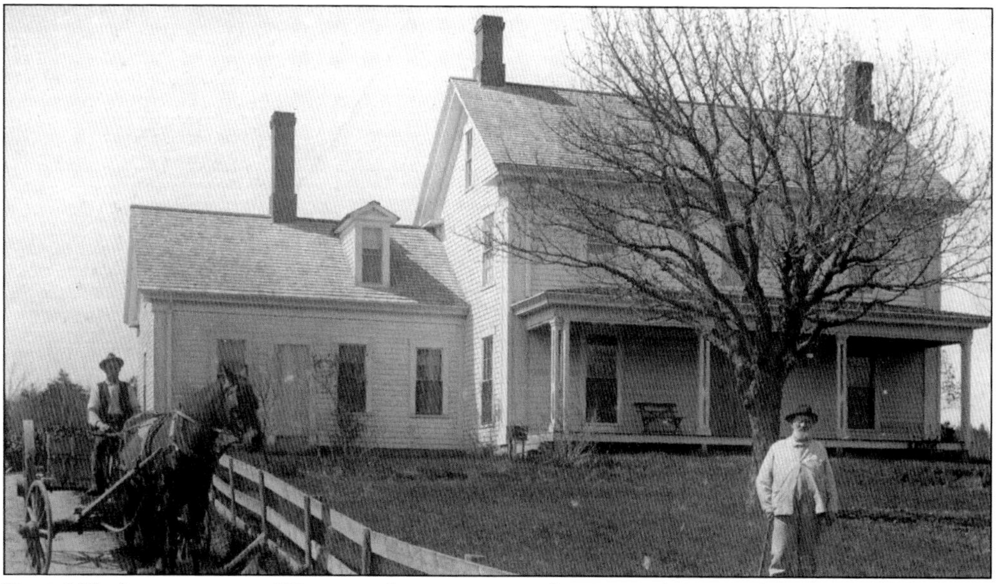

Daniel Blodgett was one of 29 original petitioners to the General Court of Massachusetts for the grant of the town of Chelmsford. He remained in town for the rest of his life, and his marriage to Mary Butterfield on September 15, 1653, was the first recorded in Chelmsford. His descendants, farmers Frederick F. (left) and Frederick W. Blodgett, are shown here at 100 Dunstable Road around 1895. (Chelmsford Public Library.)

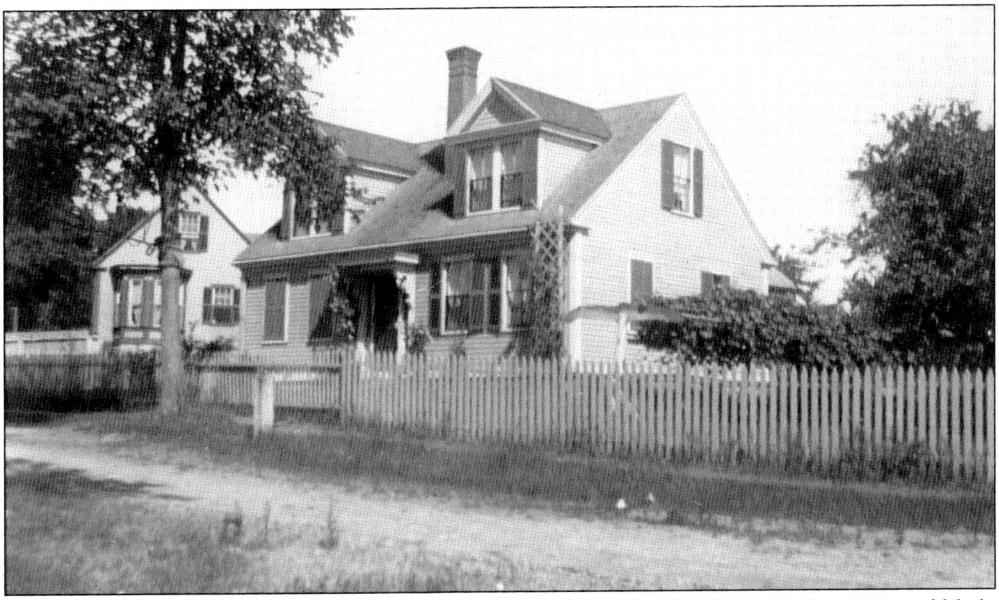

This home at 2 Edwards Place was owned by George C. Moore's wife, Ella J., in the 1890s and likely rented to mill employees. When Ella died in 1901, it became the property of her children Bessie L. Griffin and George C. Moore Jr. They transferred ownership to their father in 1911, and in 1923, the year he died, it went to the U.S. Worsted Corporation. (Chelmsford Public Library.)

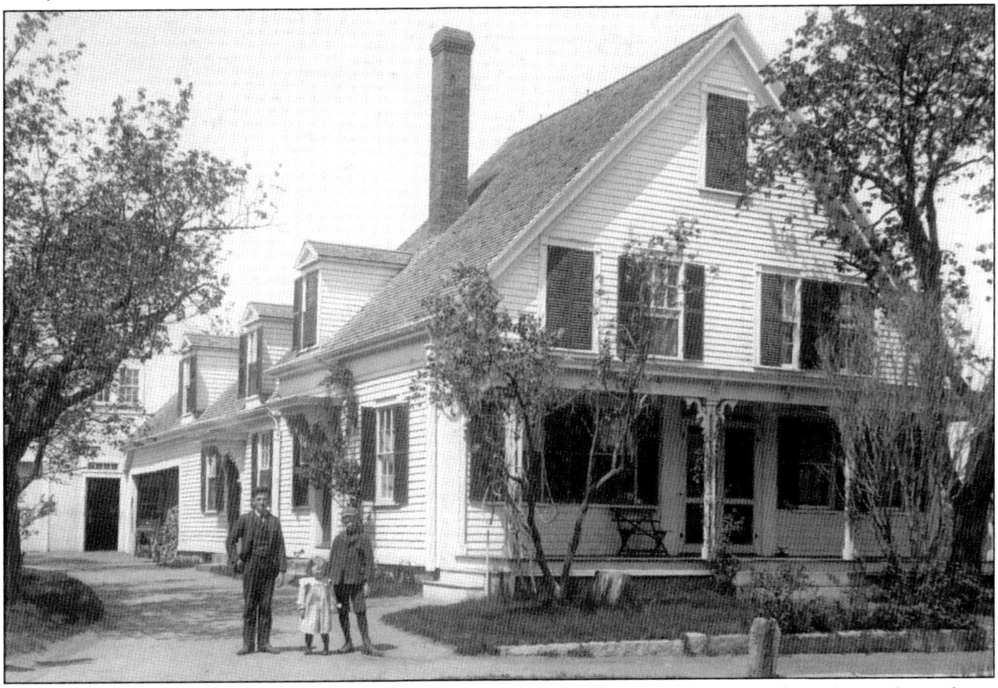

Dr. Nathan B. Edwards owned this home at 6 Edwards Place and practiced medicine here from 1854 until he died in 1893. In 1894, Dr. Fred E. Varney rented the house from Dr. Edwards's widow, Sibyl, to continue the medical practice and is shown here around 1898 with his daughter Marion and son John. By 1901, Dr. Varney had moved his practice to a new house at 34 Middlesex Street. (Chelmsford Public Library.)

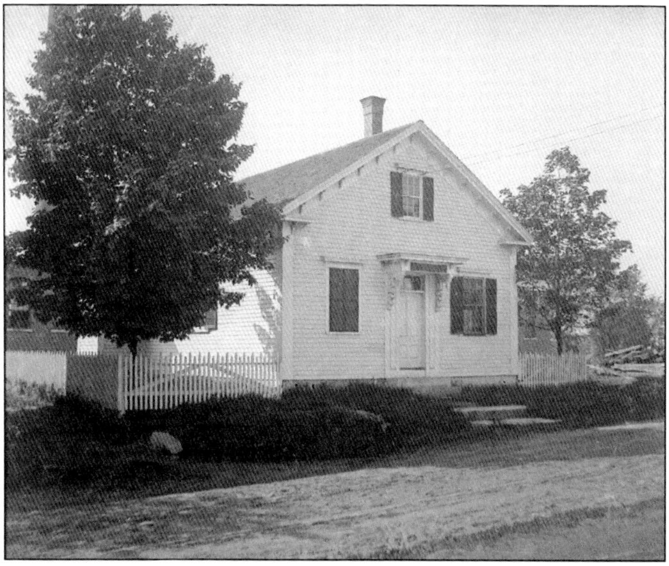

Dr. Nathan B. Edwards was president of the North Chelmsford Library Association when it organized in 1872. He sold a small lot of land he owned on Gay Street to the association in 1878 and the small library building, shown here around 1900, was built. A small closet located on the left rear was likely an outhouse when the library was built. (Chelmsford Public Library.)

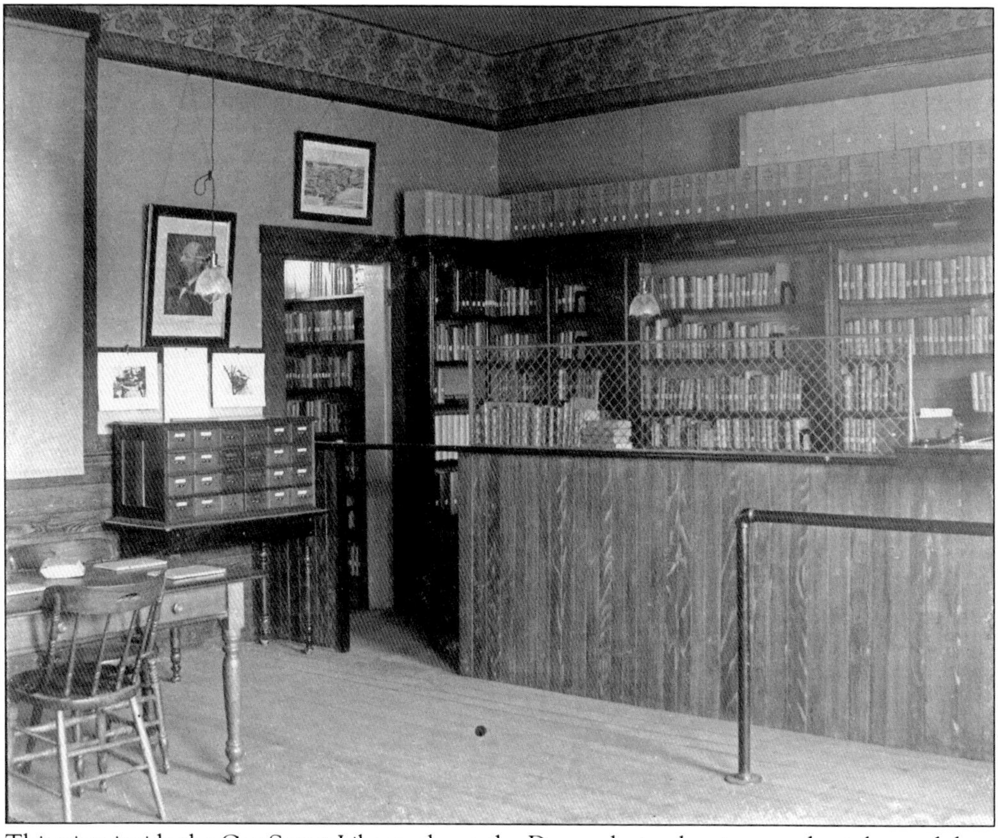

This view inside the Gay Street Library shows the Dewey decimal system card catalog and door to the closet at left and the rear wall with the librarian's check-out counter on the right. Ziba Gay, another director of the association, lived around the corner on Middlesex Street, and his unmarried daughter Emma Jane Gay was the librarian here as well as a trustee of the Adams Library. (Chelmsford Public Library.)

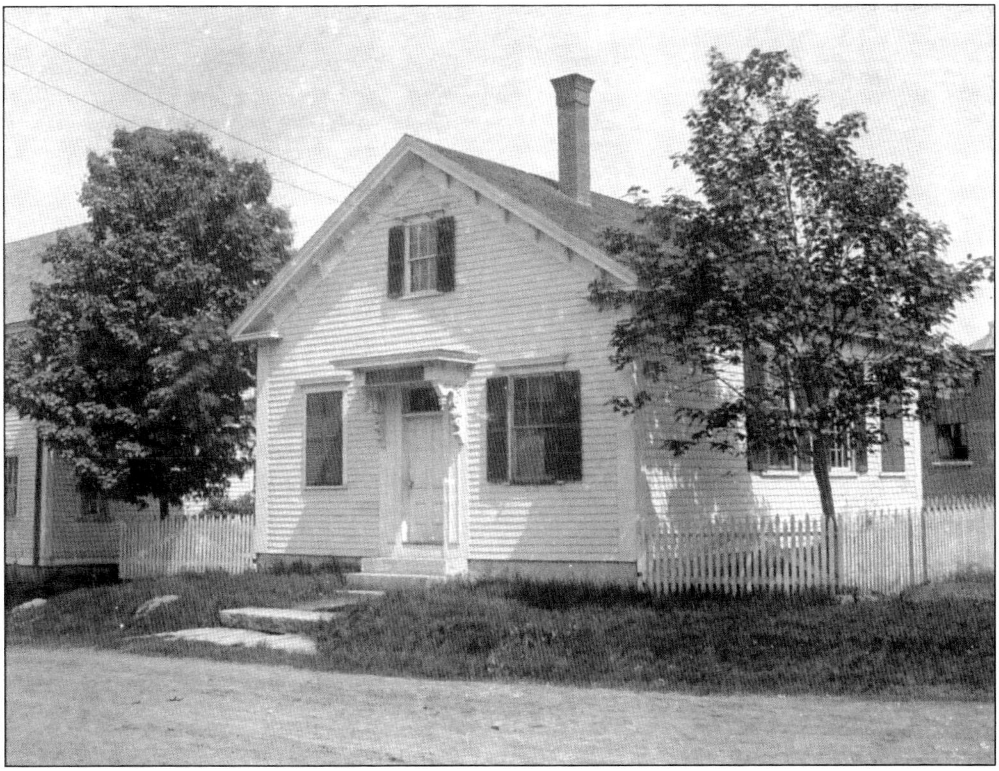

Emma Gay left her position as librarian around 1910 and was replaced by Anna C. MacKay. In memory of Anna's untimely death in 1924 at the age of 35, her older brother Stewart MacKay willed his home on Newfield Street to the town just before his own death in 1947. The Anna C. MacKay Library opened in 1949 and this site is now just a parking area. (Chelmsford Public Library.)

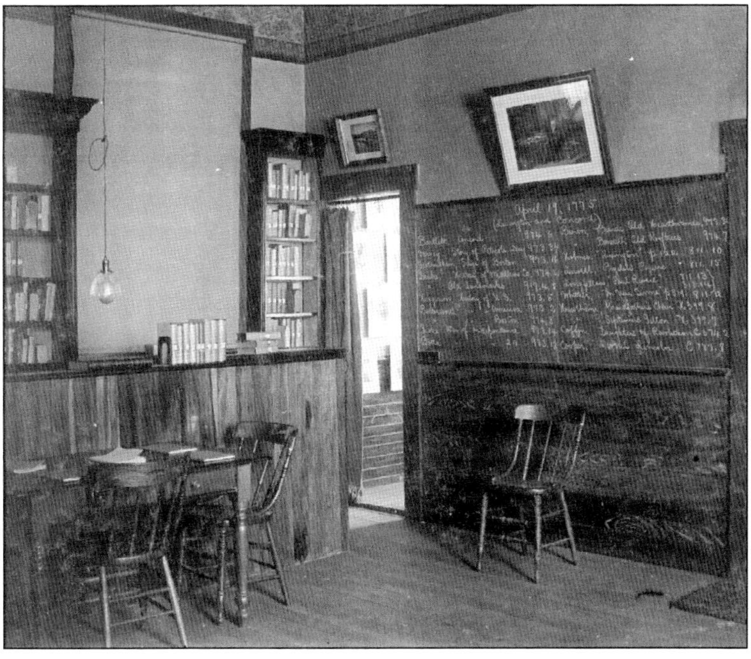

This view inside the Gay Street Library shows reading and counter space on the left and two doors to a front entry hall surrounding a blackboard on the right. Librarian Emma Gay chalked a reading list on the blackboard related to the history of the Revolutionary War. The little library became overcrowded by 1912 and was extended by 15 feet with shelving for about 1,000 more books. (Chelmsford Public Library.)

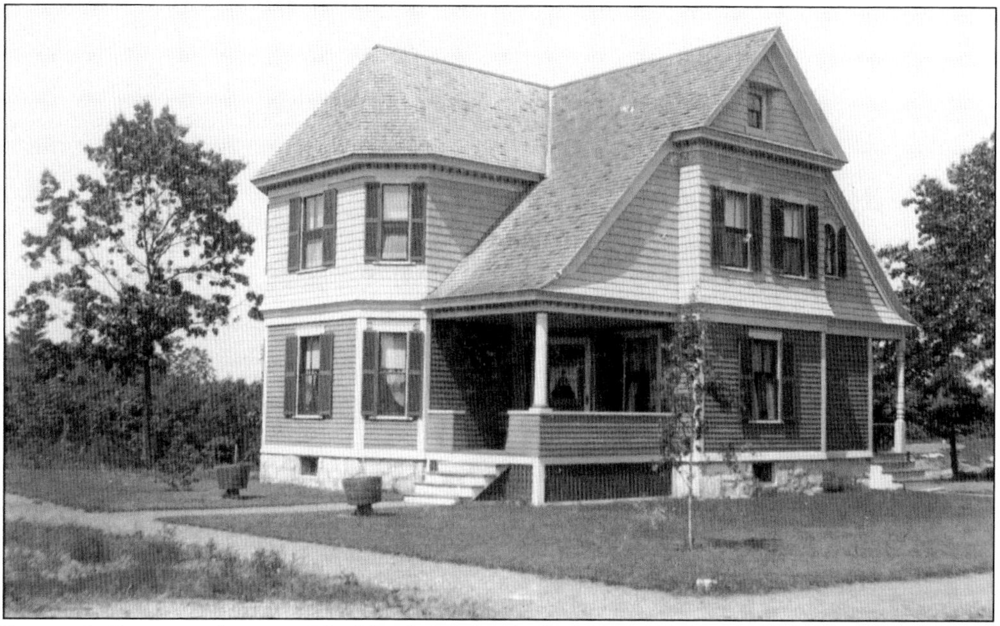

Preston L. Piggott, a director of the North Chelmsford Library Association and town auditor, lived here at 1 Mansur Street / 37 Newfield Street with his wife Bessie (the youngest sister of neighbor Hubert Bearce), daughters Arvilla and Bertha, and son Clayton. He worked in Lowell as a clerk for the Lowell Manufacturing Company until 1905, then as purchasing agent and paymaster for the Bigelow Carpet Company. (Chelmsford Public Library.)

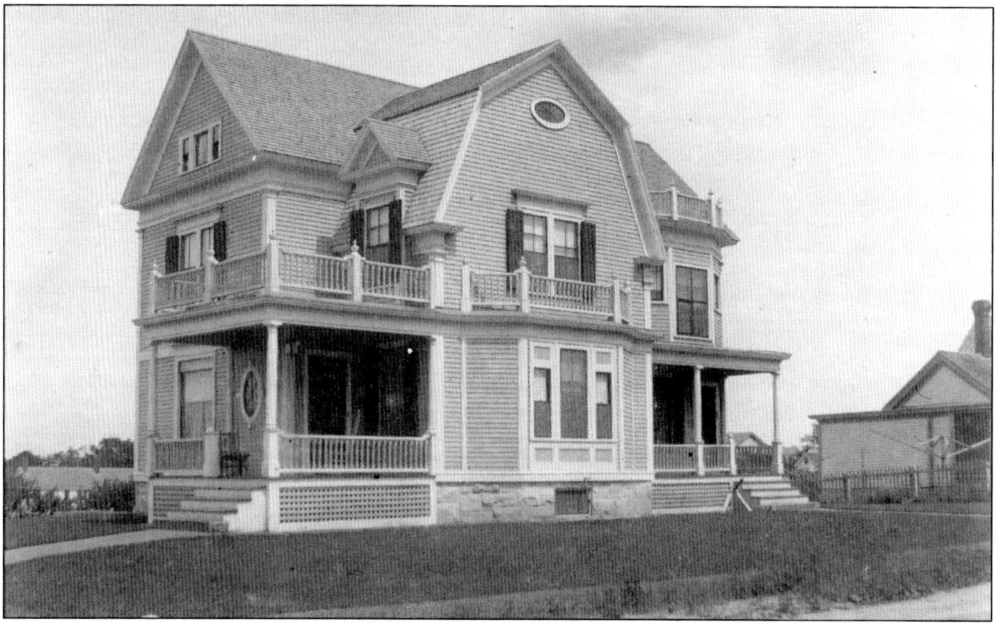

Henry T. Ripley married his wife, Georgiana, in 1898 and lived here at 44–46 Newfield Street. He worked at the Boston office of the Chelmsford Foundry Company until it ended in 1913, and started his own iron and steel company in Boston, Henry T. Ripley Inc., in 1915 with $50,000 of capital. He was also president of the North Chelmsford Library Corporation until his death in 1923. (Chelmsford Public Library.)

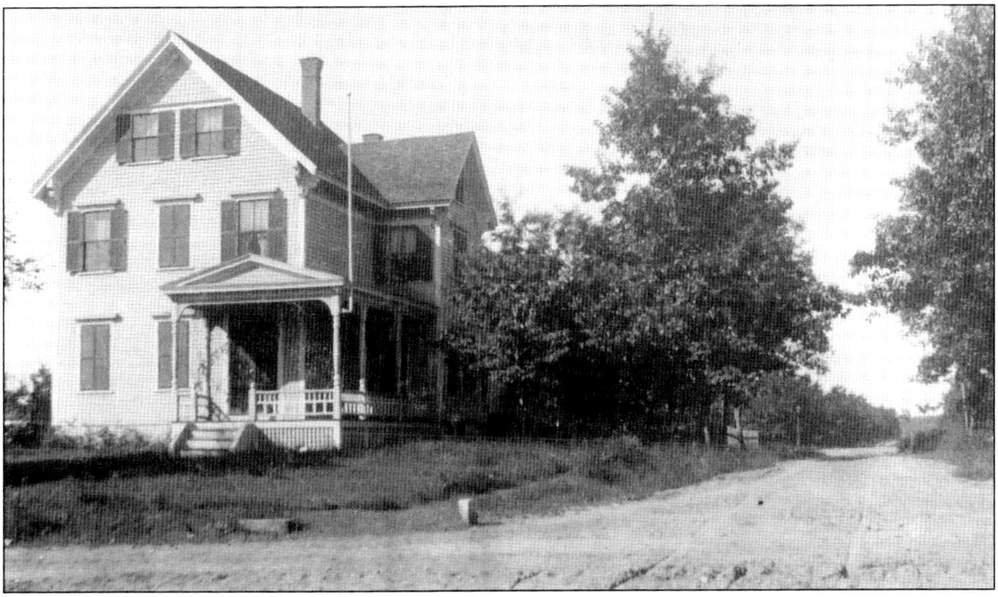

Hubert Bearce was superintendent at the Chelmsford Foundry Company and lived at 63–65 Newfield Street with his wife, Villa, son Hubert H., and daughters Esther and Florence. Hubert's father, Elijah D. Bearce, started at the foundry in 1845, working his way up to agent, then vice president. Elijah died in 1906 and Hubert moved his family to Los Angeles, California, around 1911. (Chelmsford Public Library.)

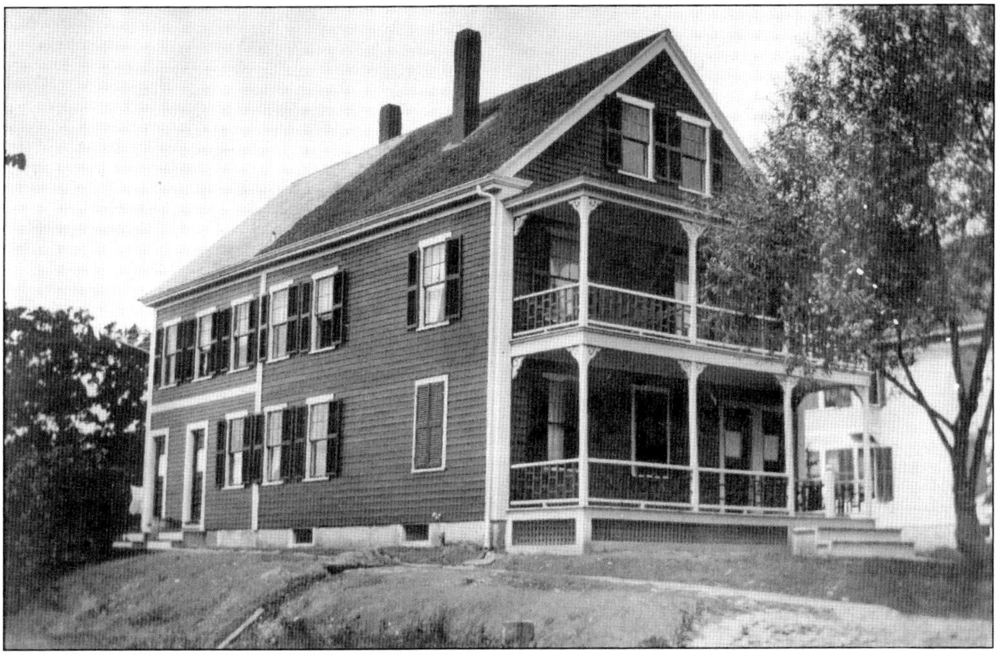

After 1883, this rental house at 69–71 Newfield Street was owned in thirds by Harry C. and Clara A. Wright and their mother, Hanna A., the widow of Samuel T. Wright. After the untimely deaths of Hanna in 1902, Clara in 1903, and Harry in 1905, the house was inherited by Frederick G. Salmon, who had married Clara in 1901. The photograph shows expansion of the two-family house. (Chelmsford Historical Society.)

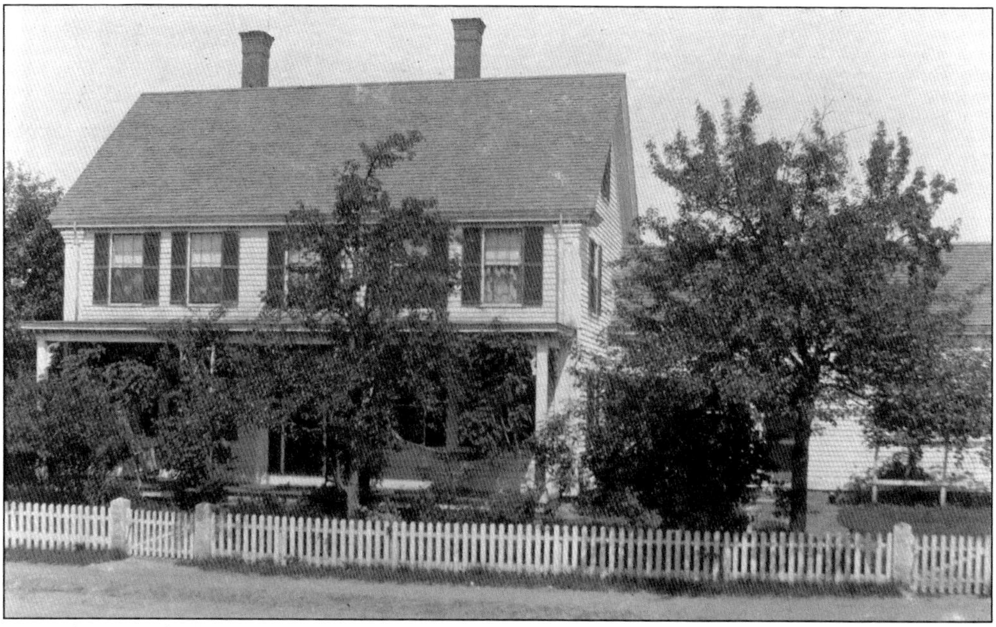

Samuel T. Wright lived in this house at 7 Washington Street behind George C. Moore's house and next door to North Town Hall. He was a trader, general storekeeper, and real estate broker, served as selectman for six years, and was treasurer of the North Chelmsford Library Association when it started in 1872. Samuel died in 1883 and his widow, Hannah, continued to live in the house. (Chelmsford Public Library.)

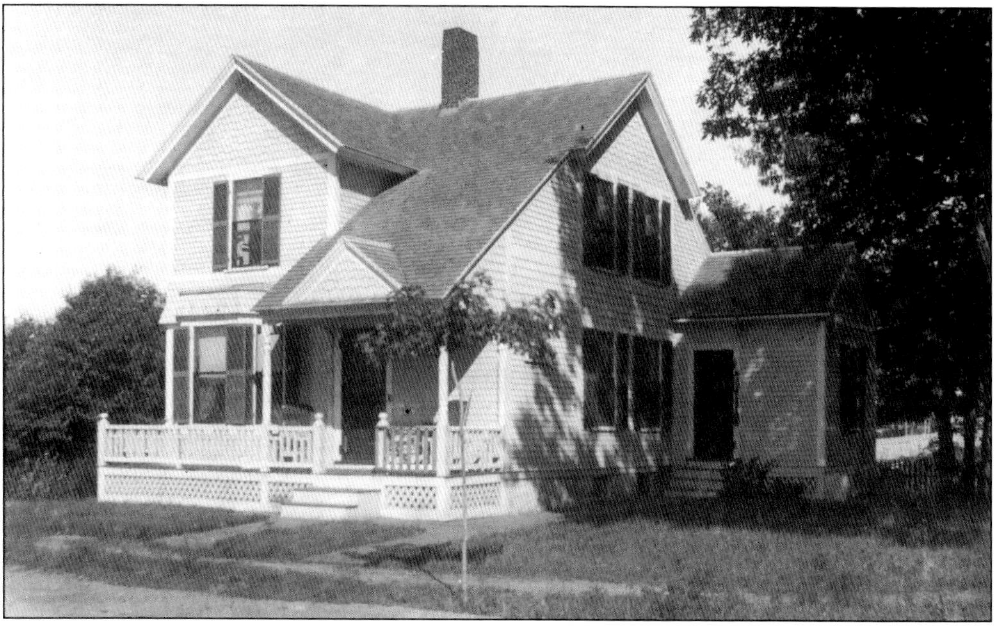

George H. Ripley, an iron worker and master mechanic in Lowell, lived here at 39 Washington Street with his wife, Edith, and daughter Helen. His father, Royal S. Ripley, was an agent for the Chelmsford Foundry Company in the Boston office. When Royal died in 1913, the year the foundry went out of business, George moved his family into 55 Gay Street with his mother, Abby. (Chelmsford Public Library.)

# *Nine*

# West Chelmsford

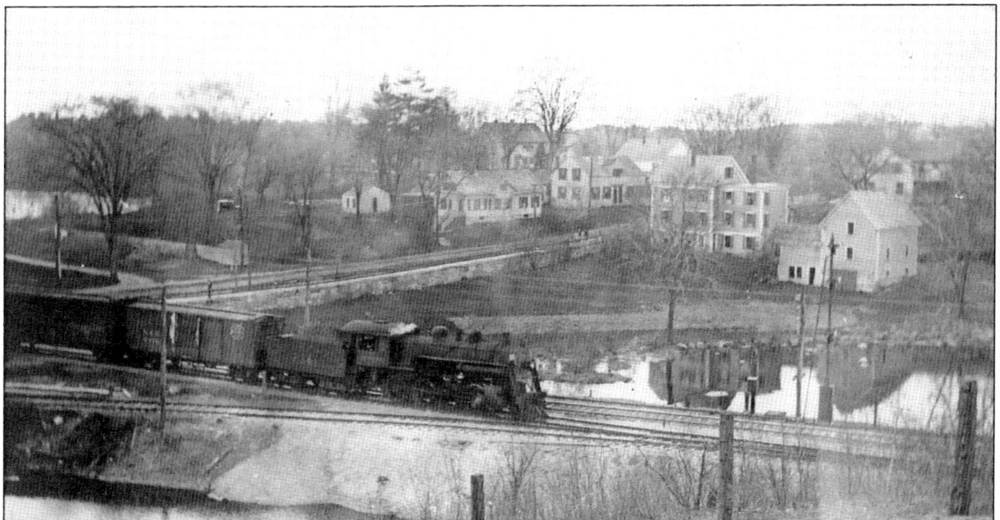

The train station and post office were the heart of West Chelmsford life for over 100 years. The last local passenger train passed through West Chelmsford on April 25, 1953, ending 105 years of service between Worcester and Lowell. The West Chelmsford post office was classified subordinate to North Chelmsford on June 22, 1962, assigned the North Chelmsford ZIP code in June 1963, and closed for good on September 30, 1964. (Thomas Collins.)

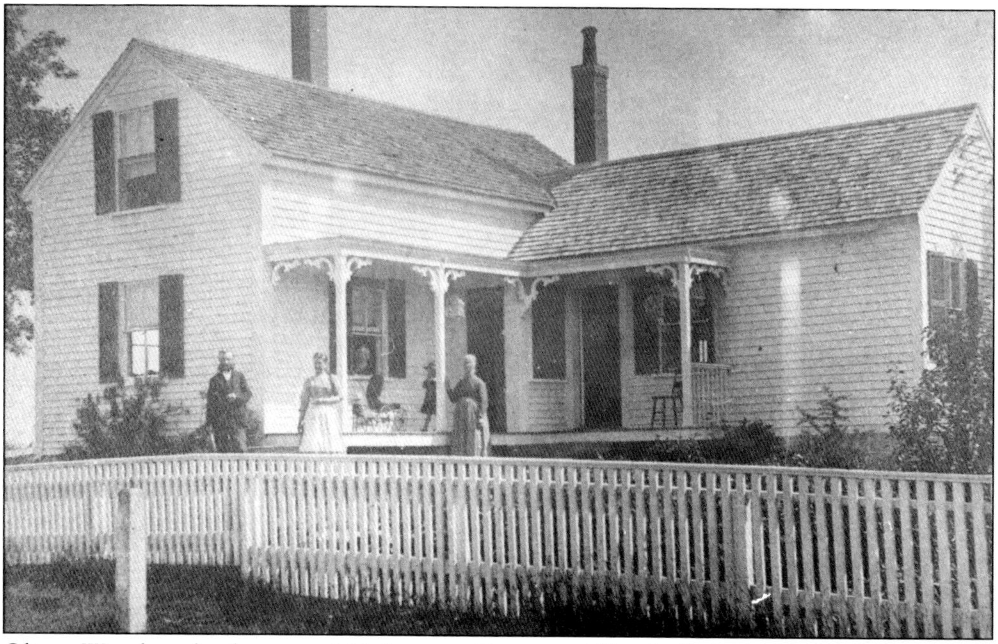

Oliver Woodward, who owned Nabnasset Grove on Westford's Nabnasset Lake, sold the grove to George C. Moore in 1874 and moved to West Chelmsford. Oliver's son William S. Woodward was employed by the Hiscox File Manufacturing Company and built houses at 164 Main Street (pictured) as well as at 168 and 170–172 Main Street. Oliver died in 1885, and this photograph may have been taken around 1888, the year William died of typhoid fever. (Chelmsford Historical Society.)

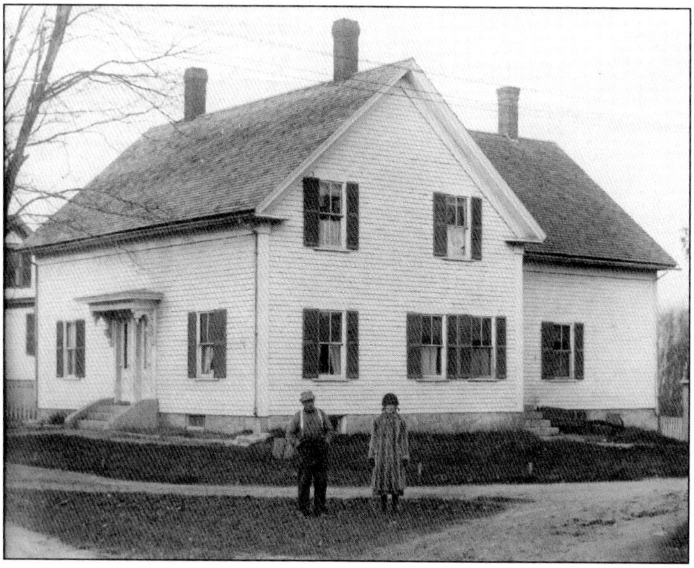

Stonecutter Carl Olsson from Sweden owned this two-family house at 170–172 Main Street with his wife, Anna, from 1910 to 1922. They raised seven children: Adina, Lydia, August, David, John, Elizabeth, and Ida. This photograph, likely taken around 1917, shows Carl and a family member or friend identified as Dida. The street at right is Wilson Lane, which leads to the control dam for Freeman Lake. (Virginia Burnham.)

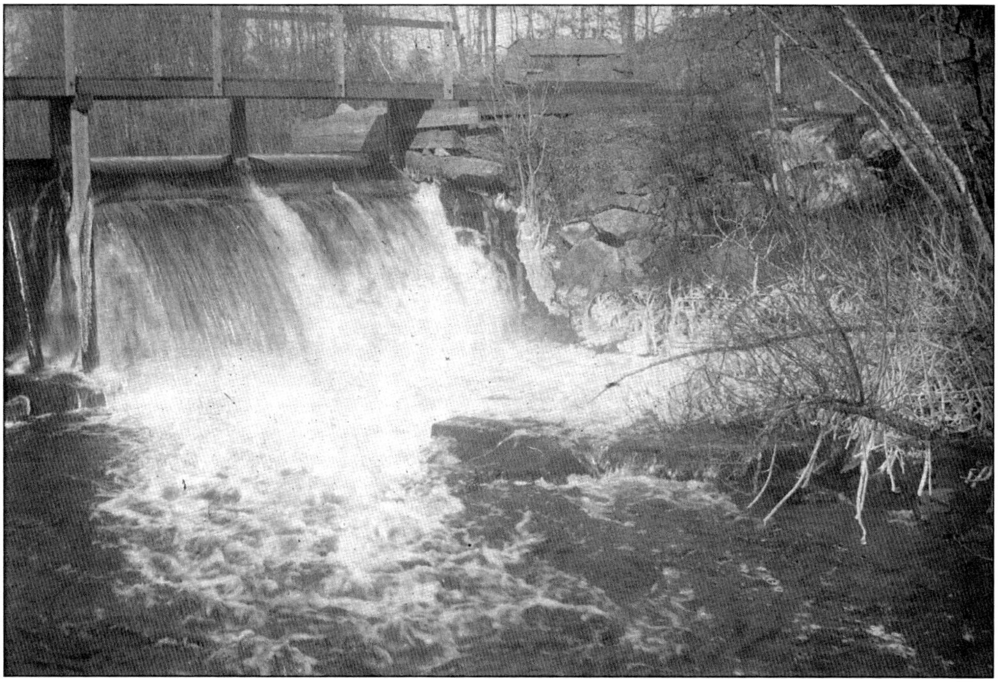

Stony Brook splits in two at the control dam behind 11 Wilson Lane. The spillway, shown here around 1900, sets the water level in a small reservoir and then drains into Stony Brook. A control gate at top right shuts off water flow to the canal. A wooden control gate shelter had four handles and was sitting on the embankment when this picture was taken. (Thomas Collins.)

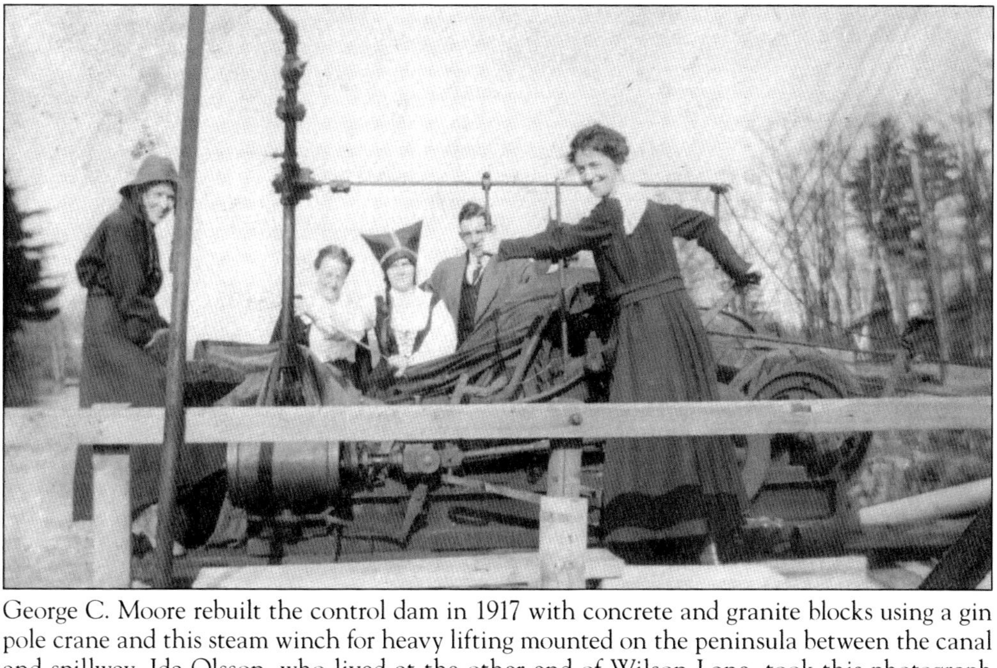

George C. Moore rebuilt the control dam in 1917 with concrete and granite blocks using a gin pole crane and this steam winch for heavy lifting mounted on the peninsula between the canal and spillway. Ida Olsson, who lived at the other end of Wilson Lane, took this photograph of her friends during a walk after church in April 1917. She died in the flu epidemic of 1918. (Virginia Burnham.)

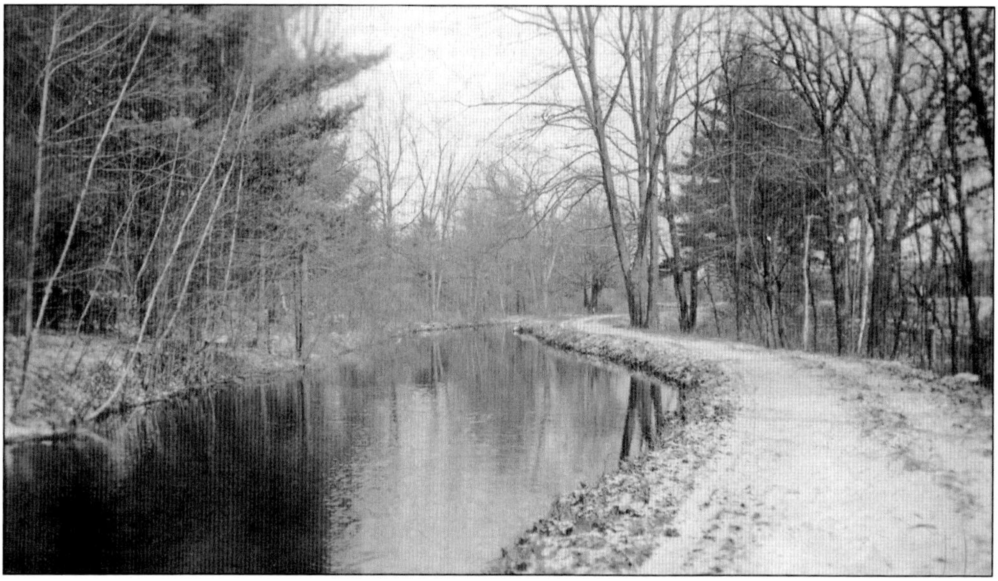

This photograph, taken after a light snowfall around 1920, shows the canal walk that resulted after George C. Moore rebuilt the dam. Stony Brook flows on the right side of the causeway for about 200 feet before passing under the railroad tracks. The canal still functions to refresh the water in Freeman Lake, and part of the walk remains passable but is overgrown with vegetation. (West Chelmsford United Methodist Church.)

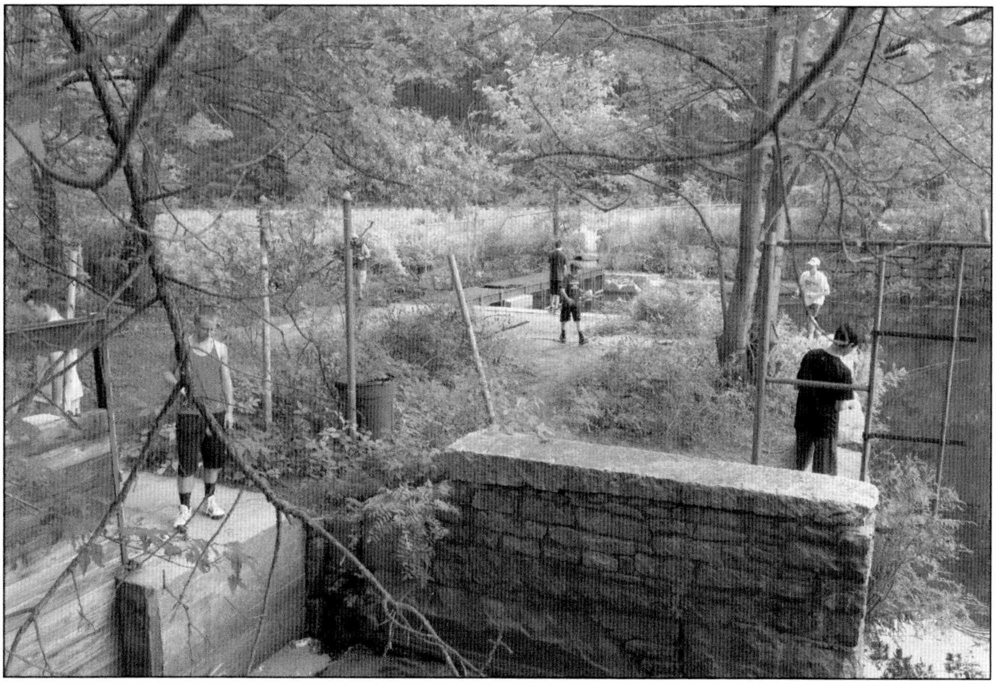

This is the rebuilt control dam as it looks almost 100 years later. The gate at far left is the canal water shutoff, and the spillway sets the water level in the canal. The Stony Brook Railroad bed runs parallel to the brook on the far side of the spillway. The site is still a popular destination and fishing hole for local boys, as shown in this recent image. (Photograph by the author.)

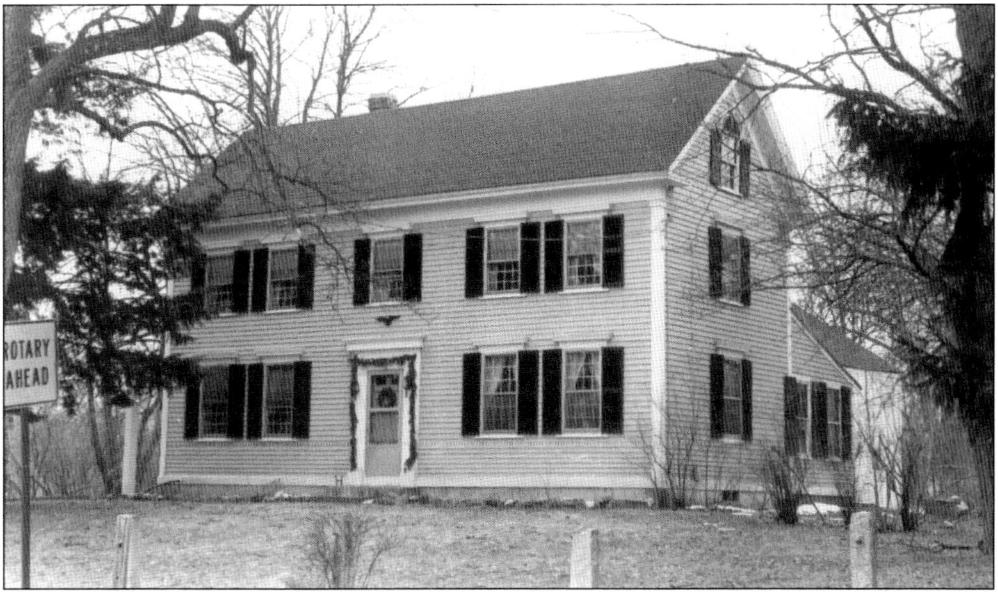

Deacon John Farwell came to West Chelmsford about 1820, first constructing a scythe mill on Stony Brook and then, in 1823, this house at 203 Main Street. Christopher Roby took over the scythe factory and three houses in 1846, including 203 Main Street, shown here in 1973. The area was known as Farwell, or Scythe Factory Village, until the railroad and post office arrived in 1848. (Chelmsford Historical Commission.)

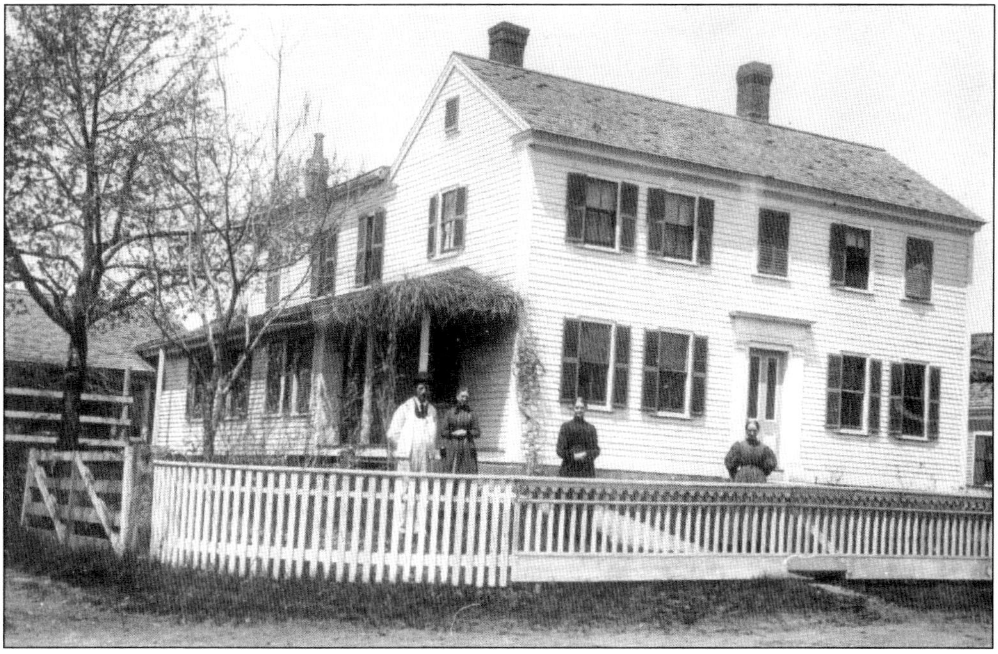

In 1850, Jonas C. Butterfield was a member of the Christopher and Susan Roby household, along with Frederic T. Sawyer. They all worked at the Roby, Sawyer & Company manufacturing scythes. Later the same year, Butterfield married his wife, Philena, and moved here to 193 Main Street. This house was built by Deacon John Farwell's son John T. Farwell. The Butterfields are pictured around 1900 with daughters Clara and Laura. (Chelmsford Historical Society.)

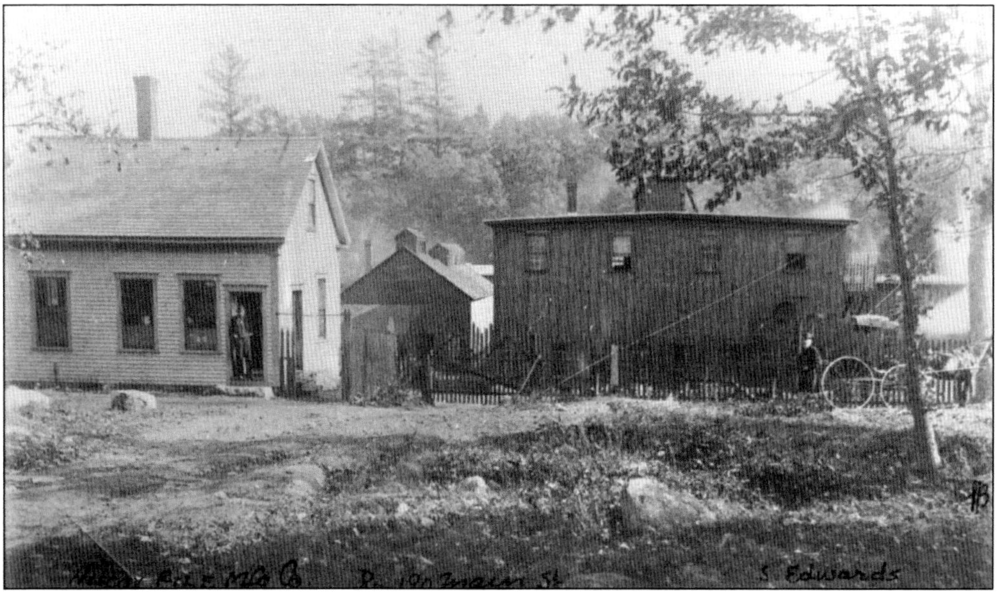


When the Civil War broke out, Christopher Roby was sole owner of the scythe mill and switched to production of swords for the Union Army. At the end of the war, he was stuck with an inventory of swords and no customers to pay for them, and he filed for bankruptcy in September 1867. The Roby Manufacturing Company continued production of industrial knives and military and society swords until 1875. (Bernie Ready.)

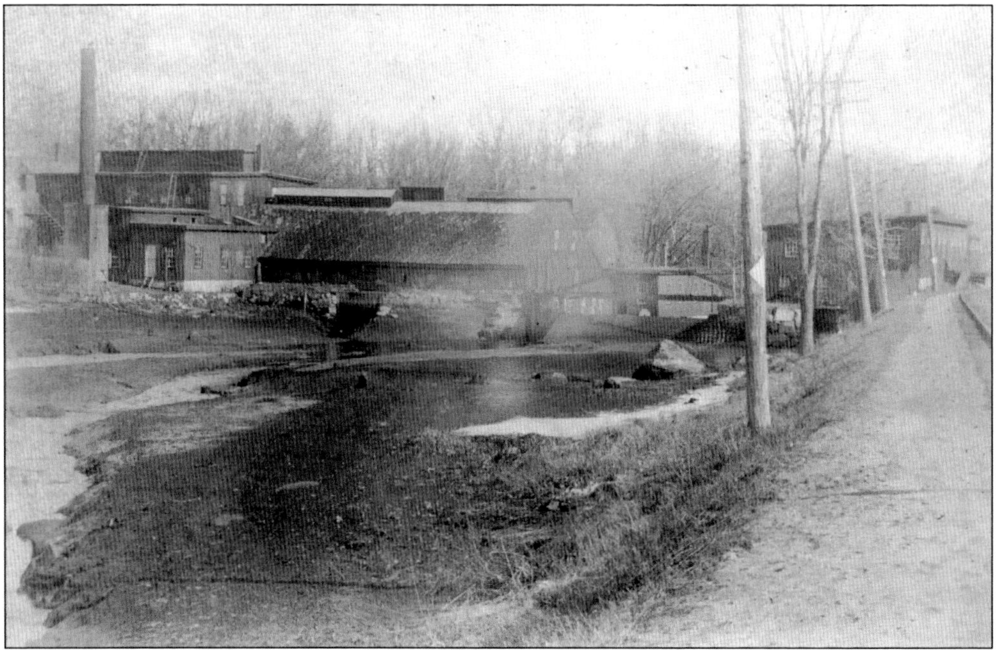

The Hiscox File Company of Lowell purchased the mill in 1875, upgrading and powering its machinery with two turbine wheels and a 60-horsepower Corliss steam engine. They specialized in planer, veneer, jointer, and butcher knives; files and rasps; and a variety of machine knives. Production ceased in 1889 when a fire partially destroyed the facility. The building on the right was torn down in 1900. (Thomas Collins.)

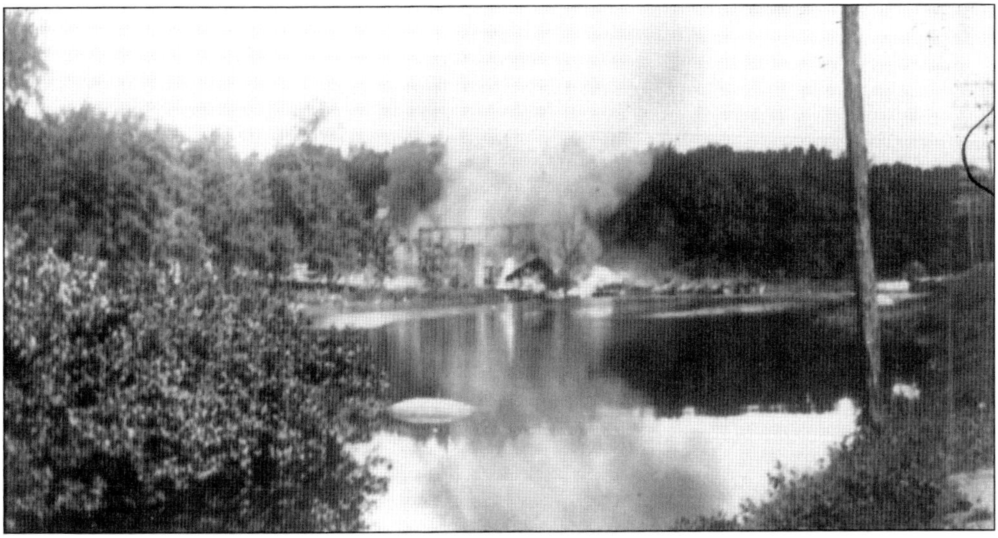

George C. Moore purchased the Hiscox mill property for the water rights in 1893 and began using the mill building as a stable with storage for hay. On September 11, 1902, a fire—possibly started by a spark from a passing train—destroyed this mill building and the nearby office. The scenic photograph below was taken about three years after the fire. Moore had some work done on the dam around 1917, when he rebuilt the canal reservoir downstream. The stone foundations shown below were replaced with thick concrete walls, which can still be seen from the railroad tracks. Rumors published at the time stated that Moore was planning a carbonizing plant, which scours wool by burning off the oils and dirt with an acid bath, but that was never built. (Above, Chelmsford Historical Society; below, Thomas Collins.)

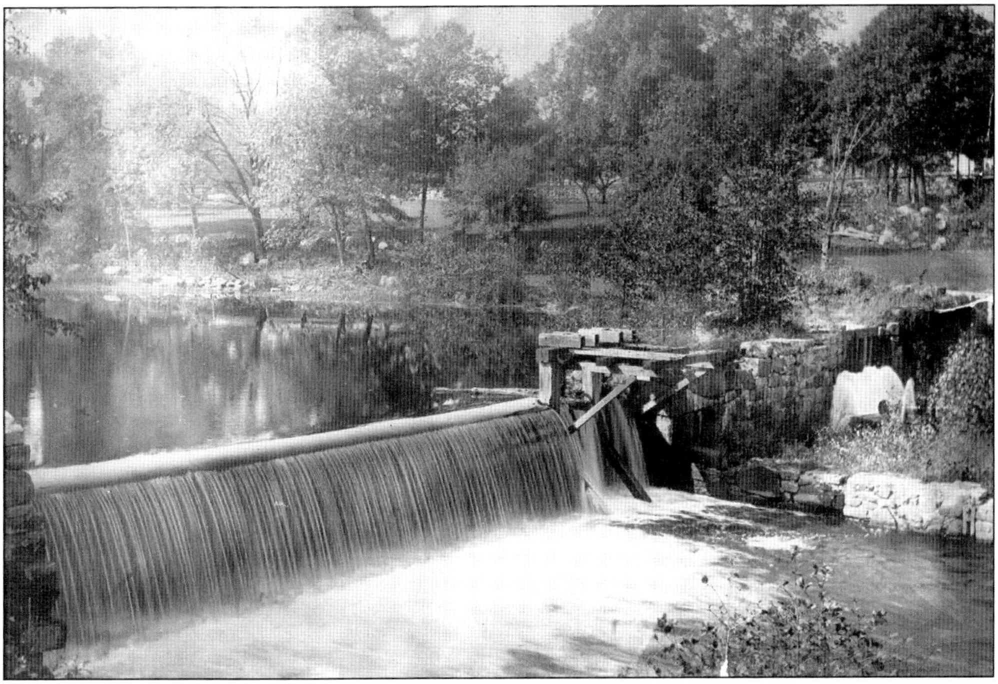

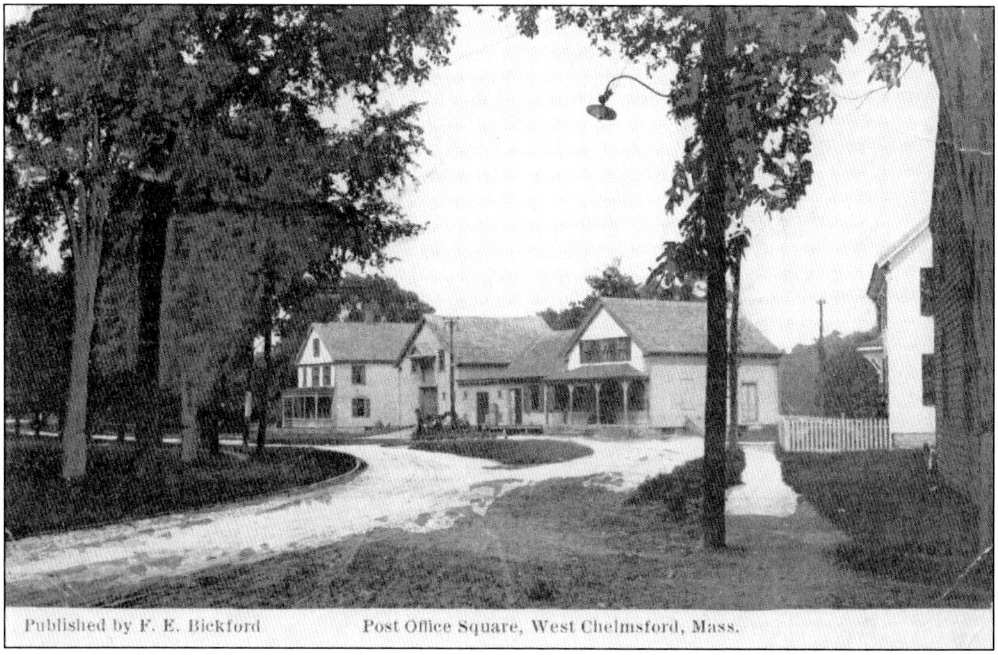


Frank E. Bickford, the son of South Chelmsford grocer Daniel W. Bickford and publisher of the postcard above, purchased the store at 212–214 Main Street from Marcus H. Winship in April 1904. He was appointed West Chelmsford postmaster in June of the same year and later became weigher of coal and hay, measurer of wood, special police officer, and distributor of books for the North Chelmsford Library Association. Bickford expanded the living quarters in front of the original store and ell, as shown below, and several of his clerks rented rooms in the building. His wife, Lillian, was appointed postmaster in 1914, and his daughter Rita G. Anderson in 1929 and 1944. He retired from the grocery business in 1931 and died in 1942. The last postmaster in West Chelmsford was Eleanor F. Ricker, appointed in 1958. (Both, Chelmsford Historical Society.)

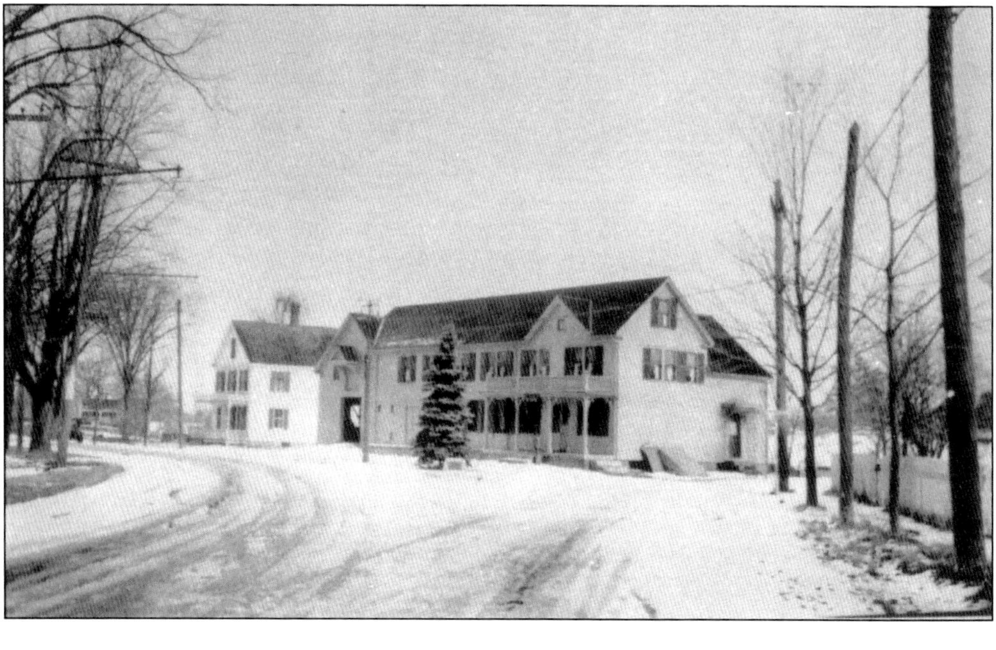

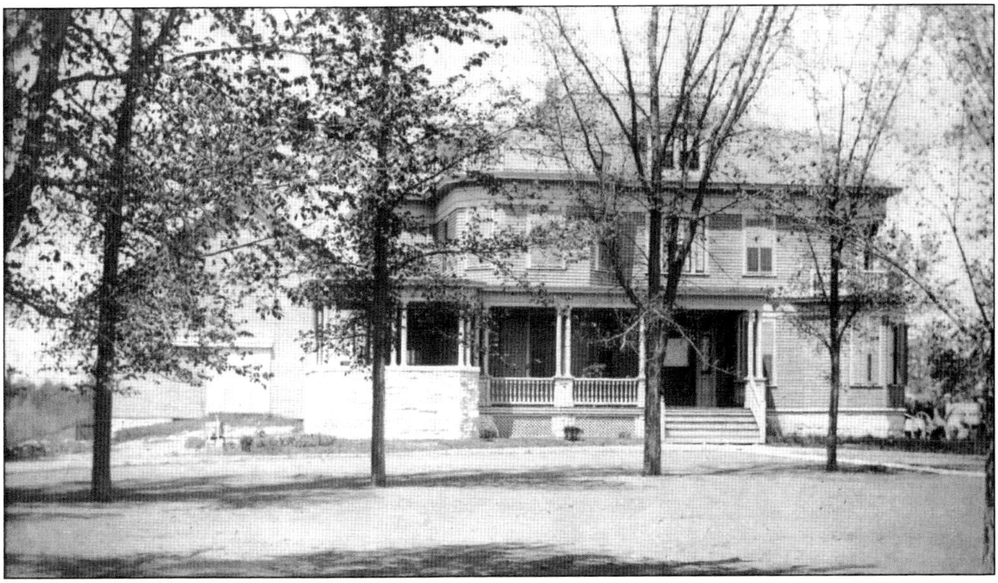

In 1869, Rev. Samuel H. Virgin, pastor emeritus of the Pilgrim Congregational Church of Brooklyn, New York, married Isadora Blodgett, the daughter of Luther and Elmira Blodgett at 209 Main Street in West Chelmsford. In 1898, Reverend Virgin had the Blodgett home moved across the street to 208 Main Street, shown at left, to make room for this grand home for his retirement. (Thomas Collins.)

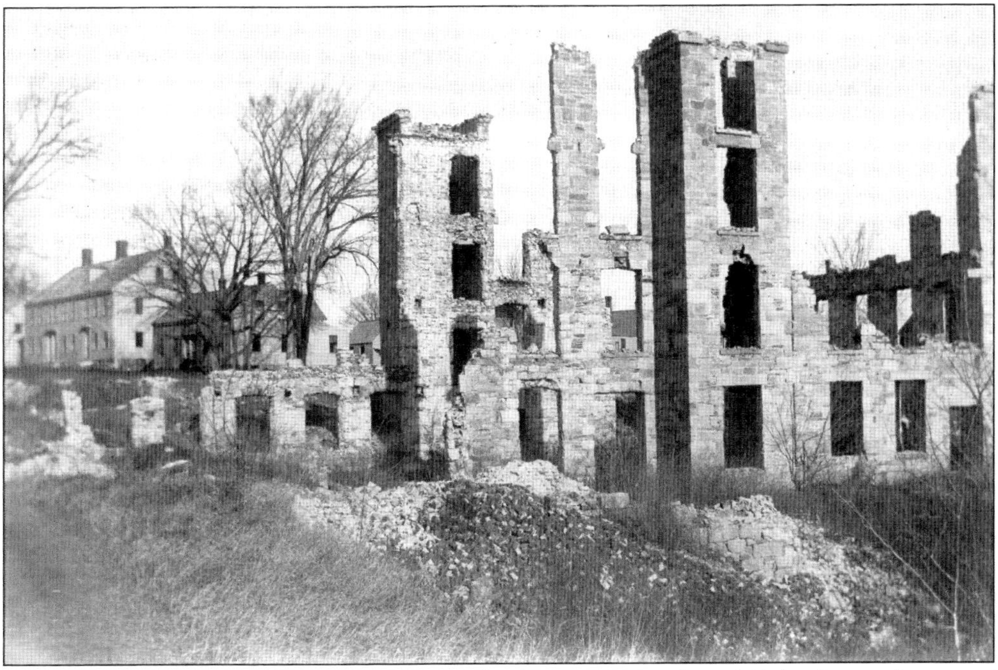

The Chelmsford Company built a mill on School Street soon after 1830 for the production of worsted yarn. That mill burned in 1863, and the complex was rebuilt as the Chelmsford Woolen Mills with the stone Eagle Mill as its centerpiece. Another fire destroyed the Eagle Mill, seen here around 1900, on December 27, 1883. The three multifamily mill tenements shown on the left have since been removed. (Thomas Collins.)

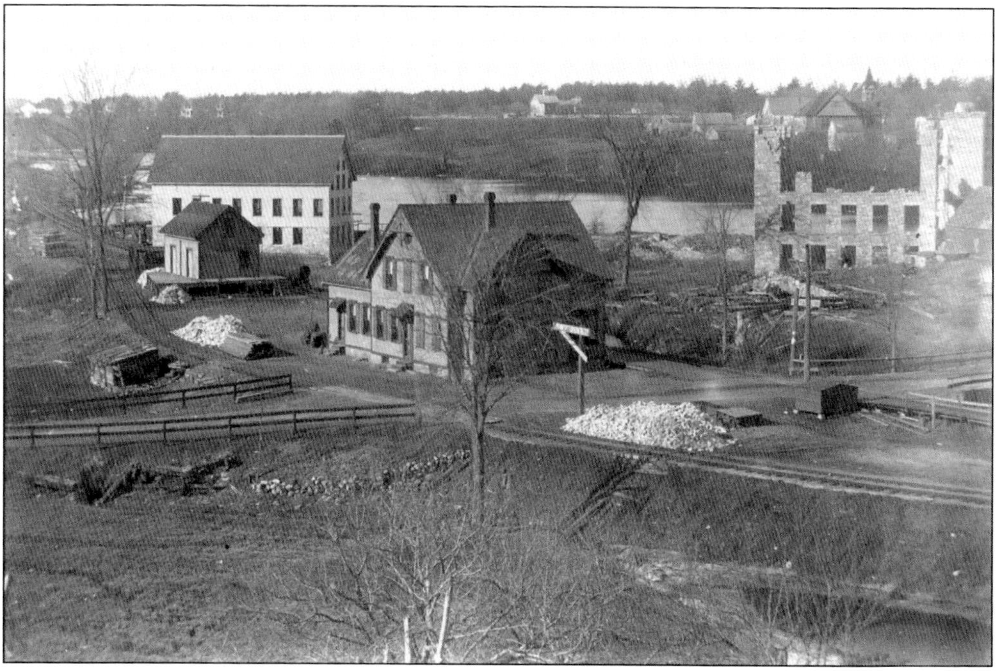

Pictured above are, from left to right, the railroad freight house, Sugden Press Bagging Company, West Chelmsford train station, Eagle Mill ruins, and West Chelmsford Methodist Church (above the ruins). Some houses on Jonas Road and Nabnasset Street in Westford can be seen across the pond and to the left of the church. School Street, in the image above, was constantly in need of repairs from washouts and was dangerous for pedestrians. William C. Edwards was one of 21 people who donated labor or material in January 1908 to improve the road and build a sidewalk on School Street, and the result is shown below. It appears that stones from the Eagle Mill ruins may have been used for the project. The freight house was moved across School Street and still exists today. (Both, Thomas Collins.)

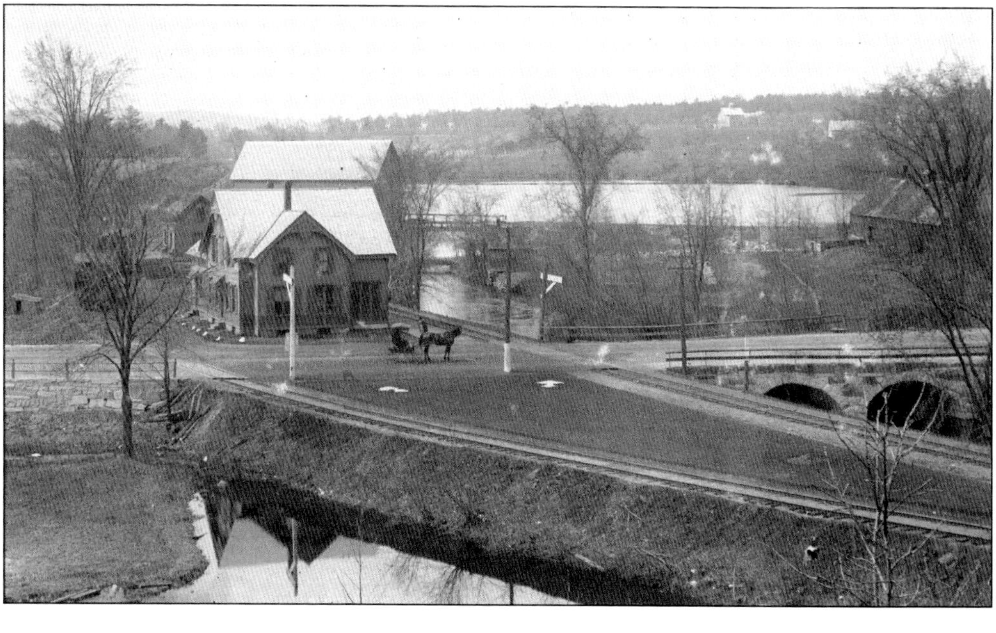

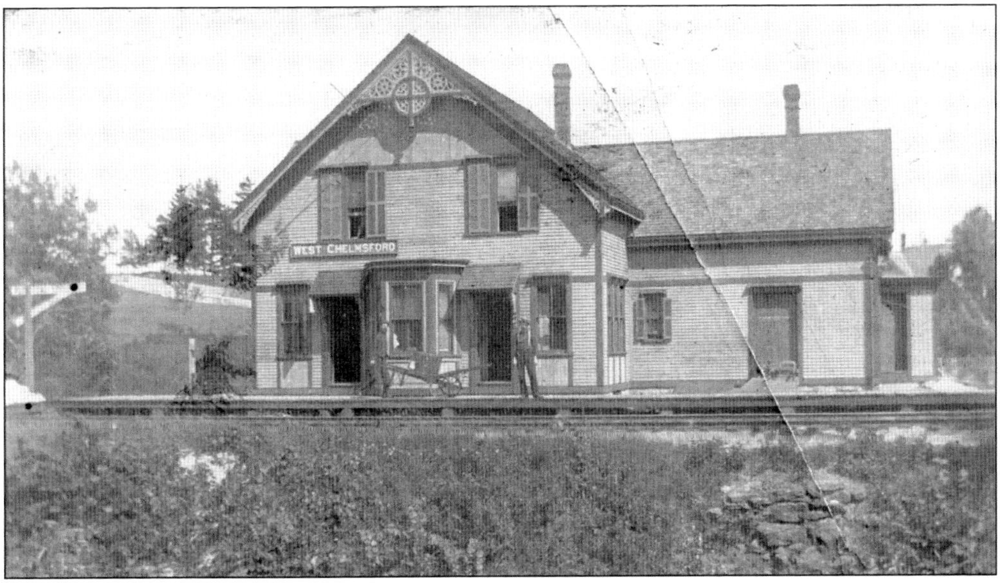


John H. Whidden, the West Chelmsford station agent, lived at nearby 32 School Street and was married to William C. Edwards' sister Sarah. In January 1886, Whidden was appointed West Chelmsford postmaster and was also serving as constable and cemetery commissioner. On August 8, 1894, John was tragically run over and killed while switching freight cars between the main line and side track. (Thomas Collins.)

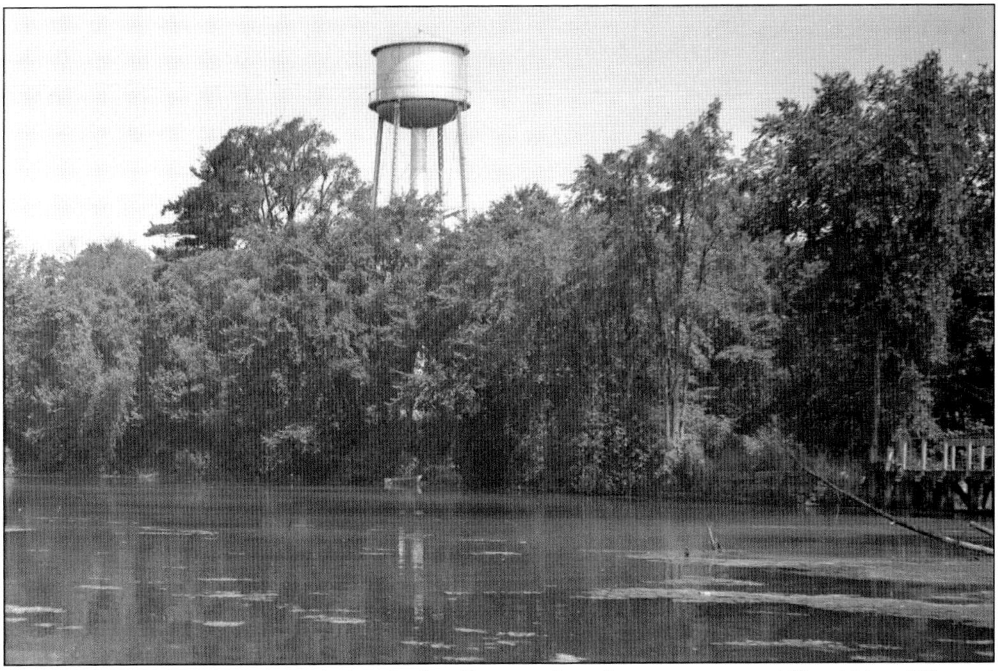

Longtime residents of West Chelmsford will remember this water tower. The Abbot Worsted Company built two towers in 1920—this one to supply their Sugden Press Bagging Company, and another on Tower Road in Nabnassett to supply Brookside Mill, which they had just purchased from George C. Moore. The West Chelmsford tower was dismantled in 1979, when the JapEnameLac plant was sold for private commercial development. (Chelmsford Historical Society.)

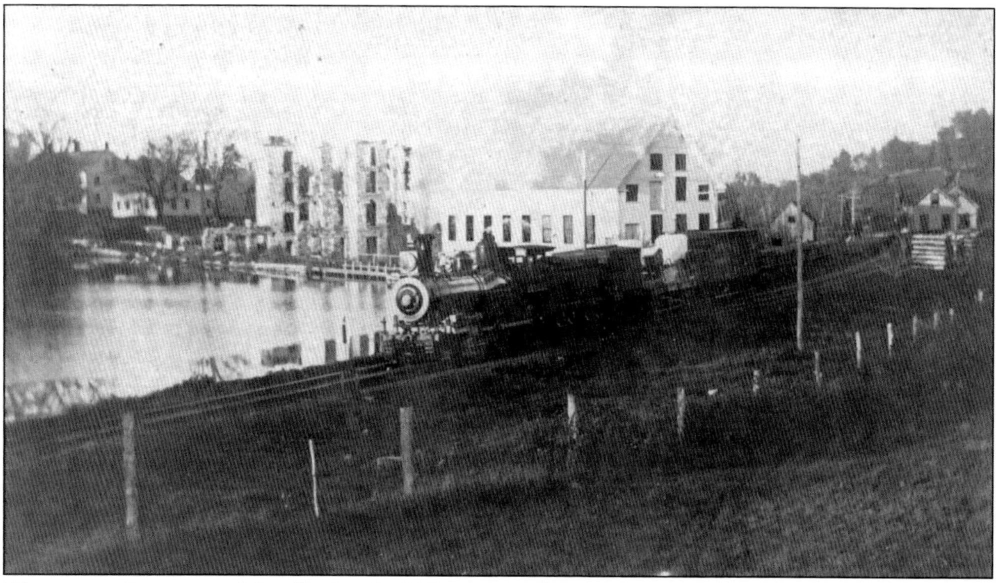

This is another view of the Chelmsford Woolen Mill tenements, Eagle Mill ruins, Sugden Press Bagging Company, Strawberry Hill, and freight house. A locomotive is headed west toward Ayer Junction. There are several horse-drawn buggies on a flatcar, and just behind that, a brakeman is riding atop a Central Vermont box car. The pasture in the right foreground is part of William C. Edwards's dairy farm. (Thomas Collins.)

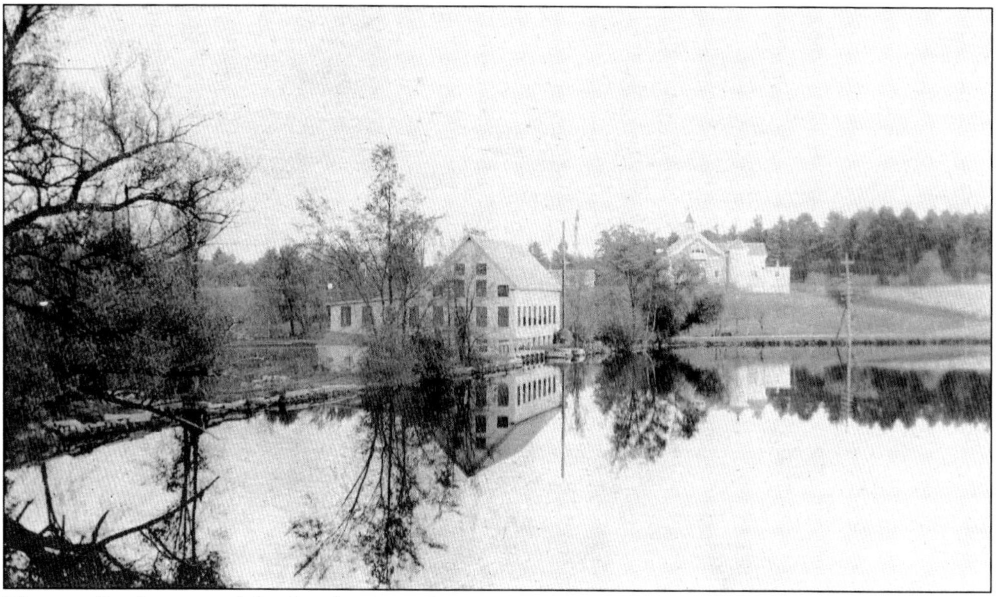

Thomas Sugden started the Sugden Press Bagging Company in 1870 for production of specialized cloth used to extract dyes, cottonseed oil, and cocoa bean products from seeds. It was located in this former Eagle Mill storehouse in 1900 when Donald M. Cameron of Westford purchased a controlling interest. Donald's brother Julian A. Cameron, president of Abbot Worsted in Westford, purchased the remaining interest in 1914. (Chelmsford Historical Society.)

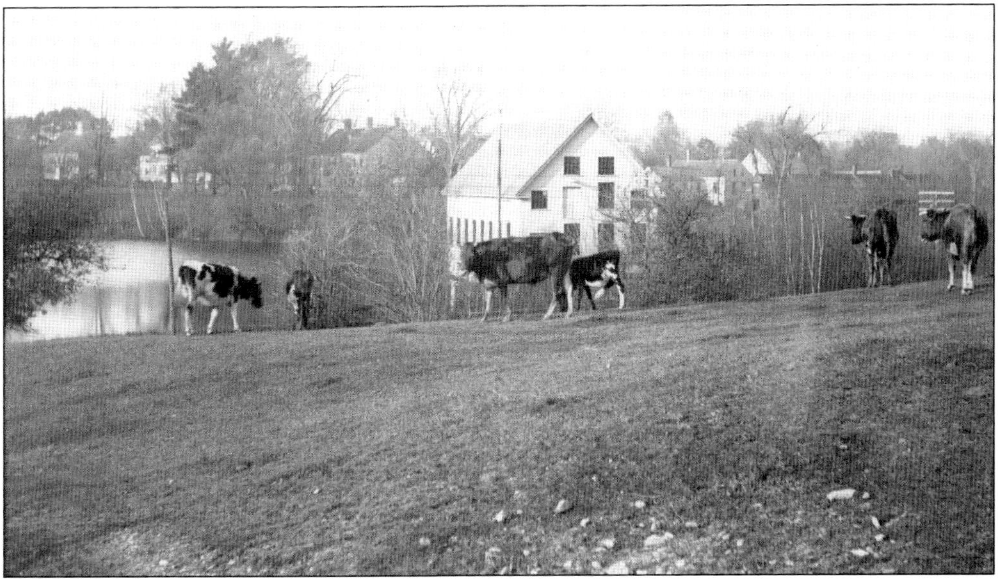

The view from the Edwards farm back across the pond shows, from left to right, the barn and residence of Rev. Samuel H. Virgin at 209 Main Street, the mill tenement houses behind 3 and 7 School Street, the Sugden Press Bagging Company, and homes on Main Street. The Edwards' pasture included nearly all the land along Stony Brook from School Street to the Brookside Mill in Westford. (Chris Ware.)

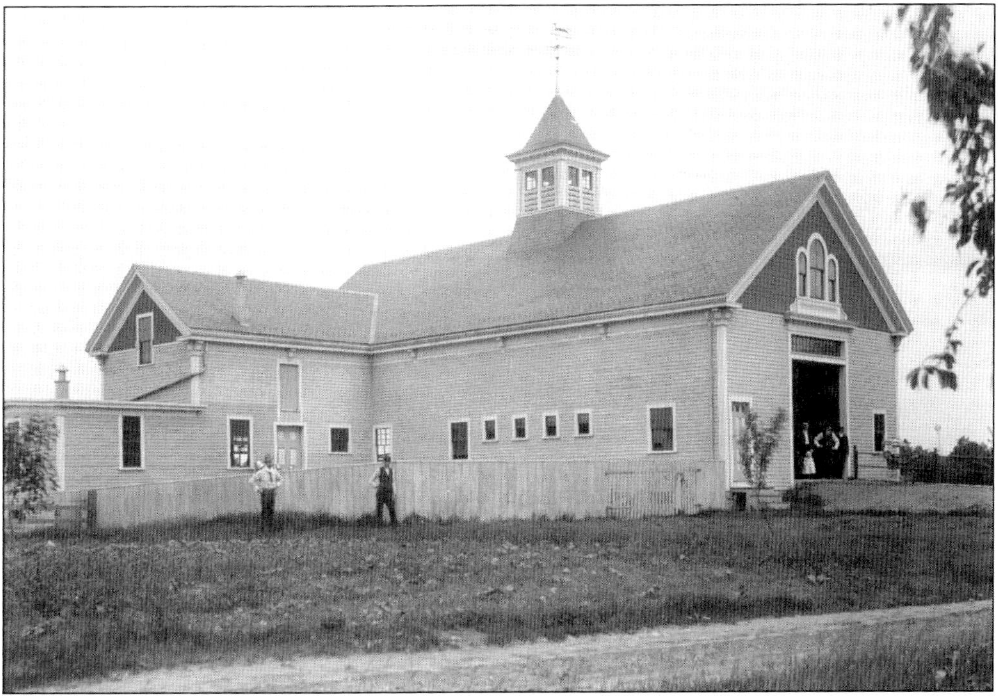

This view of the south end of the Edwards' dairy barn shows some exotic shingle, trim, and window craftsmanship. A prancing horse weathervane tops the cupola, and a windmill on Strawberry Hill is to the right of the barn. William C. Edwards is the man with his arms on his hips in the barn door, and his younger brother Charles E. is the second man from the left. (Chris Ware.)

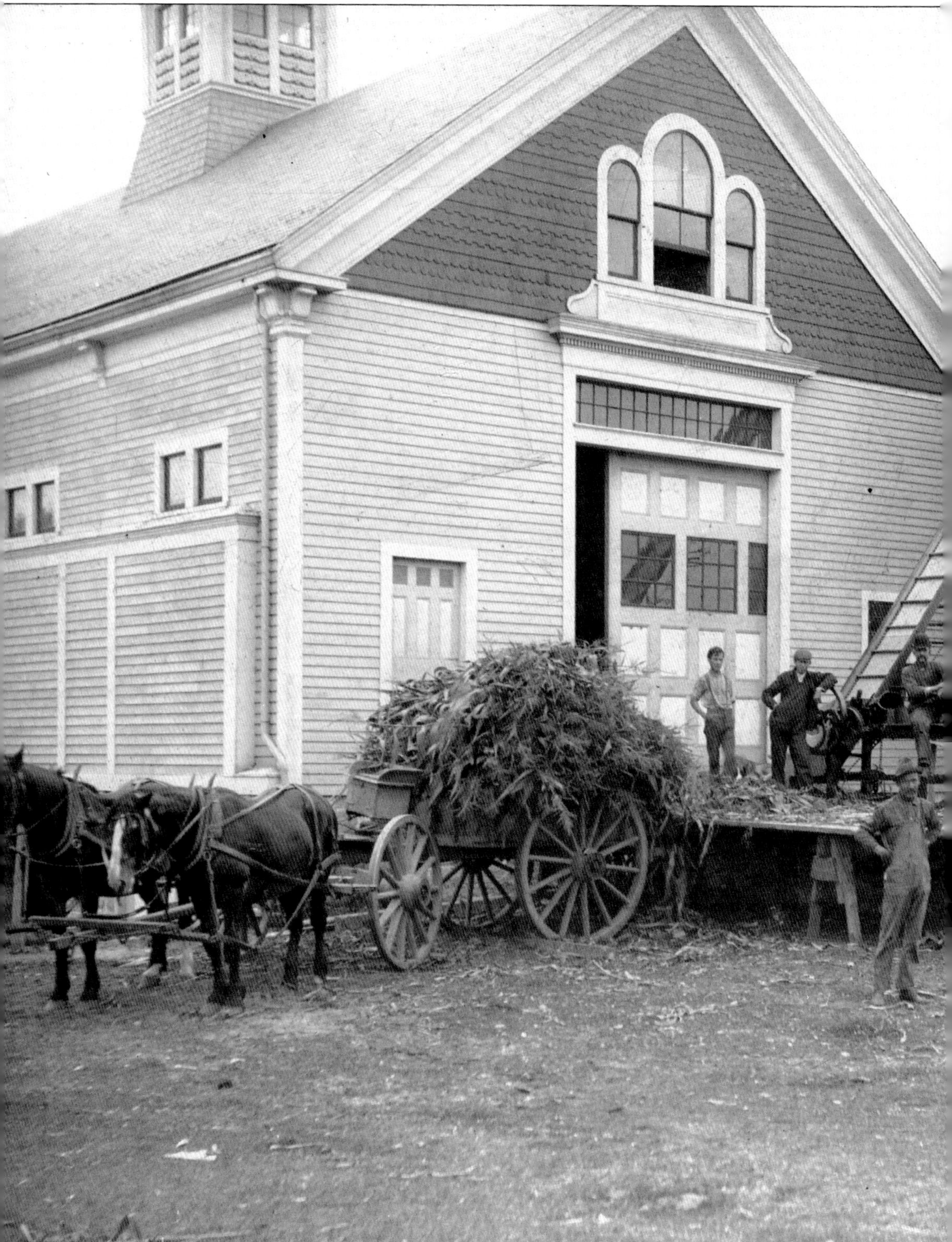

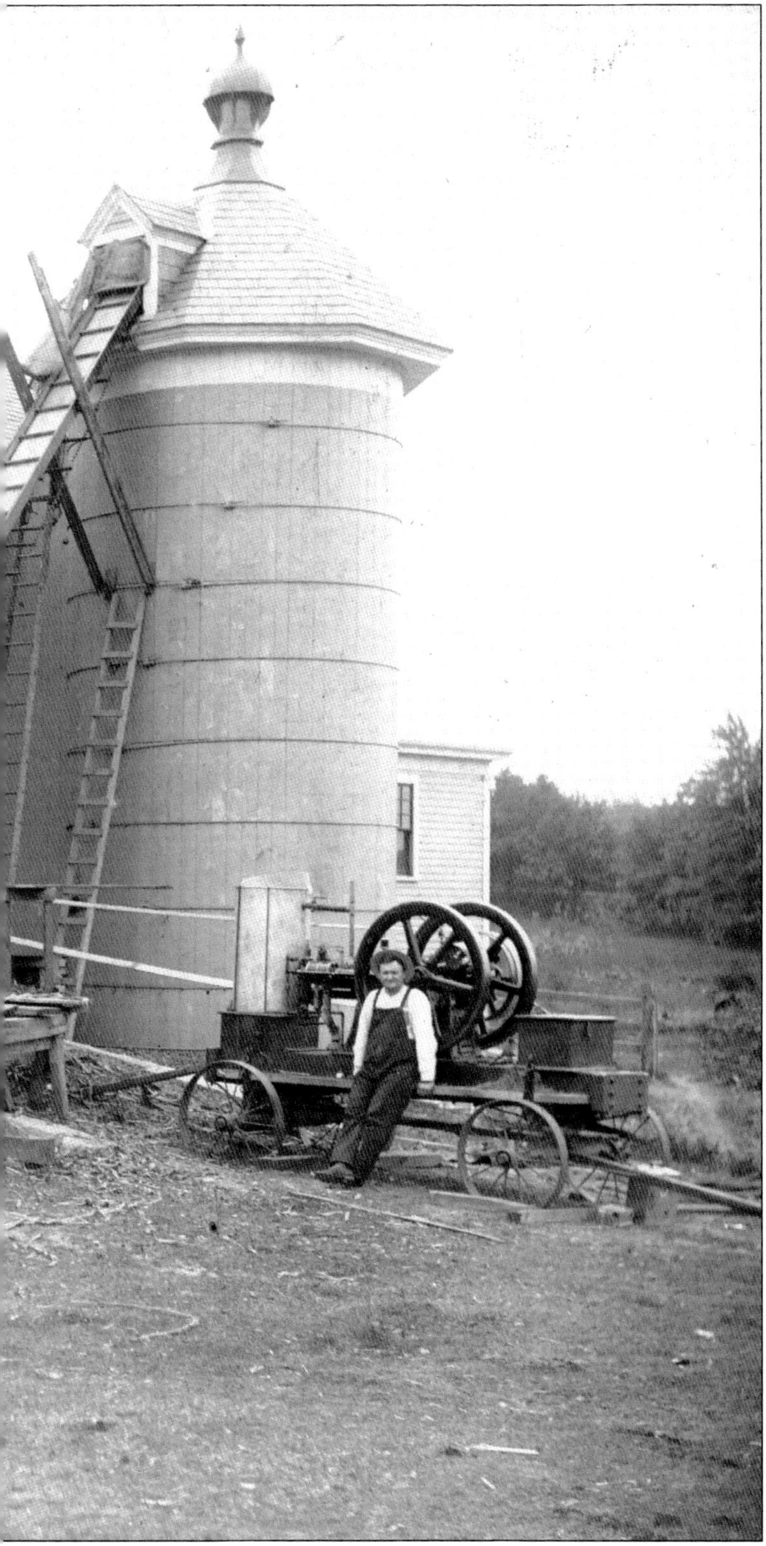

William C. Edwards, who lived just over the line at 36 Nabnasset Street in Westford, had worked as a general building contractor since 1875 with offices at 113 Devonshire Street in Boston. In 1910, he incorporated—along with John J. Monahan of 245 Main Street in West Chelmsford—as Edwards and Monahan Co. Builders in Boston and later in Lowell. A few of their projects include the J.V. Fletcher Library and Brookside mill in Westford; the Methodist church and railroad depot in West Chelmsford; Wentworth by the Sea in Newcastle, New Hampshire; and old North Station in Boston. Edwards built, and his family operated, this large dairy farm adjacent to the West Chelmsford railroad depot. Although the men in this c. 1900 photograph are unidentified, Edwards family members that year included William C. Sr. (age 55), brothers Franklin (46) and Charles E. (40), children Frederick W. (25) and William C. Jr. (18), and nephews Charles S. (18), and Arthur F. (16). High-tech farm equipment of the day included a portable steam engine linked by a leather belt to a mechanical cornstalk chopper and conveyer. (Chris Ware.)

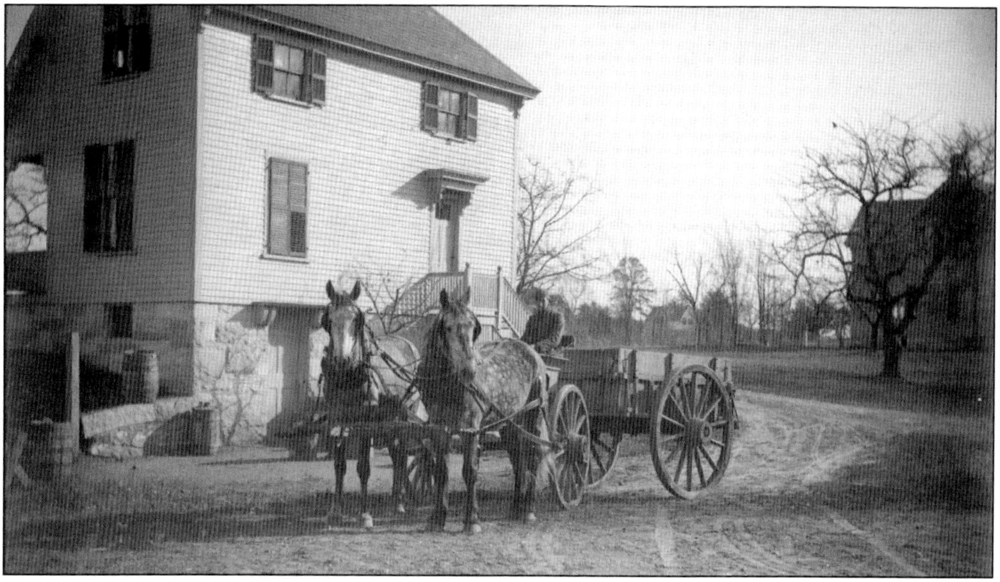

William C. Edwards's brother Charles E. was 16 years his junior and was the general manager of the family's dairy farm for several years. He was also a teamster and is shown here around 1905 with his team and heavy duty wagon. The original farmhouse on the left is at 9 Catamaran Drive, and the newer house on the right is at 12 Catamaran Drive. (Chris Ware.)

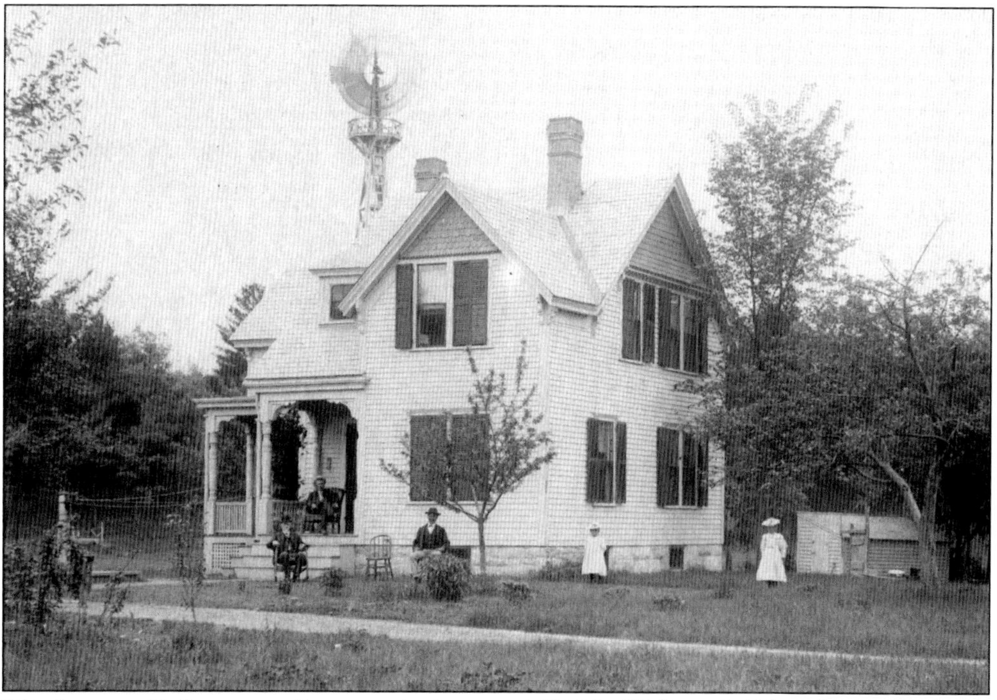

This house at 12 Catamaran Drive was built around 1900 for William C. Edwards's son Frederick W. Edwards, a bookkeeper for Edwards and Monahan at the 6 Beacon Street office in Boston. The windmill, wells, water tank, and piping on this property supplied water to the entire Edwards dairy farm. From left to right are William C. and Frederick W. Edwards, John J. and Ruth E. Monahan, and Edna L. Edwards. (William Davis.)

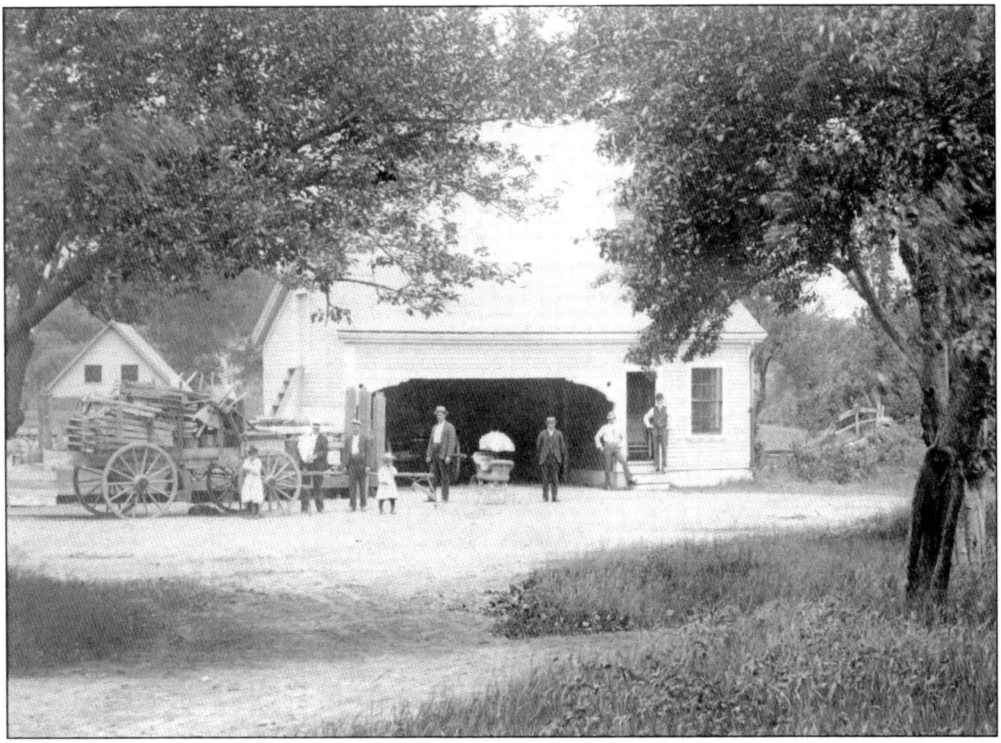

This is the Edwards farm blacksmith shop with a wagon load of construction gear loaded onto a wagon out front. William C. Edwards is on the steps at right with a bowler hat and watch chain, and his family members are dressed up for a special event. Edwards's grandson Walter converted this blacksmith shop into a residence, with a modern address of 13 Catamaran Drive, around 1950. (Chris Ware.)

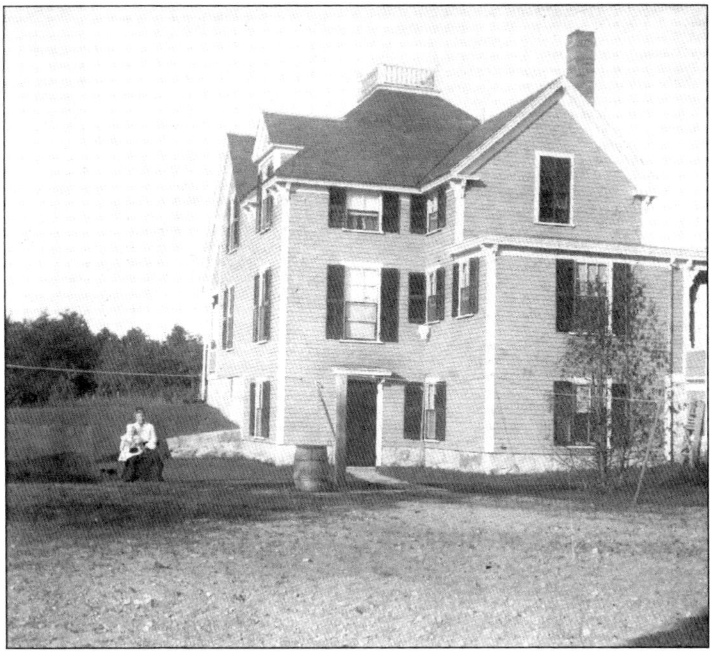

In June 1914, with World War I in progress in Europe, William C. Edwards sold his cows at auction and retired from the dairy business. The farm house at 9 Catamaran Drive was expanded to more than double its original size for William C. Edwards Jr. after his marriage in July 1915 to Margaret Brown Quist, the widow of Paul G. Quist, who died in 1914. (Chris Ware.)

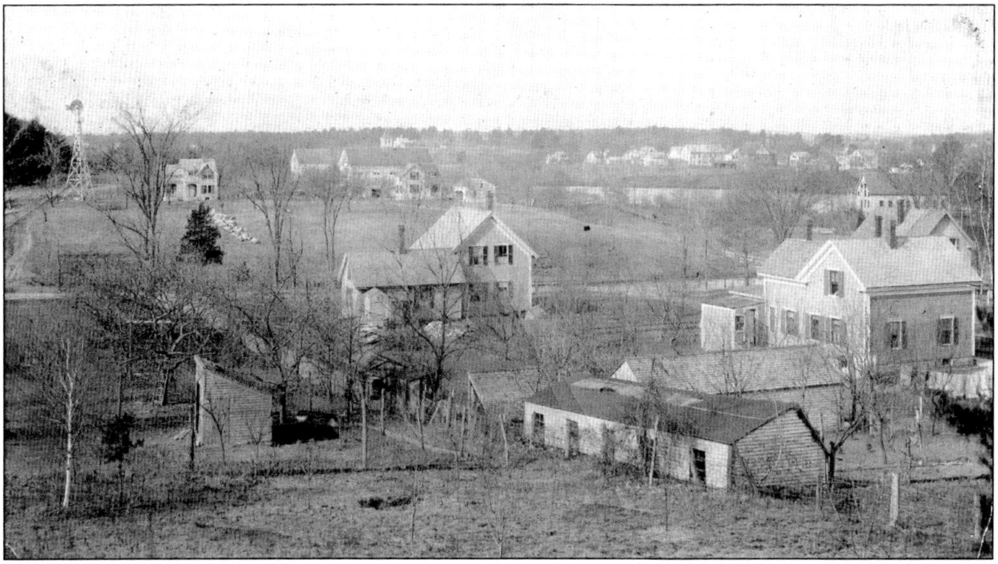

This view from the West Chelmsford Cemetery overlooks, from left to right in the foreground, 32 School Street, 5 Cemetery Road, and 30 School Street. The Edwards farm, shown in the left background, includes the windmill, the house at 12 Catamaran Drive, two barns, the house at 9 Catamaran Drive, and the blacksmith shop. Buildings in Westford, including Marshall's Hall, are visible beyond the pond and left of the Methodist church. (Thomas Collins.)

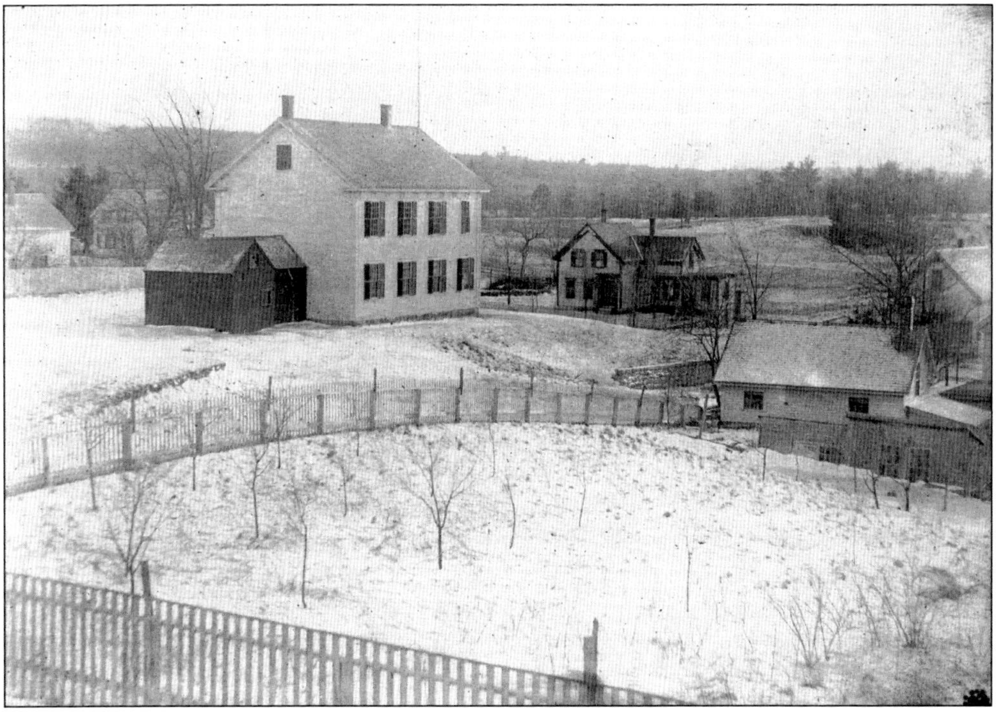

This c. 1890 image shows the West School at 40 School Street, with 41 School Street directly across and Naylor Avenue on the other side of the fence at center. Samuel Naylor, superintendent of the Hiscox File Mill, lived at 36 School Street (at far right), and Agnes Naylor, the teacher here at the time, lived with her mother, Mary, at 232 Main Street. (Thomas Collins.)

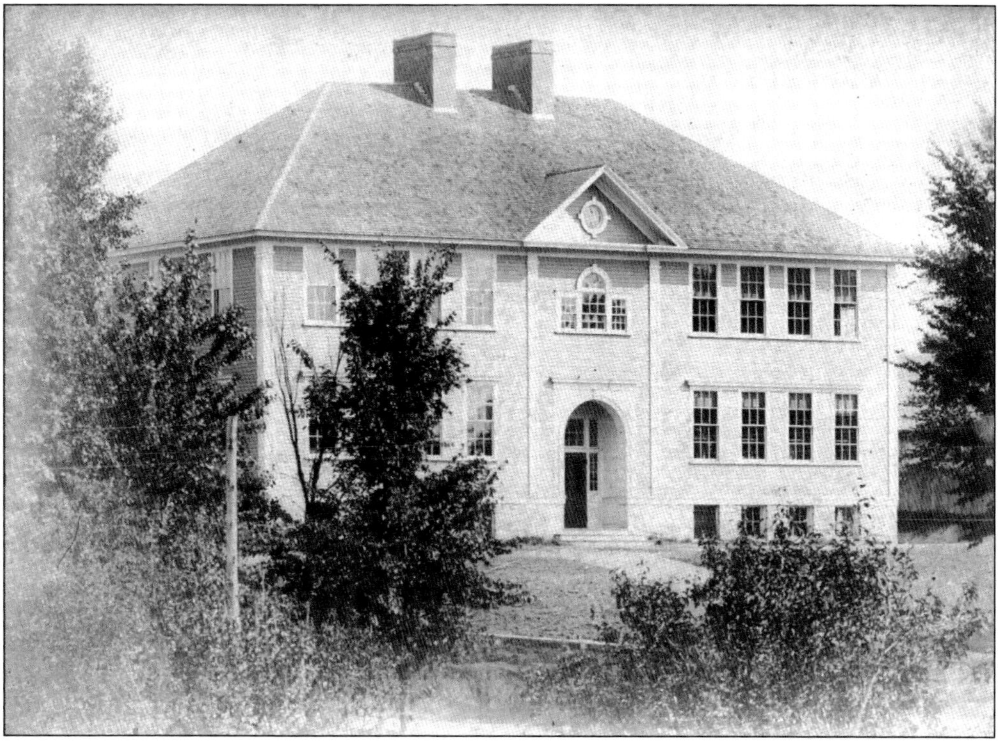

West School was outgrown by 1904, so a new school was constructed behind it for about $10,000, with William C. Edwards as the building contractor. The new West School was occupied on January 1, 1905, and in 1922 it was renamed for Corp. George R. Quessy, who was sadly killed just after the World War I armistice was signed. This school was demolished in 1980, and a residence now occupies the site. (Thomas Collins.)

George F. Snow lived in this house at 48 School Street until his death in August 1914. His occupation in 1900 was listed as farmer, but he was better known throughout town for his work as a selectman, superintendent of schools, forest fire ward, town auditor, trustee of the Methodist Episcopal church, justice of the peace, and committee on appropriations member. (Chelmsford Public Library.)

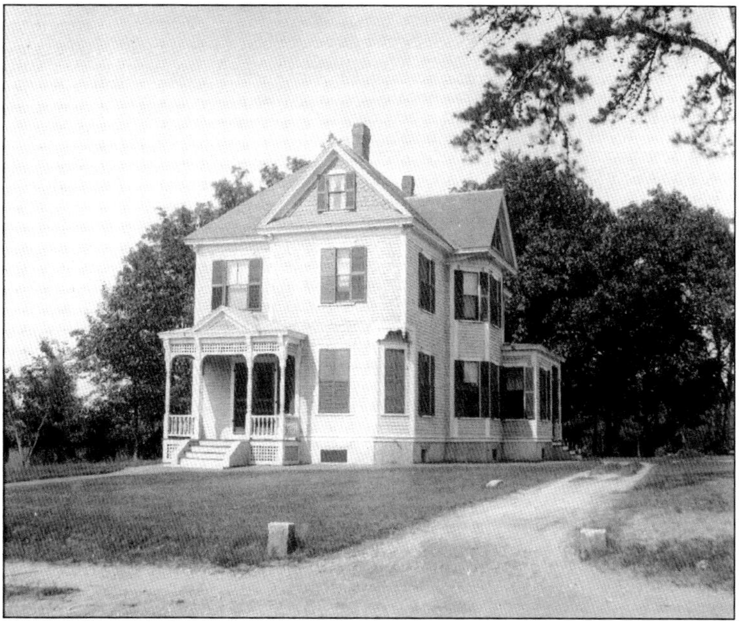

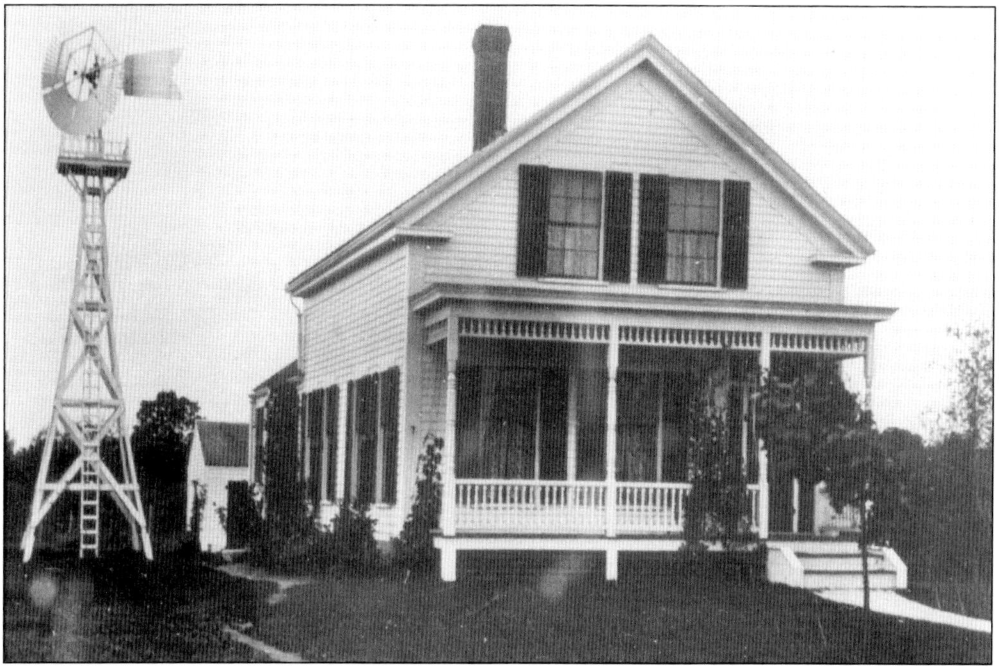

Locomotive engineer John M. Agnew purchased this 55 School Street lot from George F. Snow in 1899, and with his wife, Joann, raised their daughters Jessie M. and Lottie M. In 1937, John, Joann, and Lottie moved to 18 Adams Street in North Chelmsford. This was closer to Lottie's teaching job at the Highland School, and John, then 70 years old, began working as a locomotive fireman. (Chelmsford Historical Society.)

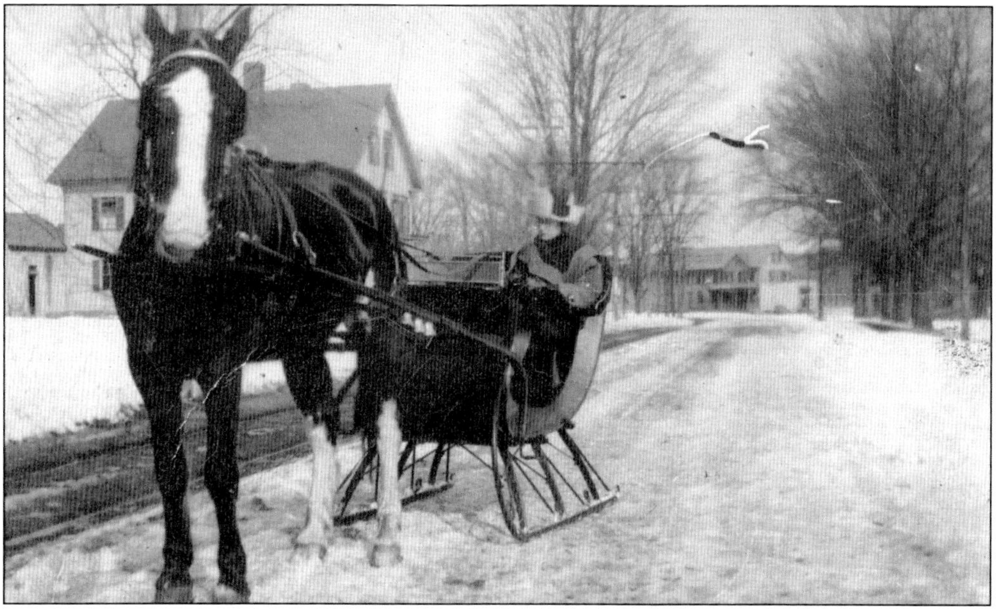

In this winter scene, an unidentified sleigh rider poses for a picture near the house of Martha Brown and her daughter Emma at 225 Main Street. The plow trolley on the Vinal Square to Brookside line has cleared the tracks, and the post office and store at School Street are directly ahead. Behind the trees on the right was a public park with benches. (Thomas Collins.)

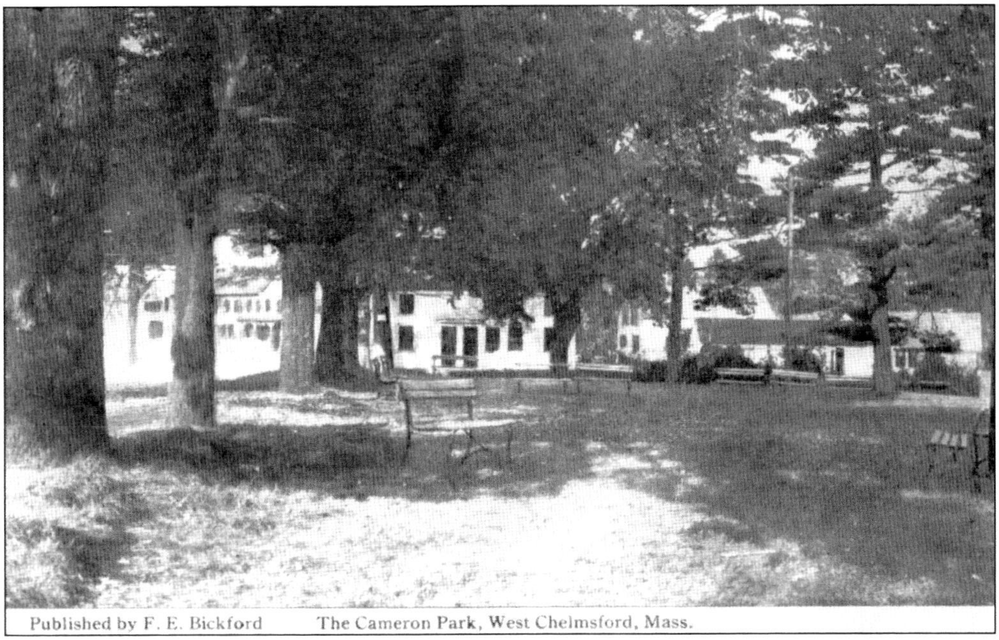


This 1917 Frank E. Bickford postcard shows "The Cameron Park" located across from 217 and 225 Main Street. The park was named for brothers Donald and Julian Cameron of Westford who were principal owners of the nearby Sugden Press Bagging Company at the time. The building at left is Bickford's store and post office, and the building at center is the last remaining Eagle Mill tenement house. (Thomas Collins.)

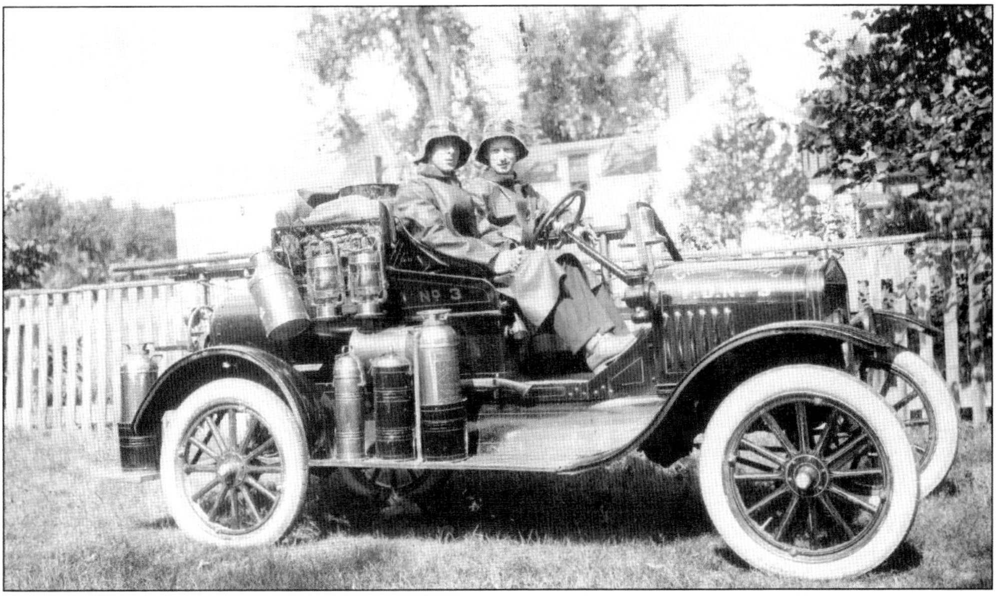


This 1921 Ford Chemical Car No. 3 is parked in front of Historical Hall at 235 Main Street with 231 Main Street beyond. Loren J. Ellinwood purchased a former store from the Marcus H. Winship estate in 1914, and after 1920, shared it with his West Chelmsford volunteer fire department. From 1930 to 1970 it was a town-owned firehouse, and is now a privately owned garage. (Chelmsford Fire Department.)

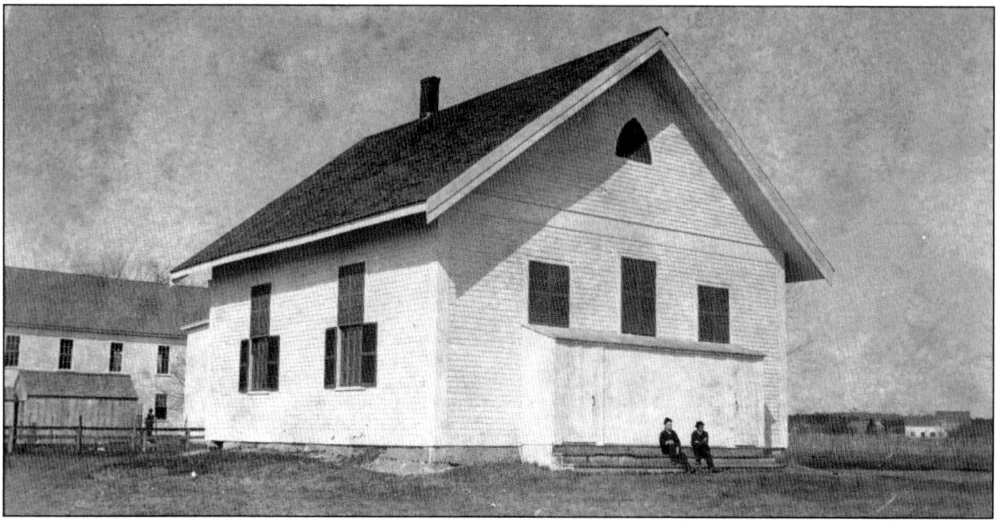

In 1854, the Stony Brook Society for Religious Worship purchased this property at 242 Main Street. A barn was acquired, converted into the chapel, and in 1872, it was deeded to the Methodist Episcopal church. In 1887, it was sold for $200 and moved by oxen and rollers to 43 Nabnasset Street in Westford. Marshall's Hall is behind the chapel, in Westford, and Main Street is on the right. (Chelmsford Historical Society.)

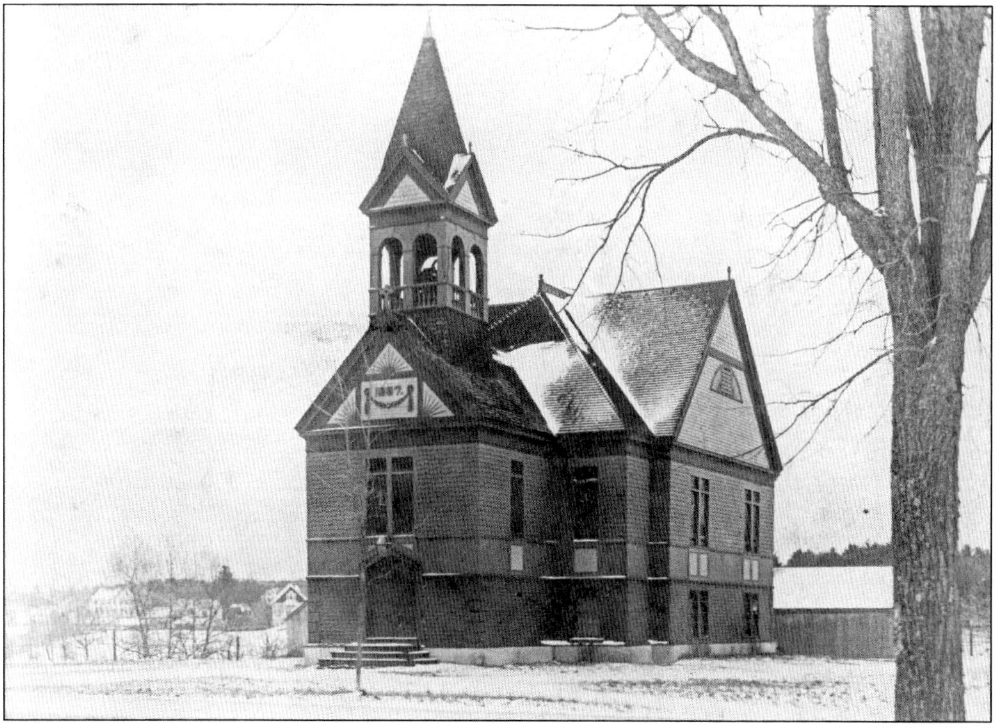


Architect Alden Frink was commissioned to design the new church, and in 1887, a $4,000 contract was signed with neighbor William C. Edwards to build the new church at 242 Main Street. Frink was known for high-profile designs in the Boston area, Thomas Edison's Florida house, and his collaboration with Edwards on Boston & Maine Railroad stations. The new church was dedicated on January 10, 1888. (West Chelmsford United Methodist Church.)

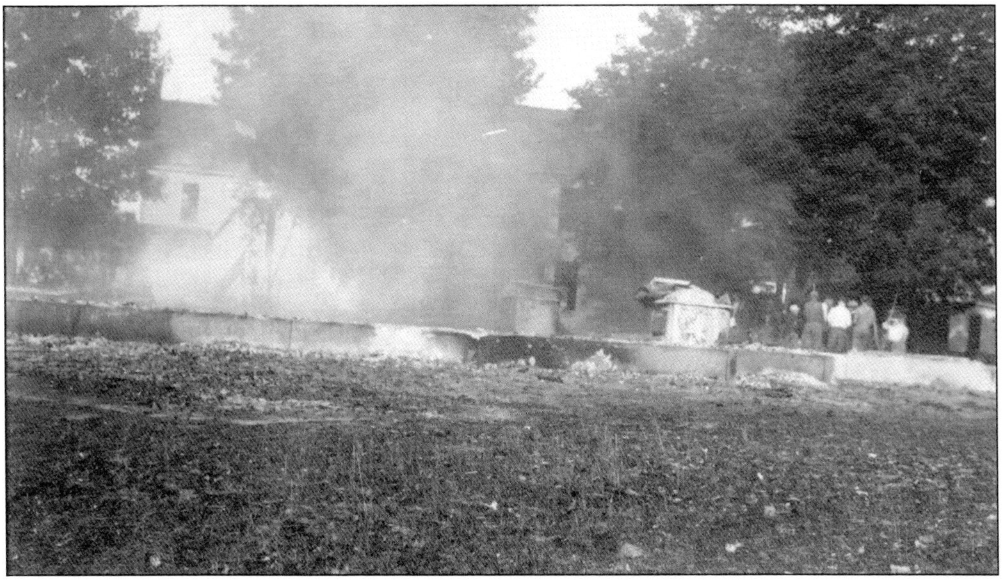

Amid a rash of arson fires in the area, West Chelmsford United Methodist Church burned to the ground on July 16, 1920, despite volunteers immediately setting up a bucket brigade to fight it. The fire department, arriving later, could only protect neighboring houses. Visible in the picture are a pair of Magee furnaces used to heat the building. Although it was never proved, arson was the most likely cause. (West Chelmsford United Methodist Church.)

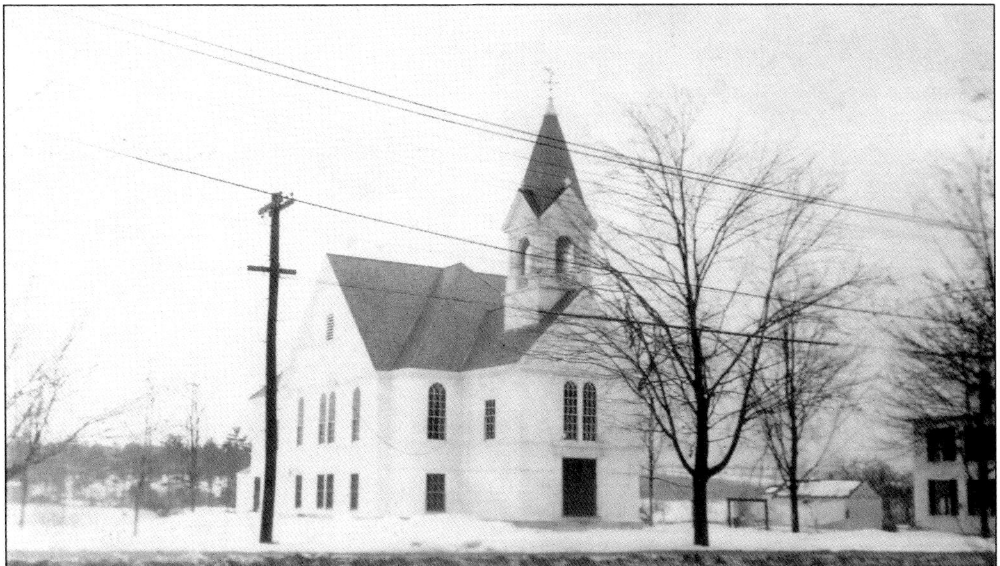

While services were temporarily held in Historical Hall, the Edwards & Monahan Contracting Company built this new church in 1921 using the original Frink design on the original foundation, with minor modifications, for about $31,000. William C. Edwards, who had personal connections with the church, supervised the construction and made sure only the best materials were used. It was dedicated on January 18, 1922. (West Chelmsford United Methodist Church.)